Alaska At Your Own Pace

Also by Bernice Beard
At Your Own Pace: Traveling Your Way in Your Motorhome

Alaska At Your Own Pace

Traveling by RV Caravan

BERNICE BEARD

ARBOR HOUSE PUBLISHING
WESTMINSTER, MARYLAND

First Edition

Every effort has been made to properly identify and capitalize trademark names used in this book. In addition, you may find some spellings that are different, but in every instance I have gone to a primary source for the correct spelling.

Tender Corporation is the owner worldwide of the trade name After Bite®. Holiday Rambler is a registered trademark of Monaco Coach Corporation. "KOA" is a registered trademark of Kampgrounds of America, Inc., Billings, Montana.

Grateful acknowledgment is made to Trails North, Inc., for permission to use their photographs and to Frantic Follies and The Days of `98 Show with Soapy Smith © 1973 through 1997 Gold Rush Productions Inc. for permission to refer to them in the manuscript.

© 1998 by Bernice Beard. All rights reserved.

No part of this publication may be reproduced, distributed, or transmitted in any form or by any means, including photocopying, recording, or other electronic or mechanical methods, or by any information storage and retrieval system without prior written permission from the author, except for brief quotations embodied in critical reviews and certain other noncommercial uses permitted by copyright law. For permission requests, write to the publisher, addressed "Attention: Permissions Coordinator" at the address below.

>   Arbor House Publishing
>   332 One Forty Village Rd., Suite 6-197
>   Westminster, MD 21157
>   Tel: (410) 857-4146; (800) 966-4146; Fax: (410) 857-3835

Ordering Information

Quantity sales. Special discounts are available on quantity purchases by corporations, associations, and others. For details, contact the "Special Sales Department" at the Arbor House Publishing address above.

Printed in the United States of America

Library of Congress Cataloging-in-Publication Data
>   Beard, Bernice, 1927-
>   Alaska at your own pace: traveling by RV Caravan / by Bernice Beard
>   1st ed   p. cm.
>   Includes appendix and index.
>   International Standard Book Number: 0-9653063-8-0
>   1. Motorhomes—United States
>   2. Alaska—Description and Travel
>   919.804929-dc21 1998
>   Library of Congress Catalog Card Number: 98-92444
>   CIP First Edition

Cover Design: Lightbourne Images
Editorial Services: PeopleSpeak
Interior Design: Joel Friedlander, Marin Bookworks
Cover Photograph, Kenai Peninsula, Alaska: John W. Warden
Cover Motorhome: Holiday Rambler® Presidential

The author and publisher assume neither liability nor responsibility to any person or entity with respect to any direct or indirect loss or damage caused, or alleged to be caused, by the information contained herein, or for errors, omissions, inaccuracies, or any other inconsistency within these pages. The author and publisher are not associated with any manufacturers of motorhomes (or other products), and are not guaranteeing the safety of these homes.

Distributed by: Seven Hills Book Distributors, Cincinnati, OH (800) 545-2005

To
Fellow RVers on the Alaskan Tour Caravan,
whose company made the adventure
exciting, enjoyable, and memorable

Ann and Louie Beeler
Ro and Bob Conway
Mary Jo and Bill Cornell
Yvonne and Wil Foreman
Lib and John Graybeal
Thel and Don Heathcock
Eunice and Fred McQuiston
Effie and Clem Swagerty
Jackie and Lyle Wrigley
Karen and Scott Bonis
Laurie and Don Peterson

and to Paul, husband,
for his love, kindness, wisdom, and encouragement
and for being a role model in learning about and enjoying RVing.

Contents

Preface ix
  1 Want to Go to Alaska? 1
  2 Traveling Cross-Country 11
  3 Getting Groceries 28
  4 Vancouver Rendezvous 40
  5 "Boondocking" at Barkerville 50
  6 Mile 0 of Alaska Highway 66
  7 Wilderness Camping 75
  8 Signpost Forest, Watson Lake, Yukon Territory 86
  9 Cleaning Up at Whitehorse, Yukon Territory 95
10 Campfire at Moose Creek, Yukon Territory 107
11 The Top of the World Highway 119
12 Welcome to Alaska! 128
13 Flight to Barrow 136
14 Fogged in at Barrow 148
15 Return to Fairbanks 159
16 The Majesty of Mount McKinley 167
17 On to Anchorage and Kenai 178
18 Captivating Homer Spit 187
19 Up Close to Exit Glacier 195
20 On the Road to Palmer 202
21 Prince William Sound 209
22 Return to Tok 218
23 Tok to Kluane Lake, Yukon Territory 226
24 Kluane Lake to Skagway .232
25 On Alaska's Marine Highway Ferry 241
26 Farewell Dinner 249
27 Reaching the Lower 48 263
28 Homeward Journey 271
29 Reflections 281
Epilogue 284
Appendix 289
Glossary 309
Index 314

Preface

MY FIRST BOOK, *At Your Own Pace: Traveling Your Way in Your Motorhome*, introduced readers to the enjoyable world of recreational vehicle (RV) travel. It received such a positive response that the publisher requested that I write a second book about my travels as soon as possible.

Since I was not opposed to the idea, and since I had on hand copious supporting notes, photographs, and videotapes from our recent trip to Alaska with several other RVers, I soon compiled a synopsis of chapters that would constitute my next book, this one. In addition, friends reading *At Your Own Pace* encouraged me to write about more of my adventures. Their faces lit up at the mention of Alaska.

I discovered that many, many people want to either go to Alaska or read about it. And there is so much to write about. My aim was to write my book in a way that would take the reader along, showing what we saw and did as we traveled, first as a two-rig caravan from our homes in Maryland to Vancouver, British Columbia; then with a tour company through British Columbia, Yukon Territory, and Alaska; and then solo back across the country to our home. Mostly, I wanted to capture the excitement of journeying in an RV to a distant place with vast wilderness and tundra.

A special dividend to writing about our journey was, of course, reliving the whole three-month, triangular trip from Maryland, with its sunny beaches beside the Atlantic Ocean, to Barrow, Alaska, bordering the mostly frozen Arctic Ocean, to Crescent City, California, with its rocky coast washed by the Pacific Ocean, and back across the Lower 48 (the contiguous United States) to our home in Maryland. Wonderful, sometimes humorous, memories of scenery, activities, and new RVing friends flowed through my mind and keyboard as I experienced again our Alaskan adventure.

Neither my husband, Paul, nor I had ever been to Alaska. As you read, you will learn of our fears and questions, no doubt similar to those that you have had when traveling to unfamiliar territory. As you journey with us, you will learn what it's like to travel in an RV with a group of other RVers and see with us magnificent Mount McKinley and other breathtaking scenes.

When I think of my original, uninformed vision of Alaska and contrast it with the real thing, I feel small and insignificant. My mind's pre-trip picture showed mostly snow, Eskimos, and polar bears. That vision was eclipsed by the real Alaska—the forty-ninth state, which is one-fifth the size of the Lower 48, with an awesome landscape that includes glacier-topped mountains, one of which is the highest in North America (Mount McKinley at 20,320 feet), 3,000 rivers, 3 million lakes, more than 5,000 glaciers, forested islands and mountains—all a part of Alaska's 586,000 square miles of wilderness. We discovered that not only were Inupiat, Yup'ik, and Pacific Eskimos native to Alaska but also Aleuts and Athabascan, Tlingit, and Haida Indians. They have been joined by people from all over the world, living and working together in an often harsh environment.

When U.S. Secretary of State William H. Seward offered Russia $7.2 million in 1867 for the territory of Alaska, it was called "Seward's Folly." Today, Alaska Day is celebrated on October 18 to commemorate the first raising of the American flag over Alaska. Following the gold rush of 1897 and later development of the timber, fishing, and mining industries and transportation facilities, on January 3, 1959, Congress granted Alaska official status as our forty-ninth state. Today Alaska is both contemporary and prehistoric, with skyscrapers silhouetted against snowcapped mountains in Anchorage and all-terrain vehicles motoring on unpaved streets in tundra communities.

One human being cannot totally capture in writing the magnificence and complexity of *Alyeska*, the Great Land, as it was called by the Aleuts. My effort here is to present those aspects of it that happily touched our caravan of RVs as we moved through its grandeur and to give some indication of the travelers' relationship with Alaska, each other, and their RVs. Not only did we experience Alaska itself, but traveling north through British Columbia and Yukon Territory to reach Alaska only added to the adventure and appreciation of the beautiful God-given panoramas in this world. I pray that reading this

Preface

volume will take you into a realm of discovery, joy, and thanksgiving.

I wish to acknowledge with deep appreciation the permission of Caravanas Voyagers® and my fellow travelers to use their names where they naturally appeared in the narrative. Bob Conway and Mary Jo Cornell graciously shared their journal entries with me. Although I purposely did not read them until after I had finished the first draft, I am indebted to these two individuals for enriching these pages.

My heartfelt thanks go also to the following: Nancy Beard for designing the delightful drawings in the page headings for the first book, which were so fitting for this second book; Joel Friedlander for his superb interior design; Jane Sharpe, for her expert library-cataloging copy; John W. Warden, for his breathtaking photograph on the cover; Lightbourne Images, for making the cover so irresistible to the eye and senses; Rachel Rice, for her excellent indexing; and Sharon Goldinger of PeopleSpeak, for her excellent editorial expertise in making sure readers were treated to a moving picture in words and for being so great to work with.

A very special thank you to all those readers who encouraged me to write a second book; to members of the Westminster Church of the Brethren Camping Group who with congeniality continue to teach and encourage me; the Western Maryland College community and other friends and relatives who warmly accept and inspire me.

In closing, I want this book to give to you a vivid image of RVing with an RV tour caravan. Whether you are a novice or veteran RVer, whether you own or do not plan to own an RV, or whether you travel solo or sign up with an RV tour caravan, I want you to gain insights that will enrich your own travel and reading experiences. I also want you to get a sense of Alaska today and of the goodness in people everywhere. I invite you now to join our caravan in a spirit of adventure as together we travel on an unknown road.

About the Author

Bernice Beard is a published writer of essays, articles, and short stories. In addition to writing, she is an active member of the Church of the Brethren. In 1989 she retired after a 27-year career in administration at Western Maryland College, a private liberal arts college, as executive assistant to the president emerita. She holds a bachelor of arts and master of liberal arts degrees from that same institution. Her favorite activities include writing, walking, and of course, traveling by motorhome.

She lives near Westminster, Maryland, with her husband, Paul. They have a son, Jeffrey, and a daughter-in-law, Nancy. The author and her husband have taken 14 major trips in their motorhome, including the 44-day RV caravan tour of Alaska about which she writes in this book.

She is listed in *Who's Who of American Women* and was awarded a Special Achievement Award by Western Maryland College for her first book, *At Your Own Pace: Traveling Your Way in Your Motorhome*.

· 1 ·

Want to Go to Alaska?

IN MY UNSOPHISTICATED imagination, I saw Alaska as a massive territory, close geographically to Russia. Most of its vastness contained breathtakingly beautiful scenery—majestic mountains with great glaciers and endless miles of snowy tundra. Its few villages and towns were scattered. Its larger cities of Anchorage and Fairbanks surely had no high rise buildings. I sensed separateness from the contiguous United States yet I felt awe toward the people, who were mostly Eskimos.

I pictured an 1800s milieu with bearded, tobacco-chewing miners coming to town for supplies, walking beside their mules. General stores carried yard goods, barrels of flour and sugar, and candy in large glass jars. Supplies were priced high and frequently ran out. Dance halls were raucous and merry with men in boots and women in swirling skirts dancing to a fiddler's music. Rugged men worked hard and played hard. Gambling and pool tables drew loud, crude men and painted, gum-cracking women to saloons.

Seals played at the edges of water in which ice floes drifted. Igloos dotted the tundra; dogsleds mushed along in wintry winds and snow. Eskimos wore fur-lined parkas and mukluks. Even so, extremely cold temperatures made their breath freeze. When they were old and ready to die, they floated out to sea on an ice floe—an image from fifth grade.

In my uninitiated mind, the Trans-Alaska Pipeline interrupted miles of gleaming, white-blanketed tundra. Prince William Sound still had a greasy slick from the famous oil spill in 1991. A short summer brought wildflowers and long daylight hours. Outside the villages, towns, and cities, a few military outposts operated, some above the Arctic Circle; their personnel in green and brown camouflage uniforms mixed with locals in the towns. Some miners set up rigs that could be seen in the foothills while other miners panned for gold in streams in summer. I saw Mount McKinley, the highest peak in North America, in all its white majesty and reminded myself of the awesome power of creation. Most of all, in Alaska I envisioned the pioneer, the person willing to risk the usual comforts and securities of life in order to explore, to adventure, and to achieve.

This mental image of Alaska came from what I had read in elementary school, seen in old movies, and fantasized about for years. Now I would finally get to see if fantasy matched reality. I wondered how much of my vision would be true and how much I would send to oblivion as Paul, my husband of 44 years, and I prepared for our first trip to Alaska in our 34-foot Holiday Rambler® motorhome.

Motorhoming friends in Maryland, John and Elizabeth (Lib) Graybeal, had set us thinking about going to Alaska and doing so in a recreational vehicle (RV) caravan under the aegis of a commercial tour company. An RV caravan tour happens when an RV organization, club, or commercial RV caravan tour company provides leaders, plans the itinerary, and makes advance reservations for campgrounds and group activities such as meals, cruises, sightseeing, and shows. Caravaners travel in their own RVs, using buses, ferries, airplanes, and trains when appropriate as supplements. Tours run from a few weeks to a few months and may include from 10 to 40 or more RVs. When on the road, the RVers travel in groups of two or three rather than as a convoy.

The previous March at church, John told Paul that he and Lib had signed up with a company for an RV caravan tour of Alaska and wondered if we would be interested in going, too. John thought the price was right and gave us a brochure that described the tour. The Graybeals had traveled previously in Alaska with another couple. John reasoned that the caravan tour would include places and provide activities and information that he and Lib had missed by going on their own.

The tour company was called Caravanas Voyagers®, located in El Paso, Texas. In addition to the "Alaska Adventure" in which we were interested, the company also offered RV caravan tours to Central America, Europe, New England, the northeast Canadian provinces, and New Zealand and Australia.

The leaflet for Alaska showed the daily itinerary starting with a rendezvous in Vancouver, British Columbia. The tour proceeded for 43 days north through British Columbia and Yukon Territory, as far north as Fairbanks in Alaska, then headed south to the Kenai Peninsula, Prince William Sound, and Skagway, where participants would board the Alaska Marine Highway Southeast ferry. The last stop of the tour would be a return to Prince George, British Columbia, after a circuitous route through British Columbia, Yukon Territory, and Alaska. Caravaners would be on their own from Prince George homeward.

Included in the base price of $4,995 (for RVs less than 25 feet in length) were campground electric, water, and sewer hookups when available; ferry fees; private cabins on the ferry; expert services of a wagonmaster and tailgunner team; four cruises (Miles Canyon, Pleasure Island, a sternwheeler, and an eight-hour Columbia Glacier cruise); a special Caravanas cap, jacket, and sew-on Alaska patch; transfers for group events; 15 meals plus potlucks; 13 sightseeing tours; *The MILEPOST*® travel guide; and four special shows.

As Paul and I talked about the trip on the way home from church, Paul said that he was interested right off the bat. Laughing, he remarked, "I can't say 'been there, done that!'"

Just thinking about going to Alaska left me breathless. I'd never thought *we'd* go to Alaska. It was always "there" and I was "here," and I'd accepted that fact. I remembered hearing when I was a little girl about a local pastor and his wife who had traveled to Alaska in the late 1930s and how brave everybody thought they were.

More recently, Fred Teeter, a close family friend, had worked as a console operator for the distant early warning (DEW) system from

August of 1976 to August of 1978. After a year in Greenland, he was transferred to Alaska where he worked at several different system locations.

One brief stint was at Point Barrow, a slip of land that juts out into the Arctic Ocean. It's the northernmost point of the United States. Ten miles southwest is the town of Barrow with a population of 3,075. The town of Barrow is one of the largest Eskimo settlements and is also the seat of the 88,000-square-mile North Slope Borough, the world's largest municipal government. Barrow was incorporated as a city in 1959, the same year that Alaska gained statehood.

Fred's reports of sub-zero temperatures, the dry cold, and the dangers of not realizing how cold it was made me marvel at his daring. He said he waited until the temperature *rose* to minus 15 degrees Fahrenheit to run for exercise and to get a break away from the station. Unlike a lot of newcomers, he easily adjusted to the perpetual night. Occasionally he saw the aurora borealis (Northern Lights), which was an awesome experience.

He said that drifting snow was the main problem at Barrow. Once a huge drift covered the door of the barracks and the people inside had to tunnel through it to get outside. I had seen a picture that he sent home of the giant, white, spherical radome that housed the radar antenna at Point Barrow. I dared to wonder if *we* might go to Barrow.

Usually not one to be hasty about decision making, Paul surprised me by urging me to call the tour company that very Sunday afternoon to see if any spaces were available. I left a message saying that we were interested in being in the same caravan to Alaska with the Graybeals.

Again at Paul's urging, I followed up first thing on Monday morning when the Caravanas Voyagers'® office opened. Paul picked up the extension; we both heard a man say that space was available.

After the usual questions about cost, cancellation insurance, and how to sign up, I asked if there would be time in the schedule and places available en route to get my hair done each week. (I had come to rely on that weekly ritual and would be at loose ends if I had to blow-dry and style my rebellious hair myself.) The man laughed, saying he hadn't had that question before but he thought it would not be a problem.

I asked if there were guardrails on the Top of the World Highway, a road with a reputation for both astronomical height and sheer drop-offs. He couldn't answer that one for sure.

We also asked, daringly in my mind, if we might plan an optional flight to Barrow, Alaska, when in the appropriate area. (It was not listed specifically in the brochure that offered, at the visit to Fairbanks, an option of flying over the Arctic Circle with a bush pilot.) Again, he thought that would be possible and said that we should tell our tour's wagonmaster, who would arrange such a side trip en route.

Over the telephone, we paid the $350 deposit by credit card. The man said that we would receive a detailed itinerary about a month before the trip. The rendezvous with the other RVers going on the same Alaskan adventure would take place in Vancouver, British Columbia, on Saturday, June 12, at Burnaby Cariboo RV Park.

We had no idea, of course, how many would be in our caravan, who they would be (aside from the Graybeals) or who our wagonmaster and tailgunner would be nor what they would actually do. In our Westminster Church of the Brethren Camping Group, which camped together one weekend a month from May through October, one couple usually shared the wagonmaster duties for a year. They made reservations at campgrounds, processed deposits, arranged camping-group activities held in our local church, and sent necessary mailings to the group. We had no tailgunner. At the weekend camp-outs, a lot of "tailgunning" went on as we talked with one another about a particular problem or special feature on our RVs.

On the Alaskan trip, the wagonmaster would make advance reservations for campgrounds and activities and somehow let us know where we were to go each day. The tailgunner would assist with mechanical and other problems on the road and would bring up the rear of the caravan so that he or she would come upon anyone needing assistance.

Among later information that came from the tour company, in addition to the final bill and itinerary, were travel brochures. A colorful brochure called "Alaska" showed a picture of Anchorage as a metropolitan city with high rise buildings. Plainly, no igloos!

My excitement mounted not only for the journey itself but for the possibility of flying to Barrow. The most northern community of the United States intrigued us because of its location on the Arctic Ocean, its Eskimo population, and the fact that Fred had worked there. We had never heard of Barrow until his experience at that outpost. How thrilling it would be to put our feet on the same remote part of North America.

At the same time, questions broke through my thrill about our longest journey yet into new regions. Would we have safe travel? Would our motorhome be ruined by rough roads? We had heard horror stories about potholes and washboard surfaces that broke axles, about stones sent flying at windshields or sides of RVs causing "stars" or "dings" in the glass and dents in the smooth aluminum sides. Would some grizzly bear or polar bear attack us?

Was there a lot of water in Alaska (after all, four cruises were included in the tour)? What was the geography of Alaska like? Would we get marooned by a mud slide blocking a road ahead of us so that we would have to camp for weeks or be airlifted out? That actually happened to friends of ours when they were on a combination cruise and bus tour in Alaska. Would anyone else in the group want to go to Barrow as Paul and I did?

Would our good health hold out? Would we know how to pace ourselves so that we didn't get overly tired and have to miss something special on the trip? What would we do if we got sick or had an accident?

The trip to Alaska would be Paul's and my first time to go on an advertised RV caravan tour and I wondered if we would really like going that way. We had, after all, been used to going on our own for long trips, just the two of us at our own pace. Would that be possible in an RV caravan? Would we fit in? An introvert by nature, would I grow weary from socializing with a group of people every day?

Would we be able to relate to others in the group? Would there be a social hierarchy according to the size and cost of one's RV? Would there be some people who would want to spend money extravagantly so that we would feel pressure to keep up? Would we, who do not smoke or drink alcoholic beverages, be accepted as equals? Would we accept the others as equals?

A big question for me was whether we would travel on Sundays. I usually went to church on Sunday and observed the Sabbath for the most part as a day of rest and worship. Yet I knew that when traveling one had to accommodate to one's situation. Still, I wondered how the tour company would handle different religious affiliations and practices. Surely not everyone would belong to the Church of the Brethren as the Graybeals and we did. My questions would be answered in time.

Paul wrote a check for the final payment for the trip, which included the base price of $4,995 for two persons per rig and an additional $589 because of the length of our 34-foot Holiday Rambler® motorhome. The additional fee covered the cost for our longer RV to be carried on the Alaska Marine Highway ferry at one stage of the trip.

To reach the rendezvous site, Vancouver, British Columbia, the Graybeals and we would travel in our RVs from our homes in Maryland. As a former campground owner and veteran motorhomer, John planned a likely itinerary for the four of us to travel across the country. That travel plan would take us across the northern states and would include a stop at the Mall of America (Lib's and my enthusiastic input) in Minnesota and sightseeing in Montana's Glacier National Park.

The Graybeals invited us to their home (about five miles away from us near Manchester) to go over our plans and talk about the trip. Afterward, I notified Caravanas Voyagers® to send any mail for the four of us before May 27 because after that date we would be en route to Vancouver.

Using the tour company's information and his computer, John printed out a customized, detailed itinerary with telephone numbers, dates, and places so our families and friends would know where and when to reach us if necessary and to give them the fun of traveling vicariously with us. It also helped me to feel in touch with them when I was far away on the road knowing that they had some idea of where I was.

Since our route west started closer to our house, John and Lib planned to meet us on the morning of our migration at the end of our road, which intersects Route 140. From there we would go to Taneytown, a small town about ten miles northwest, where at the main traffic light we would turn southwest toward Frederick, Maryland, a large city that we would bypass, and soon afterward take a turnoff onto I-70 West, and begin our Alaskan pilgrimage.

To prepare for the trip, I followed a checklist that I had created when we bought our motorhome almost six years earlier. My checklist is formatted by categories: kitchen and dining area supplies and equipment, bathroom supplies and equipment, bedroom supplies and equipment, wardrobe accessories and equipment, handbag items, living room supplies and equipment, driving area supplies and equipment, and items to do before leaving home such as "Leave telephone numbers, addresses, and license plate number with Jeff," "Arrange with post office to forward mail," "Call neighbors on either side," and "Get groceries."

Paul's checklist also has categories: bathroom supplies and equipment, wardrobe accessories and equipment, driving area supplies and equipment, living room supplies and equipment, outside storage supplies and equipment, and items to do before leaving home. Some of these are "Check on gasoline for motorhome and tow car," "Check on propane gas," and "Obtain supply of oil for motorhome engine." Basically he checks all the systems of the vehicle to make sure they work and adds supplies as needed.

Using my list, I simply made sure we had a good supply of the items usually kept in the RV, such as paper napkins, bathroom tissue, and laundry detergent. In our bedroom in the house, I set up a folding clothes rack. As I made decisions and as I laundered clothes, I hung on the rack the blouses, pants, shirts, sweaters, and coats that I wanted to take along. I purposely kept them in the house until a day or two before we left so that I could see what I was taking and think about what I wanted to add.

In addition, we followed the instructions in the tour company materials. Paul and I checked with our health care insurance companies to learn what to do if we should need medical attention in Canada and Alaska.

A drop leaf table and straight chair in the living room near the front door of the house were unofficially designated as repositories for items going to the motorhome for the trip. Our motorhome was parked in its own driveway beside our house. We simply took along an armload whenever we walked out the front door and turned left onto the front pavement and around the corner of the house to the motorhome. (I must say that each time I stepped up into the motorhome with my cargo a thrill streaked through me—it was as if I were a modern Lewis or Clark about to set out on a journey of discovery. Sometimes I'd open my arms in a wide arc, breathing in deeply as if I were taking in fresh air in the springtime, then I'd relax and say out loud, "Hello, Motorhome! We'll soon be on the road again!" Just being inside the motorhome somehow sent my thoughts into a realm of freedom and adventure.)

Overall, we felt better prepared for this trip than previous ones. Following our first dream journey to Arizona three years earlier, Paul had installed two swing-arm wall lamps for brighter lighting inside the motorhome, an electric can opener, and an additional electric outlet for my laptop computer under the dashboard in front of the passenger seat.

For the Alaska trip, he assembled a small computer desk (which I painted ivory to match the decor) and fastened it to the carpeted floor just behind the passenger seat where a swivel easy chair had been. He also moved the dinette table two and a half inches toward the window to give more aisle space, which allowed us to pass one another at that place without cheek-to-cheek dancing. In addition, he ordered a special transmission overdrive unit and had it installed by a local RV dealership just in time for the trip. (The unit would cut down on the motorhome's appetite for gasoline and give it more zest for climbing hills.) We had not had time, however, to test it for leaks by taking it on a short jaunt before the long journey to Alaska.

Paul wanted the motorhome to be shipshape. He keeps a maintenance log and tries to change the oil and do other such tasks on the schedule recommended by the manufacturer. He handles immediately whatever problem comes up, although it sometimes takes a while to fix the problem permanently. He upgrades the quality of accessories in the motorhome, for instance, replacing the plastic bathroom sink with a porcelain one. He makes the RV more comfortable with such projects as renovating the bed platform base so that there is more toe space around it at the floor level. He grew frustrated when taking a shower from having to adjust the hot and cold water spigots and replaced them with a mixer valve that he could adjust with one twist of his hand. He did the same thing with the bathroom sink. The kitchen sink came equipped with a mixer valve.

His overall philosophy is to solve as many problems as possible himself—he learns more that way, he says. When he hits a snag, he reads, rereads, asks questions of people, and thinks about it until he gets to the bottom of the problem and simultaneously gains a thorough knowledge—whether it is of the motor or the auxiliary generator or the plumbing and electrical systems or any other part of the motorhome. And he does it all with the dignity, courtesy, and persistence of a Paul Newman.

The night before our departure, we slept in the motorhome so that we could pull away in the morning without the usual last-minute check of the house. Also, I could transfer breakfast foodstuffs like milk, bread, and cereal from the house to the motorhome the evening before and eliminate that last-minute rush in the morning.

Before the Alaska trip, Paul and I had always traveled as solo RVers. Now we would be going across the country with another couple and later on, after our rendezvous in Vancouver, with a larger caravan. My mind murmured continuous questions, all related to how the trip's people, places, and the tour itself would soon unfold.

· 2 ·

Traveling Cross-Country

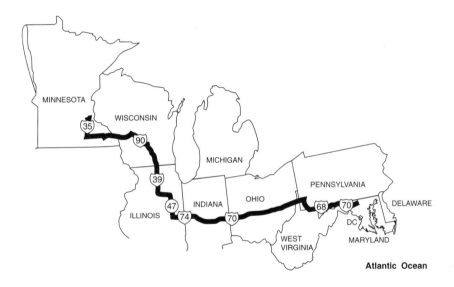

"THEY'RE LEAVING in three minutes!" Paul announced as he hung up the telephone in our motorhome on Friday morning, May 28. "They" were friends Lib and John Graybeal with whom we were about to set out on a cross-country journey in our two motorhomes.

We would travel from our homes in Maryland to a campground in Vancouver, British Columbia, where we would rendezvous with other, unknown RVers for a six-week, tour-guide-led, caravan odyssey to Alaska. All of my pre-trip questions now would begin to find answers.

Paul and I would have 3,445 miles and about 15 days to practice and test our caravaning abilities before we reached Vancouver. This would be our first caravan with the Graybeals.

Lib grew up on a dairy farm, as I did. We both graduated from New Windsor High School, she as a member of the class of 1945 and I a year earlier. Lib's family's farm was located along the Uniontown Road that led from Westminster to Uniontown, Maryland. My family's farm was several miles away and off of Springdale Road, which ran from the Uniontown Road to the small but old town of New Windsor, Maryland. Different yellow school buses took Lib and me to New Windsor High School, which had one homeroom for each grade of high school. Pupils changed classes according to whether they took the academic, commercial, or general course. For a few years following high school, we both worked for the local gas and electric company. Then our paths went in different directions for many years, yet we greeted one another happily at special events that brought us together.

Both Lib and John lost their first spouses through death. Miraculously, they combined her four and his three children and their ten grandchildren into a loving unit. They talked openly and lovingly about their former spouses, yet their love for one another shone brightly in the way they related to each other. John was a former principal and supervisor with the public school system. After early retirement, being excellent with math, he became a volunteer income-tax preparer for senior citizens in the area. He had also previously designed and built his own successful campground, no small feat, and was a member of the Campground Owners Association, serving as a director on its board.

John and Lib attended the same Westminster Church of the Brethren that Paul and I did. They were already veteran RVers and a vital part of the church camping group when we joined it. They had traveled to Alaska once before with another couple, making their way on their own. This time John wanted to experience going with a tour company guide. Paul and I had never been to Alaska and would not have attempted it on our own.

Traveling Cross-Country

Paul had retired from the Chesapeake and Potomac Telephone Company of Maryland (later Bell Atlantic-MD) as a long-distance technician. His interests lay in electronics, mechanics, woodworking, land genealogy, and motorhoming.

At 7:39 A.M., with the house locked, the door to our motorhome locked, and both of us in our seats watching for traffic, Paul steered out of our driveway and swung the coach into the right-hand lane of the country road that went past our house. As we descended the hill toward Route 140, I wondered excitedly how it would be to caravan. What if our friends wanted to stop at a place of interest and we didn't, or vice versa? Or what if they wanted to start out in the morning at a time that we didn't, or vice versa? The trip from Maryland to Vancouver would be just a sample of what might happen on the later Alaskan quest.

At the bottom of the hill, we parked well off the road in a vacant lot. We waited only a few moments before we saw the familiar, 34-foot, green-and-white Pinnacle belonging to the Graybeals gliding toward us on Route 140 and then parking on the right shoulder of the road. Lib and I smiled broadly as we waved to one another from our passenger seats.

"Do you want to take the lead?" John asked over the citizen's band (CB) radio.

This could be a problem, I thought—would they both want to lead or follow? Then I heard Paul say, "I'll give it a try," and we pulled onto the highway with the Graybeals behind us. We always kept enough space between the RVs so that other vehicles wanting to pass did not have to try to pass two motorhomes at one clip.

"We're on our way!" I said. Paul accelerated toward the 55-mile-per-hour speed limit. Our two RVs headed for Taneytown.

How smoothly the "lead" question was handled! Perhaps later on we would switch and the Graybeals would lead. Perhaps the compatibility of the moment would be the touchstone for the trip.

At Taneytown we turned left toward Frederick, which we bypassed, and soon found ourselves on I-70. On that interstate, we rode past lush green trees and brush of blooming honeysuckle on the

13

roadsides near Hagerstown, Maryland, as we headed for Zanesville, Ohio, our first overnight. That would be followed by subsequent stays at campgrounds in Illinois, Wisconsin, Minnesota, North Dakota, Montana, Idaho, and Washington. Our itinerary called for a major stop of three days at the Mall of America in Minnesota, the second largest shopping mall in North America, and a swing around the southern rim of Glacier National Park in Montana.

Having adjusted to the process on previous trips, I typed into my laptop computer as we rode along. On the carpeted hump (covering the engine of the motorhome) to my left lay a clothbound journal. On my right was an orange mechanical lead pencil easily available in a section of a brown cup holder hanging from the window frame. Sometimes it was handier to use the pencil and journal to jot down notes.

In addition, I kept a record of the nitty-gritty information such as date, odometer reading, weather, time, places stopped, items bought, and gasoline purchased. For this I had created a chart on legal-sized paper, made a lot of copies, and fastened them into a tablet. I kept that trip log handy by placing it on top of the television set that was to my left on the carpeted hump.

But for the moment, I sat in the tan plush-upholstered passenger seat with the computer on a turkish towel on my lap. In front of me was the tan vinyl dashboard with its ample glove compartment and a huge windshield. Above the windshield and high across the inside front of the motorhome were two oak, roll-top storage cabinets. Near the center of the front, hanging from the bottom of the cabinets, were the rear view monitor and the CB radio and microphone.

Paul sat behind the adjustable steering wheel and a bevy of instrument panel dials, some of which he had installed himself, including a tachometer, transmission oil temperature gauge, and vacuum gauge. His chair matched the passenger's; both were adjustable electrically. To his left was an exit door that led to outside ladder-like rungs on the side of the motorhome used to reach the street.

Behind us was the living room, which contained a three-cushion sofa, convertible to a bed, that was covered in a soft blue tapestry material with a dainty pink/peach design. Across from the sofa was a small computer desk and a tan plush upholstered chair on a metal pedestal that allowed the seat to swivel. On both sides, above the windows, were oak storage cabinets.

The entry door, with one step inside, was located between the living room area and the kitchen on the curb side of the vehicle. Across from the kitchen counter, which had oak cabinets above it, was the dinette table. It comfortably held place settings for four people. Bench seats with detachable pillows in the same blue tapestry as the sofa completed the dining area.

On the curb side next to the kitchen counter was a gas stove with slide-out pantry drawers beneath and a microwave/convection oven above. Adjacent to the kitchen were four wardrobe closets, floor to ceiling, which formed part of the center hallway that led to the rear bedroom. A queen-sized bed, whose platform could be lifted up for storage, dominated the space. How glad I was that Paul had earlier renovated the bedroom and provided easy access to the large area under the platform. We found this extra storage space handy for storing folding chairs and tables and other bulky objects.

Paul also created more walking and toe room around the three sides of the bed, which made moving about in the bedroom less awkward. At the head of the bed was a large, four-paneled, beveled glass mirror, which added sparkle and spaciousness to the area. End tables with cabinets beneath fit into the corners on either side of the bed and were handy for tissues, a traveling clock, and on mine, a journal. Above the mirror on the rear wall hung closets in which we kept extra bed linens. Large windows with both Venetian blinds and lined draperies flanked the bedroom. We usually kept these blinds and draperies closed, even when traveling during the day.

In front of the rear bedroom on the street side was the bathroom. It contained a wash basin, a combination tub/shower, and a toilet on a carpeted platform. The faucets were the ones installed by Paul. What satisfaction that project has brought him. He loves comfort!

Next door to the bathroom on the street side was the refrigerator/freezer. It held a week's supply of groceries. Adjacent to the refrigerator toward the front of the motorhome was the dinette.

Stretching the length of the motorhome from below the front carpeted engine cover (the "hump") to the bedroom was a tan and gray tweed aisle runner. We had laid it, holding it in place with double-sided tape, over the tan carpet that came with the vehicle as protection for the carpet. That preserved the carpet's newness that eventually some new owner will appreciate.

The outside of the motorhome was cream-colored, smooth aluminum siding. Spanning its length on both sides was a broad stripe of silver, red, white, and blue.

As we headed west on that first morning out, a station wagon stuffed full of suitcases and travel gear passed us.

"Remember when you used to travel in a station wagon that was filled up like that one?" Paul said to John over the CB.

Over the CB, John told us how he and his young family had traveled like that for several years before they bought their first motorhome. Paul responded by CB with his own story of a four-week trip we took to the West Coast with our teenage son, Jeff. Paul had to get up early to unpack and repack things after staying in a motel or tenting at a campground.

"I think today's pace is a little bit better," concluded John, referring to traveling by motorhome.

Traveling on, we left I-70 about 30 miles west of Hagerstown when it turned due north into Pennsylvania and we continued instead on I-68, which went west. After about two hours, we were ready for a travel break and pulled into the Sideling Hill Exhibit Center beside I-68. In the May sunshine, a Maryland ranger stood outside talking about a live exhibit of birds, a turtle, and snakes. As I passed the ranger and walked over to the main exhibition building, I heard flapping overhead and bird cries. A black buzzard that had been tethered to a post had freed itself. It flew to the nearby balcony of the exhibit building, its tether dangling as it perched.

Through my video camera, I watched as the ranger leaped across an open area that was about 35 feet above a concrete apron. Once on the balcony, he rescued and recaptured the bird.

Traveling Cross-Country

"[At Sideling Hill] in the parking lot, we snapped our first photographs of ourselves in front of our two motorhomes." (L-R: John, Lib, and Paul)

The crisis over, I caught up with Paul, Lib, and John inside the building and shared their fascination with exhibits of the geology of Sideling Hill as well as mounted animals, such as the black bear, fox, turkey, and beaver, native to Maryland.

Back in the parking lot, we snapped our first photographs of ourselves in front of our two motorhomes.

Our interlude lasted only a half-hour; then we were back on the road. Soon we were driving through the beautiful Appalachian Mountains, headed toward Morgantown, West Virginia. When we stopped for lunch in our coaches at a truck stop, the parking lot was so dusty that only Paul ventured outside to check the tires and see if all appeared to be in order with the motorhome. Conscientious person that he is, he voluntarily retrieved the whisk broom from under the skirt of the chair beside the entry and swept the dust from himself before stepping inside.

During our afternoon drive, to keep from getting stodgy, I got up from the passenger seat several times to get a soda for us or do whatever tasks came to mind. It kept my circulation going. I had learned a long time ago that inactivity causes lactic acid to accumulate in the body, which in turn causes fatigue.

As Lib and I talked over the CB, she said she had brought along four books to read and was into one already (although she never read while riding along). I had brought magazines I wanted to get caught up on.

She also said she wanted to lose weight during the trip (not that she needed to in my opinion), whereas I hoped not to add to my 123 pounds. Alas, I knew not what delicious temptations awaited!

After going through a long traffic backup on I-70 and driving all afternoon, we turned into the KOA® Kampground at Zanesville, Ohio, at 5:13 P.M. John had made reservations weeks earlier because it was Memorial Day weekend. We had driven 364 miles our first day on the road.

Relieved not to have suitcases to carry into a motel, Paul soon hooked up the motorhome to water and electricity. To hook up to water, he simply retrieved the water hose from the outside compartment on the street side, screwed one end to the receiver at the motorhome and the other end to the spigot at the campground. He carried an extra length of hose for those times when the water supply was farther away than one white hose would reach.

To hook up to the electricity, he pulled the heavy black electric cord from its outside storage compartment at the rear of the motorhome and plugged it into the campground outlet—as simple as plugging in an electric toaster! He also carried an extra heavy-duty extension cord just in case the main cord wasn't long enough.

With our refrigerators full, it was a given that we would dine at our own tables that evening. Later, as John and Paul were outside checking tires and generally looking at our vehicles, they agreed to start out about 7:30 the next morning. I totaled the columns of my nitty-gritty trip log chart for the first day on the road (Spent Today, Spent to Date, Miles Today, Miles to Date) and wrote in my journal, while Paul relaxed on the sofa in front of the television. Tired from the excitement of the first day's travel and with another full day coming up, we headed to bed early.

Traveling Cross-Country

Our second day out, we drove from Zanesville, Ohio, across Indiana to Mahomet, Illinois. As we made our way across Indiana, for a while we became part of the heavy traffic headed toward Indianapolis for the Indy 500 speedway races that weekend—a famous Memorial Day event.

Then we left I-70, went around the north side of Indianapolis to I-65, and took a shortcut on Route 32 that led us westward to I-74. On that shortcut, young corn plants grew in long rows in level fields. Other level fields appeared to be disc plowed and seeded. Cows stood knee-deep in fields of abundant grass. The farms looked productive and successful.

As we passed a church on that Memorial Day weekend, people lingered at a grave site. White peonies along the outside border of the cemetery bloomed in bursting fullness. At another cemetery, pink peonies and other flowers, cut and placed in containers, decorated grave sites. Two men walked among the tombstones, hands in their pockets, heads up, looking for familiar names beyond where they stepped.

We drove on—my eyes scanned green and brown fields. Signs said Do Not Pass on the two-lane road, but almost no traffic came our way. That state route (32) was the kind of escape that a traveler longs for to relieve the pressures of crowded interstate driving and to regain serenity.

"You get a little more flavor on this than you do on the interstate," John said on the CB.

"Oh, this is pretty. I really do appreciate this. It takes away all the frustration of the interstate. This is true flavor, I think. There are nice-looking homes along here. I mean people really care. They mow out along the road here," said Paul.

Too soon, it seemed, we turned onto I-74 and left the peaceful, intimate countryside. Although planted fields extended on either side of the dual-lane interstate, the busyness of the highway took away from the sense of communing with nature.

At 4:36 P.M., after 383 miles, we pulled into Tincup Campers Park, Mahomet, Illinois. We ate dinner in our motorhomes and then did what a lot of campers enjoy: explored the camp store, laughing as we met one another there.

"Would you like to take a walk?" I asked Lib. After riding all day, it seemed like a good idea. So she and I walked for exercise on the campground road while Paul and John discussed what time we would leave the campground the next morning. In our planning session at the Graybeals' before the trip started, we easily agreed that leaving about eight o'clock most mornings would be comfortable all around. We knew, however, that some mornings we'd want to get an earlier start or relax and leave later. So each evening, we checked with each other to confirm our departure time.

It must have been during that conversation that Paul told John that he (Paul) had placed cash in his shoe for safekeeping and that he wanted someone else besides me to know about it. (On later trips, he carried less cash and used more debit card purchases.) Paul and John both had a good laugh as Paul said, "If something happens to me, be sure they give my shoes to my wife!"

The next day, Sunday, we rode on Route 47 heading north through the corn belt of Illinois. Our travel goal for that day was De Forest, Wisconsin. As we drove on the almost lonely country road, I felt glad we were traveling with another couple. Traveling in twos gave me a feeling of safety and security that I had not expected.

We passed another lavishly decorated cemetery on that Memorial Day weekend. A warm glow came over me as I thought of the love of the people placing flowers on the graves of their families and friends. That love seemed to flow out to me from the profuse red, pink, and white blooms. Never before had I been so touched by love just from seeing flowers in a cemetery. It made me realize that although my mother was cremated, I continued to think of her and honor and love her. It reaffirmed my own decision for cremation and my belief that the form in which a person was buried had not a whit to do with the love of one's family and friends.

As we traveled the countryside with its vastness and serenity on that Sunday morning, I gave thanks, silently, for the many blessings

Traveling Cross-Country

we experienced. Giving thanks seemed especially important on that day set aside for worship and rest.

We set our watches to central daylight time, except for Lib, who had her own policy of never changing the time on her watch.

After traveling north on Route 47, west on Routes 17 and 18, we turned north again onto I-39, which blended into I-90. It was raining when we pulled into the Kampground of America (KOA) at De Forest, Wisconsin, in mid-afternoon (2:48 P.M.). We parked our RVs side by side.

By nightfall, the intermittent rain on the roof of the motorhome brought a sense of coziness as we stayed inside. Paul read a newspaper that he'd bought earlier at the camp store and I wrote in my cloth journal; both of us watched television.

Overnight, the thermometer dipped to a chilly 46 degrees and skies were overcast. To cope on that Monday morning, May 31, I put on a warm aqua-colored sweat suit.

"I'm going to wear my rain jacket. It really cuts the wind. There's a real breeze blowing out there! That wind chill factor is *low!*" Paul said.

Paul put on gloves and a yellow slicker when he went outside to take our trash to the trash bin and to disconnect the black electric cord from the campground outlet. With enough freshwater in our tank for overnight use, Paul had not bothered to hook up to water at the campground spigot the previous night.

As we were about to pull away from the campsite, I looked across and waved good morning to Lib, who sat in the passenger seat holding a cup of coffee. She wore a white "grandchildren" sweatshirt. It sported red apple designs with the names of her ten grandchildren written in white on them.

We headed for Backstretch RV Park at Shakopee, Minnesota, southwest of Minneapolis, where we planned to stay three nights.

Lib and I had to see the new Mall of America, the largest in the United States and second in size in the world only to the Edmonton Mall in Canada. It was advertised as the nation's largest fully integrated retail/entertainment complex, featuring Bloomingdale's, Macy's, Nordstrom, and Sears plus hundreds of specialty shops.

Knott's Camp Snoopy, a seven-acre theme park, featured over 23 rides and attractions, 15 food venues, and specialty stores. The first Lego Imagination Center; a two-level, 14-screen General Cinema; and over 40 restaurants and nightclubs, including America Live, Gatlin Music City Grill, Fat Tuesdays, Knuckleheads Comedy Club, and more, were part of this grand attraction. The Mall also offered over 13,000 free parking spaces, ample bus and RV parking, group tours, information centers, and helpful guides. Lib and I could hardly wait to tackle it!

"How do you feel this morning?" I asked Paul as we rode along.

"Not too bad. I mean, I really don't feel totally rested yet."

"Why not?" I asked.

"I hardly ever get caught up. That's just my makeup," he said. "I've been that way most of my life and I really don't expect it to change."

The morning travel on the divided highway in Wisconsin was uneventful except for seeing two instances where state troopers had stopped cars and another instance of an anxious pheasant trying to walk across the road. We moved on into Minnesota with scenic farmland and great acreage but, unlike Illinois's level fields, on gently rolling terrain. Cumulus clouds seemed to stand still beneath the blue sky. Several herds of cows lay down in their pastures.

"Anybody need this rest area up ahead?" asked Paul over the CB. We continued to be the lead vehicle.

"No, we're probably all right," responded John on the CB.

"Okay. I'll keep on going, then," replied Paul, as he laid the CB microphone on the dash. CB communication worked great between our two motorhomes. We used channel 13 to keep in touch with each other.

That evening, at Backstretch RV Park in Shakopee, Minnesota, Paul put on his long, gray-striped denim coat, which he had inherited from his father. It looked like an old-fashioned duster. He shoved himself under the motorhome to add transmission oil to the overdrive unit. He had discovered a leak earlier that day when we made a fuel stop. Taking the bull by the horns, he had immediately arranged to have the unit examined and repaired at a service center in Coeur

Traveling Cross-Country

d'Alene, Idaho, next Tuesday, eight days away, when we expected to be in that area.

During that same afternoon as we drove along, John saw steam coming out from under the front of our motorhome on the driver's side, where the motor is located. Over the CB he told Paul, who immediately pulled off the road. As Paul and John looked under the hood at the front of the vehicle, they saw that the radiator hose had come off. Paul soon replaced and reclamped the hose to the radiator and we were on our way again.

Having mechanical trouble on the road was unusual for us. Prior to traveling, Paul worked on maintaining our motorhome, as well as upgrading it and making it more comfortable. He enjoyed learning about how the motorhome worked. I was thankful for his interest, knowledge, and persistence in keeping the motorhome in good shape. Unlike many people, Paul believed in correcting the minor things before they became major. That kind of work may seem tedious to others, but I knew it paid off in the long run.

The newly installed transmission overdrive unit began leaking transmission oil the fourth day on the road. (We later learned the leak was caused by a rough area on the metal overdrive output shaft that abraded the rubber seal.) Each evening after that, Paul would "scrooch" himself under the motorhome and refill the unit with transmission oil until we got to Idaho, where the unit would be serviced by a certified transmission overdrive technician.

"Give me a few more paper towels, honey," I heard Paul say in a muffled voice from beneath the coach.

I snapped them from the roll above the kitchen counter, went outside the motorhome, and stooped way over with my head almost touching the ground. When I did so, I saw an outstretched hand dripping with pale red liquid.

"Is that blood?" I asked.

"No," Paul laughed. "It's just transmission fluid." He took the towels and continued to check the fluid level. The two mechanical problems to date—a radiator leak and the transmission oil leak—were under control, thanks to Paul's diligence.

John and Lib were both patient and supportive. I told them how much we appreciated their understanding. "You would have done the same thing for us," Lib said.

Earlier on the trip, John's new motorhome developed its own problem with the mud flaps going forward over the tires instead of hanging behind them. He had tried tying the flaps to the understructure of the motorhome, but they continued to wear against the fender guard. That Monday he decided to remove them completely.

So much for the problems. We were there to see the mall!

The next day, Tuesday, June 1, it was cold but sunny as the four of us boarded the Graybeals' Pinnacle. John drove us to the famed Mall of America, where he parked in an adjoining lot. As we walked up a ramp from the garage level to an upper level, I asked Lib if she thought she and John would want to go to Barrow. She said they would talk about it, of course, but she was not sure. She was not keen on flying in what might be a "puddle-jumper."

Feeling like tiny ants in the spacious mall interior with its high-domed central hub, Lib and I each optimistically bought a $1 Mall of America shopping bag. Then pairing off with our spouses, we decided to meet for lunch at 12:30 at a food court on the third level of the great mall.

Paul and I went searching for things on the list I had been compiling since well before leaving home. In Bloomingdale's third-floor domestics department, he sat on a wooden ledge while I looked for cotton towels for him. (He's allergic to polyester.) When I asked him which of two washcloths he preferred, he said, "I'd like one that's not too bulky. This one would be all right."

By the time we rejoined the Graybeals at 12:30 for lunch, we had explored Bloomingdale's and several specialty shops, as our packages attested. As we ate in the food court, the screams of people on amusement rides in the adjacent Camp Snoopy punctuated our conversations.

After more shopping in the afternoon and marveling at the cavernous rotunda and all of the offerings for amusement, entertainment, and shopping, we returned to the campground.

24

Traveling Cross-Country

"As we ate in the food court [at the Mall of America], the screams of people on amusement rides in the adjacent Camp Snoopy punctuated our conversations." (L-R: Paul, John, and Lib)

"I don't think we'll need to walk tonight," laughed Lib. My feet and I agreed. Besides, Lib and I were going to the mall again the next day.

Lib and I took the shuttle from the campground for another turn at the mall on Wednesday morning, June 2. We decided to each go our own way in the morning, meet for lunch, and shop together in the afternoon.

My first stop was a Regis hairstylist, which I had scouted out the day before, where a young woman shampooed and blow-dried my hair. During previous trips, I had come to depend on the experienced stylists in Regis salons, which are in many malls across the country.

When Lib and I shopped together that afternoon, we each bought a pair of linen pants, white for me and black for Lib. That was the extent of my purchases that day, whereas Lib bought some other clothes.

Back at the campground, I asked Paul, "Would you like to take us out to dinner somewhere around here where there's parking space for the motorhome?"

"Yes, that would be a good idea. It'll give me a chance to see how the motorhome behaves." He had taken it to a nearby RV service center that day to have the upper radiator hose connection repaired.

And so about 5:30, the four of us pulled into the parking lot of Dangerfield's, off Route 101. Paul parked our motorhome near a black stretch limousine.

"People come here in everything from a motorcycle to a motorhome," I commented as we walked past all the vehicles toward the restaurant.

The four of us sat relaxed beside a window that overlooked the backwater of a river. Soon a slim, nimble waiter came over to our table. In formal attire, including white shirt and green bow tie, he was every inch the correct butler one sees on television. I thought of my cousin Frank, no longer living, who both looked and acted like this man. I wonder what *his* name is, I mused about the waiter.

"Would you like cocktails or something to drink?" he asked.

"No, thank you," we all replied to the cocktail portion of his question. Then John ordered two iced teas and the waiter turned to leave.

"What is the blue plate special?" I asked, having seen it mentioned in the menu.

"That's over at 5:30," he said quickly.

"But it says on the menu 6:00 P.M." I countered.

He looked at my menu. "Oh, let me check," and away he went as fast and agilely as he had first appeared. He was soon back again.

"It's barbecued ribs, mashed potatoes, and veggies. I'll be back to take your order." And away he went again.

Something about him—perhaps the gray hair combed straight back and a small white mustache or perhaps his focus on his job—made me think that he must be a retiree in a second career. I knew that many retirees diverted their energies into a new field.

When he came to take our order, he started with me.

"I'd like the seafood stir-fry entree," and he wrote it down.

And then I asked, "Does the seafood have monosodium glutamate in it?" I had found that the preservative MSG gave me a headache.

"What?" he asked quickly, cocking his head toward me.

"Does it have—"

He interrupted, without smiling, and said with a Mr. Belvedere–dryness. "We can put some Geritol in it for you. How would that be?"

Laughing hard, I said, "That would be *great!*"

By the end of the meal, I looked for an opening to ask his name—somehow I wanted it to be Frank like my cousin. John and Paul paid the checks in one of those leather folders and our fleet-of-foot, taciturn friend returned to our table with the change. As he turned to leave for the final time, I asked him directly, "What is your first name?"

"John," he said with an arched eyebrow.

"I thought it would be Frank," I said.

He gulped.

"My wife's writing a book and you'll probably be in it," Paul tried to explain away my question.

"I hope it's x-rated. That'll give me something to live for!" he said victoriously. He turned on his heels and was gone, having had the last word and leaving us laughing.

What did not leave us laughing was the leaking transmission fluid in the motorhome and Paul's having to refill it every night after a day of travel. That was the first time that we had had such a constant problem with the motorhome. I hoped it wouldn't continue the whole trip. It could spoil everything.

· 3 ·

Getting Groceries

HOLSTEINS LAY contentedly in meadows of tall grass, chewing their cud, no doubt. From our two-vehicle caravan, we saw hundreds of acres of farmland on either side of the divided highway, I-94, in Minnesota on that Thursday morning, June 3. Stretching to the distant horizon, some of the fields were covered with young green leafy plants that I couldn't identify. Tall silos and farm buildings met the baby blue sky with its low-floating puffs of white clouds.

Only the steady thump of our wheels going over bulging seams of the concrete highway disturbed the peaceful, pastoral scene. And then as he drove, Paul noticed that our cruise control no longer worked.

"I can fix that," he said. "It's probably the dump valve." It was the leak in the transmission overdrive unit that really baffled and nagged at him.

It was at a Perkins Family Restaurant that Paul's usual beverage order received the label "clear coffee" from John. By four o'clock that Thursday, we had registered at the Grand Forks Campground, North Dakota. Shortly afterward, the four of us traveled in the Pinnacle to the Columbia Mall and to the Perkins Family Restaurant.

Getting Groceries

To appreciate what I'm about to tell you, you need to know something about Paul. He drinks ordinary hot water, usually heated in the microwave about two minutes, to which he adds cream or skim milk and two packs of granulated sugar per cup. He always drinks it at breakfast at home.

When we go to a restaurant, he orders it saying, "Hot water, just plain hot water, with cream and sugar, please." Usually the server looks unbelieving, so Paul adds, "Just bring me hot tea without the tea bag." He has both baffled and educated countless servers in restaurants by this strange request.

His mother-in-law (my dear mother) and his digestive system got him into the habit. My mother always drank hot water instead of anything stronger. She sometimes called it "contentment," sometimes "Cambridge tea," but mostly just plain "hot water." Paul began drinking it when we still lived at my home during the first six months of our marriage. He continued to drink it because the doctor told him he would be better off staying away from caffeine. Even decaffeinated coffee disagreed with him.

During the preceding days of that trip Paul, as usual, had ordered "hot water" with his meals in restaurants. John and Lib took it all in stride, laughing with us at the reactions of the servers.

That night at dinner at the Perkins Family Restaurant, Paul ordered his usual hot water. The waitress, after the usual hesitation and acceptance, brought him an insulated carafe filled with it. Paul prepared several enjoyable cups during his dinner.

While we waited for the waitress to clear the table so we could order some of the delicious-looking strawberry pie that we had seen on the way in, Lib said, "I notice that this nonsmoking section is crowded whereas the smoking section has hardly anyone in it."

We all looked through the etched-glass divider and confirmed her observation. The conversation then went from the airlines being one of the first businesses to ban smoking to the Amish growing tobacco to sell but not using it and to other inconsistencies, which led to Paul's comment: "And now we have *clear* things like clear soap, clear beer—"

"Clear coffee!" quipped John, referring to Paul's hot water. We all laughed and laughed. After that, Paul started asking for "clear coffee." Alas, the servers thought that he meant decaffeinated coffee. So Paul was back where he started, but from then on, the rest of us thought of his hot water as clear coffee.

We kept migrating west. From Grand Forks, North Dakota, we moved steadily across the state on U.S. 2 to Williston, also in North Dakota, where we camped at Buffalo Trails Campground on Friday, June 4. The next day, Saturday, June 5, we continued on U.S. 2 rolling along in northern Montana through the Great Plains. From the radio a classical piece by a string ensemble wafted above the motor and road noise. The big sky folded its gargantuan arms around us. Against the horizon lay acres and acres of short grass on which cattle grazed, replacing the buffalo of older times. Occasional white crosses planted beside the highway reminded us of traffic fatalities at those places.

"Oh, my. What a tragedy that must have been!" I said as we passed four white crosses beside one another. "They were just over that brow of the hill. Maybe somebody was trying to pass on the hill."

I thought of the possible victims and how life goes away, and I wondered fleetingly when our turn would come. But for now, like the road itself, we went on. I would try to apply the lesson and drive carefully. Paul always drives gently, looking ahead, usually braking in plenty of time. He remembers well the routes and towns from reading the map the night before.

With the road easy to maneuver on, we drove with dark blue-black clouds facing us, rain spattering the windshield, the sun shining over my shoulder, and behind us, white-gray clouds hanging low under the light blue sky. What the terrain lacked in change, the weather made up for.

After 448 miles, a very long day's travel for us, we reached Shelby, Montana, where we registered at the Lewis and Clark RV Court. It was after six o'clock. With steak being a favorite of John and Lib's and eating out being a favorite of ours, we dined at a local steakhouse.

Getting Groceries

On Sunday morning, June 6, we continued crossing Montana on U.S. 2 and arrived at East Glacier Park, the eastern gateway to the spectacular Glacier National Park. It was about 50 degrees and sunny. We drove along the southern edge of the park over the Continental Divide and Marias Pass, elevation 5,216 feet, up mountain slopes and down to valley floors. In the distance we could see mountains of even higher elevations, some with snow on them. Where we traveled, lush green bushes, pines, and deciduous trees grew next to one another on steep hillsides; two white-tailed deer disappeared among the trees; little creeks and rivulets, clear aqua, flowed energetically alongside the road; blue wildflowers bloomed on roadside banks; and large patches of white Indian pipes inhabited glens.

On a morning when we would normally be in church, I wrote a prayer of thanksgiving in my journal as we drove through that inspiring green passageway of trees, mountains, and brooks. Even the undersides of leaves blowing in the breeze sparkled in the sunshine. I was thankful for that scenic feast and for the loving care that went with it.

We arrived at West Glacier, the main western entrance to the park, where we ate an early lunch and got information on where to go next. From there, we drove to the visitor center at Apgar, deeper inside Glacier National Park. We visited the store and walked around the grounds. I watched a small group of people feeding prairie dogs until a park ranger told them that it was against the rules to feed the animals in the park.

In a quiet moment, Paul sat on the shore beside Lake McDonald looking around with his binoculars. "Old Man and the Sea," quipped Lib.

John drove us in their motorhome on the beginning section of Going-to-the-Sun Road, which winds across the width of the mountainous park. We knew that vehicles longer than 21 feet were restricted from traveling on major portions of that road as it climbed higher into the mountains. After driving through a wooded area adjacent to Lake McDonald, we turned around at McDonald Lodge, went back to Apgar where Paul and I had parked our motorhome, and resumed our day's journey together.

By evening we had arrived at the KOA in Troy, Montana, almost on the border with Idaho. I used the microwave oven to thaw and reheat frozen dinners that I had prepared at home and brought along. After a quiet dinner, I did my usual trip-log tallies and wrote postcards. I got inspired and baked and frosted a German chocolate microwave cake from a box mix that I had bought that day in a store at the West Glacier Park entrance. It was almost nine o'clock when I took Lib and John each a piece. Then I joined Paul in watching television.

On Monday, it was a short drive to Post Falls, Idaho, where we registered for two nights at Suntree RV Park. We received campsites side by side, our usual request. And wonder of wonders, just across the highway from the campground was a factory outlet shopping center. Lib and I spent the whole afternoon there.

Meanwhile, Paul talked both by telephone and in person with the technician in nearby Coeur d'Alene who would be working on the overdrive unit of the motorhome the next day at one o'clock. Back in Post Falls, Paul bought a distributor cap as a spare at a Chevrolet dealership. At some point that afternoon, Paul and John each washed our motorhomes in the large truck facility at the campground.

Later that evening, Lib and John knocked at our motorhome door. Smiling broadly, Lib wanted John to see what I had bought for Paul at the Famous Brands Store that afternoon. I had purchased a unique item just for the fun of it—a white plastic plunger tool with four tiny wire claws that protruded when the plunger was pushed in. It was about the size and shape of a click ballpoint pen except the wire prongs at the point end were about an inch long when extended.

"Do you know what that is?" I asked John, who is a whiz at figuring out things.

He proceeded to push the plunger and to study it. Libby asked, "Do you know the name of it?"

"You pick up something with it," he mused.

"What did you put on my plate?" she tried to help, apparently referring to something during their evening meal.

Getting Groceries

"Pickles—it's something to pick up pickles?" he guessed.

"From a jar," I said. "It's a picker, er, er," I stammered.

"A pickle picker," Lib, John, and Paul said in unison.

John began a litany of alliteration. In the end someone said, "It's Paul's pickle picker-upper," and we all exploded with laughter. After more conversation about our afternoon's purchases and what we would each do the next day, the Graybeals went next door to their motorhome.

Paul and I were both tired and went to bed early, sometime after nine o'clock. It was the first evening he had not felt obligated to crawl under the motorhome to check the transmission overdrive unit and to add transmission oil. The next day was his appointment to get it fixed.

During the next morning, Tuesday, June 8, at the campground, Paul and I went through our usual morning routine of getting our own breakfasts. Each of us always ate a bowl of cereal with fruit and skim milk and drank a cup of hot water. We may not eat at the same time, but we always fixed the same menu for ourselves.

When I retired from Western Maryland College, an independent liberal arts institution, Paul was already retired. We fell into a routine of getting our own breakfast and lunch or supper, with me preparing the main meal of the day and Paul doing the dishes for that meal. Because we had different projects and schedules, that flexibility worked well for us.

On the road, that routine was modified according to whether Paul was driving, in which case I often prepared both lunch and the main meal and we usually did the dishes together. Paul had no hang-ups about doing dishes or about making the bed. On the road, we seldom got up at the same time because only one of us could use the bathroom at a time. After we were both up, at some point we usually made the queen-sized bed together. That task was much easier for two people to do together than for one to maneuver several times around the bed in order to get the linens and bedspread just right. (On our earlier trip to Arizona, we had resolved the question of whether to pull the bedspread straight over the pillows, as Paul liked to do, or to tuck it under the pillows for a *House Beautiful* look, as I preferred. One morning he surprised me by leading off with the way I liked and we have been making the bed that way ever since.) And with a view of the bedroom from the front of the coach (unless we closed the folding door), we always made the bed as soon as possible.

That same morning, I did the laundry at the nearby women's shower room that also contained washers and dryers. When I returned, Paul surprised me by having set up the computer and printer at the small computer desk he had installed prior to the trip. He had also retrieved a wood-slatted folding chair from beneath the lift-up bed. And so I did my favorite thing, writing in the computer journal, updating and printing out what was going on with us.

About 9:30 A.M., Lib and John pulled out slowly from their site, happily smiling and waving to us as they headed out to play golf, one of their favorite activities. They had a 10:24 A.M. tee-off time. It was a cloudy, windy day, and I hoped it would be better by the time they got on the course.

Paul read *USA Today* at the dinette table while I pecked away at the computer center. Even with traffic on nearby I-90, it was quiet inside our coach. Leaves moved vigorously on the maple trees that shaded our campsite. It was a nice, peaceful campground.

A red light appeared on the laptop computer. I discovered that although the computer was plugged into the surge protector, the surge protector was not plugged into electricity. I had been typing all morning on battery power. Had I lost everything?

Immediately, I plugged in the surge protector and turned its toggle switch to On. Seconds seemed like minutes. Finally, the green power light appeared on the computer. A close call! I would not have wanted to repeat all that I had put into my journal that morning—I couldn't have. Another lesson: check to be sure the surge protector serving the computer is plugged into electricity.

At the service center in Coeur d'Alene about one o'clock, the technician directed Paul to drive the motorhome about halfway into a work bay in the building. I stayed inside the coach while Paul stood

Getting Groceries

around outside watching. Using hydraulic jacks, the serviceman raised the front end of the motorhome about 14 inches. Since the inside of the motorhome was dark at the front end, I walked downhill to the rear bedroom and opened the curtains for light. That part remained outside the building. Sitting on the bed, tilted of course, I began editing one of the journal entries I had printed out earlier in the day.

Meanwhile, the technician removed the drive shaft, the emergency brake drum, and the old seal; looked to be sure of where it was leaking; put in a new seal; replaced the emergency brake drum and the drive shaft, and made sure the overflow vent was not clogged. Even though the technician could not find anything wrong, Paul was pleased with the workmanship.

On the way back to the RV park, we stopped at a discount food store, a huge warehouse-like place, where I took the opportunity to stock up on supplies for Alaska.

Later at dinner in the nearby campground restaurant with our traveling companions, I said, "We got groceries for Alaska. It took longer than I planned. I spent a lot of time thinking about what to get for the potlucks and other meals we'll be having on our trip."

"Did she ever!" Paul said. "She bought $106 worth!"

"A hundred and six dollars!" exclaimed Libby, a shocked look on her face. "What did we tell you about Alaska that made you think you couldn't get any *food?*"

By this time we were all laughing so hard that we couldn't stop. Every time I thought about Lib saying "a hundred and six dollars," I doubled over. My stomach muscles hurt. Someone commented that when everybody else runs out of food they will know where to get some. Wiping away tears of laughter, I said I wasn't sure about where we were going to put all those groceries. More guffawing! Giggling, Lib sensibly offered to find some space in their vehicle if we needed extra room.

From the restaurant, we walked back to our motorhomes. Paul and I then left our campsite in the motorhome to look for an ATM machine so we could withdraw some cash. We did not find one, but

35

we stopped for gas back at the campground so we would be ready to go the next morning.

Before coming in for the night, however, Paul went next door to the Graybeals' to discuss our departure time in the morning, how far we would go the next day and the day after that, and when and where we could stop for my weekly hair appointment and Lib's bi-weekly manicure and still get to Vancouver on Friday. And what was I doing? Putting away groceries, of course!

I removed from the shelves all of the groceries we had on board and stacked them on the dinette table in categories—fruits, vegetables, soups, and so forth. To these groups I added the seven-paper-bags-worth of foodstuffs that I had bought at the warehouse. Together, they formed several Great Pyramids, but it showed me how much space the various categories needed. In the end, the items that Paul and I would use regularly went into our pullout pantry drawers. In a nearby stationary cupboard, I crammed the reserve stock plus what I had bought for potlucks.

In the process, I realized I needed dishwasher and laundry detergent! I didn't dare mention that to my traveling companions. I could hear Lib say, "What! More groceries? You spent $106 and you need *more* groceries?" and giggle in the asking.

In my defense, I should mention that I had read and heard that prices in Alaska were very high, which is why I was ready to stock up in the Lower 48 (a term used by Alaskans when referring to the contiguous United States).

On Wednesday, we left Post Falls, Idaho, and drove on U.S. 2 under cloudy skies. As we drove into Spokane that morning, the highway was so bumpy that Paul remarked, "You could do your laundry on this trip just by putting it in the tub and letting it shake." We visited the Ginkgo Gem Shop at Vantage, Washington, at the Ginkgo Petrified Forest State Park, and ate lunch in our motorhomes in their parking lot.

In intermittent rain, we drove 246 miles on U.S. 2 and then I-90 from Post Falls, Idaho, to Easton, Washington, that day and camped at RV Town, Inc., for the night.

Getting Groceries

The rain continued that evening and we stayed indoors after dinner in our motorhome. Paul looked over some of his motorhome maintenance books while I did the usual trip-log calculations and wrote in my journal. We watched some television and then got ready for bed.

At home, Paul liked to watch the ten o'clock news before turning in, and this habit continued to some degree on the road. It worked out great because I could take my shower and then, after Paul turned off the television, the bathroom would be free for him. Some evenings, when we were both too tired from a full day's travel to watch television or when the television reception or programming were poor, I would just ask Paul if he wanted to use the bathroom first or if I should go ahead. Some of our other caravaners used the bathhouse facilities at the campgrounds for their daily showers. For me, it was more convenient and comfortable to use the shower in the motorhome.

Some evenings on the road Paul liked to relax and nod as he leaned against a pillow at the corner of the sofa, his legs stretched out in front of him. This left the dinette table free for me to work on my writing projects. If he needed to use the dinette table to spread out his electrical systems charts, other motorhome resource materials, or even the newspaper, the surface was large enough that he could use one side of it while I used the other. Often I kept on the cushioned seat beside me and next to the window a collection consisting of my Bible, dictionary, postcards and stationery, or whatever I might be working with at the moment. By keeping those things on the seat, I could easily reach them and yet keep the table surface free for other uses. And they rode on the wide seat without spilling.

The next day, Thursday, about 8:00 A.M., we left the wet pine grove of our campground and drove northwest on I-90 and then due north on I-5 to Lynnwood. We sought out Alderwood Mall, the largest shopping center in the state of Washington. Once again the mall came through for us—a manicure for Lib and a shampoo and blow-dry for me. In addition, Paul got a haircut and bought coveralls so that he could look more presentable when working on the RV on

37

the road as well as protect his traveling clothes. John already had a nice-looking pair of dark green coveralls.

By 3:15 P.M., we had arrived at Ferndale Campground, Ferndale, Washington, from which it would be only a short drive to the Vancouver rendezvous site.

Unfortunately, the leak in the transmission overdrive unit continued. Paul couldn't figure out what was causing it. In the Ferndale laundry room, at a telephone where he could sit down, Paul talked with the people who had serviced the unit in Idaho. He then called the people who had installed the unit in Maryland. He also telephoned the company that manufactured and sold us the overdrive unit in the first place. From these calls, he learned that the overdrive manufacturing company would replace the rough shaft at one of its authorized dealers, which for us would be in Portland, Oregon, after our tour of Alaska. He also learned that the fluid in the overdrive unit had to be replaced *only* every 1,000 miles, not every day.

I was so relieved I could have wept. Now we could really get on with our vacation! Paul would have the hassle of keeping an eye on the mileage and getting under the vehicle to refill the fluid every 1,000 miles, but that was much better than every day.

With that problem under control, we enjoyed delicious grilled chicken legs and turkey fillets that John prepared on his portable outdoor grill. We ate inside in our "house" because it was too cold outdoors. I cooked fresh broccoli in the microwave. Lib brought rolls and a fresh apple pie from a nearby bakery.

She and John had found a grocery store in Ferndale after arriving at the campground, using their motorhome for transportation. They shopped while I did laundry and Paul made his three telephone calls about the overdrive unit.

Amidst our congeniality at supper, we decided we could just laze around the next morning because we were only about an hour's drive from Vancouver. We should not arrive at the Burnaby Cariboo RV Park too soon, we had been told, or the park would charge an extra day's rent.

Getting Groceries

Our rendezvous with the other RVers on the caravan tour of Alaska was the next day. I would soon begin facing the challenges and adventures of relating to a large group on a planned tour in new territory. I looked forward to it, yet couldn't help wondering how it would go, which was part of the excitement of this trip.

· 4 ·

Vancouver Rendezvous

MALLARDS AND OTHER DUCKS waddled and quacked on the banks of a man-made pond at Ferndale Campground, Ferndale, Washington. I sat leisurely at the dinette table in the motorhome looking out at them fluffing their feathers and digging into their down with their bills. The water moved in arcs across the surface of the pond. It was the morning of Rendezvous Day, June 11.

John and Paul were outside putting air in the tires of both motorhomes using John's small air compressor. It was only about 55 miles from our campground at Ferndale to our rendezvous site across the Canadian border at Burnaby Cariboo RV Park in Vancouver, British Columbia. I was anxious to go yet couldn't help feeling apprehensive about what we would find when we got there.

We left Ferndale at 11:14 A.M. At the Canadian border, the customs officer asked us a few questions and then told us to have a good trip. When we looked back, however, we saw that our traveling companions had been asked to pull into an area to "verify their vehicle." I saw an officer moving about inside their motorhome. In the end, our

VANCOUVER RENDEZVOUS

friends had to relinquish some tasty apples they had just bought in the state of Washington.

By 12:51 P.M., Paul halted our motorhome at a stop sign in front of the surprisingly modern two-story office building of Burnaby Cariboo RV Park in Burnaby, British Columbia. *Trailer Life Campground/RV Park & Services Directory* gave the campground a 10/10/9 rating, with 10 being the best. The first number refers to completeness and quality of facilities, the second to cleanliness and physical characteristics of rest rooms and showers, and the third to visual appeal and environment quality.

John and Paul went into the office to register. People walked about everywhere. I saw a multitude of RVs to my left parked as if they were attending a convention. Soon we backed into one of the 217 paved, landscaped sites with full hookups (water, electricity, sewer) and became part of that huge aggregation of recreational vehicles of all sizes, brands, and descriptions.

"The wagonmasters and tailgunners are here, but I haven't seen them yet. They're supposed to come around to see us with a goody bag sometime," Paul told me.

"Soon . . . we became part of that huge aggregation of recreational vehicles of all sizes, brands, and descriptions."

41

During the sunny afternoon, while Paul was somewhere else on the campground, a woman with light blonde hair and a contagious smile knocked on our screen door. With a lilt in her voice, Laurie Peterson introduced herself and Karen Bonis, who smiled beside her. Laurie and her husband, Don Peterson, would be the tailgunners. Karen and her husband, Scott Bonis, would be our wagonmasters. The four of them were employed by Caravanas Voyagers®, El Paso, Texas.

I invited them in, of course, and they suggested that we sit at the dinette table. They had brought with them a plastic bag that contained instructions, an orientation booklet, a list of people on the tour with the sizes and brand names of their RVs and their assigned numbers for the tour, a blue nylon jacket for each of us, patches to sew on the jackets if we wanted to, a small plastic squeeze-type coin case, two pairs of brightly colored decals with the number "1" for our motorhome, a calendar that showed daily destinations, and hard plastic identification badges.

Karen told me that we should wear the badges *everywhere* we went as a group, even to departure meetings. She said we should attend an orientation meeting at 9 A.M. the next day on the second floor of the office building in the RV park. We should bring a notebook and *The MILEPOST®* travel guide that had been sent to us earlier.

I asked about free time each week to get my hair done. Karen said that would be possible, that there were other women on the tour who had the same request.

"Paul and I would like to go to Barrow where a friend of ours once worked. Do you think that will be possible?" I asked.

She said she would be glad to make those arrangements. We could fly out of Fairbanks during the tour's three-night stay in that city. We might have to miss either a bus tour of Fairbanks or a boat cruise that was already scheduled for the group (which was a disappointment to me since I wanted to do those also), but a flight to Barrow was certainly an option. She and Laurie did not yet know if anyone else was interested in going on the flight. At the appropriate time, Karen would make the flight plans.

Before Karen and Laurie left our motorhome, Karen said that we should make sure we had a highlighter pen and a notebook, and exchange some of our money for Canadian currency at a bank that was in a nearby mall.

Shortly afterward, as I was filling Paul in about the goody bag and instructions, we had another visitor—Mary Jo Cornell, who with her husband, Bill, would be on the tour with us. Vivacious and outgoing, Mary Jo, I could tell immediately, would by nature be the fun-loving, question-asking spokesperson among us. She and Bill had left their home in Fairfield, Connecticut, on May 9 in their 27-foot Conquest motorhome. They had followed the Oregon Trail as much as possible. We invited her and Bill as well as John and Lib to go with us in our motorhome to find the bank at the mall. Mary Jo and Lib also wanted to find a grocery store.

Somehow Paul found the way—I was quite turned around and couldn't have found my way back to the campground if I had tried. At the bank, we exchanged $500 into $631.50 worth of Canadian money. Nearby was a grocery store. I bought only $18.01 worth of groceries, milk, and fresh fruit, not just because our cupboards were already well stocked, but because I never did get the hang of the price comparisons of Canadian/U.S. currency. It all seemed unintelligible to me.

By 3:19 P.M. we were back at the RV park. Paul and the other men in our tour group, with the tailgunner's help, placed decals on each RV so that we could identify our fellow caravaners on the road. They positioned the decals on the flat surface near the front and rear roof lines on the street (driver's) side of the vehicles. The decals had "Alaska" printed in white letters on a bright blue rectangle below a drawing of a motorhome. The other important decal that the men placed just below the Alaska one contained the number assigned to each vehicle. That number was printed in white on a bright red background. The two decals together, placed one above the other as a unit on each vehicle, were about 12 inches wide and about 10 inches high.

The wagonmasters had assigned a number to each RV according to an alphabetical listing of the last names of those going on the tour. Beard happened to be at the top of the list alphabetically and so Paul and I became Number One. The Graybeals became Number Six. We would use those numbers as we talked with one another on the Citizens Band radio when on the road. We would also use them to easily identify the rigs in our caravan when we passed one another on the road or stopped to sightsee.

While Paul was involved in the "decal party," I walked the few steps to the store at the park office. Following the wagonmaster's recommendation, I bought a highlighter and an 8½-by-11-inch, lined, spiral-bound, three-ring notebook, some postcards and stamps, some small packs of facial tissue (they had no regular-sized boxes, which I would have preferred), and a newspaper.

The next morning, Saturday, a motley group of strangers assembled on the second floor of the office building. Most of us appeared to be in our 60s and 70s except for Eunice McQuiston and the Bonises, who looked younger. The 20 of us were scattered around the room by couples, just as our homes were scattered across the United States. During the introductions, we learned that Louis (Louie) and Ann Beeler (Number Two) lived in Montana; Bob and Rosemary (Ro) Conway (Number Three) in New York; Bill and Mary Jo Cornell (Number Four) in Connecticut; Willis (Wil) and Yvonne Foreman (Number Five) in Louisiana; Donald (Don) and Thelma (Thel) Heathcock (Number Seven) in Massachusetts; Fred and Eunice McQuiston (Number Eight) in Arizona; Clemitt (Clem) and Effie Swagerty (Number Nine) in California; and Lyle and Jackie Wrigley (Number Ten) in Florida.

And our RVs were just as varied: The Beelers drove a 27-foot Tioga® motorhome, the Conways a 23-foot Tioga® motorhome, the Cornells a 27-foot Conquest motorhome, the Foremans a 21-foot Tioga® motorhome, the Heathcocks a 23-foot Southwind motorhome, the McQuistons a 22-foot Ford pickup with a Coachman camper, the Swagertys a 31-foot Cross Country motorhome, the Wrigleys a 33-foot Holiday Rambler® motorhome, the Petersons a 36-foot combination of Chevrolet pickup/Comfort fifth-wheel, and

VANCOUVER RENDEZVOUS

the Bonises a 40-foot Allegro® motorhome. As I've already mentioned the Graybeals drove a 34-foot Pinnacle motorhome and we drove our 34-foot Holiday Rambler® motorhome. Scott and Karen had recently bought their coach, which they had ordered with many custom features since they lived in it full-time. They towed a Dodge 4x4 Raider. The rest of us had been discouraged by the tour company from taking a tow car on the Alaska tour.

Wearing a green Irish hat and grinning from behind a graying mustache and short brown-and-gray beard, Scott greeted everyone and said that his hat was one of many different toppers he would wear at every get-together. The caravaner who had kept track of the exact number of his different hats worn on the trip would win a prize—it had to be the *exact* number in order to win.

After introductions all around with one person from each couple sharing some brief biographical information, the wagonmasters oriented us for the tour. In my new spiral-bound, three-ring notebook with the words for notebook in both English and French on its royal blue laminated cover, I began the first page of many notes to be made by either Paul or me at almost daily departure meetings at campgrounds.

That morning, Saturday, June 12, the wagonmasters told us to get dried milk or flashed milk (which does not require refrigeration and has a long shelf life) and to stock up on paper products such as facial tissues. (I had already done that since Karen and Laurie mentioned it in their introductory visit in our motorhome the day before.) They acquainted us with the Canadian metric system and buying gas by the liter at the pumps. (That went in one ear and out the other for me.) They also said that our excursion had been extended an extra day (to 44 days instead of 43) because of ferry scheduling.

They said that the CB numbers for the tailgunners would be "Voyager 40" and for the wagonmasters would be "Big 50" for the Allegro® and "Little 50" for the Raider tow car. When we left the campground in the morning we were to tell Voyager 40 by CB that we were leaving. We were not to leave the campground in the morning before the wagonmasters. They needed to get a head start in order to assign sites and be prepared for our arrival at the next campground.

45

Departure meeting times would be posted on the portable bulletin board attached to the side of the Allegro®. At least one of every couple was expected to attend every departure meeting with a notebook to take down directions and other information for the next day's travel.

When we reached Yukon Territory, we were to drive with our headlights on at all times in accordance with the law of that province. Although it had been known for so long as the Alcan Highway, they told us that that was no longer the correct name; it was the Alaska Highway. Indeed, I had to get used to its new name.

The wagonmasters stressed the importance of using *The MILEPOST®*—it would be our travel bible. We would actually see small posts with numbers marking the miles alongside the roads; these "mileposts" were the basis for the travel guide called *The MILEPOST®*.

That reference manual not only identified specific mile markers but was loaded with information on local places of interest. It was like having a tireless, informed travel guide in the RV with us. By reading ahead in *The MILEPOST®*, for example, we could determine whether or not we wanted to stop and visit a particular place or how many miles it was before we would get to a pull-off (an area at the side of the highway specifically graded for vehicles to park for a brief time) or a place to eat. It even warned of road dangers such as narrow winding stretches and told of wildlife in the area.

During departure meetings, our wagonmasters would use *The MILEPOST®* to go over the next day's travel, asking us to highlight with our markers specific points of interest or special road warnings. I would learn as we went along how essential a reference tool *The MILEPOST®* would become.

That afternoon, our group of initiates boarded a sightseeing bus for a grand tour of the city of Vancouver. The tour ended with an elegant dinner in the revolving restaurant (Cloud Nine) atop the Landmark Hotel. What a spectacular panoramic view of the city!

At dinner, Paul and I felt a connection with Don and Thel Heathcock when we learned that Don was retired from the telephone com-

Vancouver Rendezvous

pany as was Paul. We learned also that Don loved ice cream and played a trumpet in the Chelmsford, Massachusetts, community band. He and Thel had a Dalmatian, Bumper, whom they dearly loved and missed so much because he was back in Massachusetts.

The McQuistons, on the other hand, brought along their little schnauzer, Pepper. Pepper was already a great comfort to Don and Thel. Since many RVers travel with pets, campgrounds accept them. The McQuistons follow the local animal laws such as requiring that pets be on a leash or contained in the vehicle and that droppings must be put in a plastic bag and then put in the trash can. Highway rest areas provide grassy plots for caretakers to walk their pets.

After returning to our motorhome at the RV park, I felt the excitement of beginning to know our fellow voyagers. Wil and Yvonne were newlyweds, having tied the knot in April. A bachelor and a merchant marine most of his life, Wil had suffered a stroke in February, walked with a cane, and spoke haltingly. He and Yvonne had planned their wedding and the Alaskan tour before his stroke, so they decided to go forward with both. Yvonne thought that being on the tour would be good therapy for Wil, that his recuperation would be faster because of the motivation of daily travel and being with people. I marveled at their spunk and good cheer. Eunice and Fred had been married less than a year and the rest of us were fairly to very long-time married couples.

The next day our adventure would begin with these people, who so far looked like strangers with the potential of becoming friends. Our cross-country caravan with the Graybeals had shown us that caravaning worked, at least in a twosome. Now we would learn if it would work over the long haul with 11 other couples and their vehicles.

At 6:40 the next morning, Sunday, June 13, the CB crackled as the wagonmasters and tailgunners checked in with one another on channel 13. At 6:45 promptly, we saw Wagonmasters Karen and Scott leave the campground in their huge tan-and-brown motorhome with the Raider tracking behind.

Soon we heard other voyagers checking in with Tailgunner Laurie by CB saying that they were leaving the campground.

47

After looking to see that the Graybeals were ready to pull out, Paul reached in front of the steering wheel for the CB microphone hanging beside the rear-view monitor. I sat in the passenger seat with the trip log in my lap, ready to write down our departure time from Burnaby Cariboo RV Park, according to my usual custom.

"Number One's going to move out," Paul said over the CB, referring to our assigned vehicle number.

"All right, Number One. See you down the road," responded Laurie in her cheerful, laughing voice that would gladden us throughout the entire trip.

"Followed by Number Six," said John over the CB.

"Got it, Number Six," answered Laurie. She also responded to Number Nine, the Swagertys.

"This is exciting!" I said to Paul as I felt our motorhome move forward. I wrote 6:56 A.M. as our departure time in my chart-like trip log. The odometer showed 45,628 miles. The weather was a cool 46 degrees and sunny.

Behind us drove John and Lib; Clem and Effie followed them. As we left the RV park and reached Trans-Canada Highway 1, Paul followed Karen's written directions that he had copied the day before from the bulletin board on the side of her motorhome.

Our route for the now-44-day excursion would take us north and northwest through British Columbia and Yukon Territory, then west on the Top of the World Highway into Alaska. Our first major city in Alaska would be Fairbanks, from which point Paul and I hoped to fly to Barrow. Upon our return to Fairbanks, the tour would take us south, stopping near Mount McKinley in Denali National Park and Preserve, then it would go on to the Kenai Peninsula, Prince William Sound, and south to Skagway where we would drive our RVs aboard the Alaska Marine Highway ferry for the last leg of the trip to Prince Rupert, British Columbia. From there we would go to Smithers and then to our final overnight together at Prince George, British Columbia. Our destination that first day, however, was Cache Creek, with stops en route at Minter Gardens for a group breakfast and at Hell's Gate for a ride on an airtram across a rocky gorge.

Vancouver Rendezvous

In his reserved way, Paul was excited about the trip. I could tell by the way he had participated in the orientation—volunteering to take others in our motorhome to the bank and grocery store, walking around the RV park getting acquainted and helping others, and copying the travel directions for our first day out. And by the way he had competently radioed to Tailgunner Laurie that we were leaving the RV park, using our vehicle number like a pro.

While I was more timid about getting acquainted with others, as I sat safely in the passenger seat inside our motorhome I felt in high spirits and excited to be on our way. I hoped that both of us would rise to whatever challenges lay ahead, that we would be good caravaners, and that we would be glad we had gone when it was over.

I looked at the plastic identification tag that hung around my neck. The tag called the tour an "Alaskan Adventure." With our motorhome problems under control and our trip orientation at the RV park, Paul and I were probably as ready as we could be for whatever lay ahead. Along with our other caravaners, the two of us were heading out on a sunny morning into the unknown and the untraveled.

· 5 ·

"Boondocking" at Barkerville

OUR THREE RVS continued along in bright sunshine toward Abbotsford on Trans-Canada Highway 1 on Sunday, that first day of our 44-day tour by caravan of Alaska. Paul was behind the steering wheel and in calm control, as usual. John and Lib followed us but not too closely. Two voyagers passed us, including the Swagertys.

"Nice to have a pretty day to start," I said.

"Yes," Paul said quickly. "Well, I guess Don and Laurie are leaving the campground by now."

I looked at my watch. "Yeah. 7:35. They were supposed to leave at 7:30," I replied and added, "Do you think this will be an 'Alaskan Adventure' as our nametags say?"

"Boondocking" at Barkerville

"Well, I don't know how you define adventure, but if you mean that we'll be doing something different from what we usually do, then I think it will be an adventure. How exciting an adventure it will be remains to be seen. I think that if we go to Barrow, that will be a real adventure. That's something I really hope we can do."

An hour and a half later, we pulled into the parking area for Minter Gardens, at Chilliwack, British Columbia. Someone in our tour group had said that these gardens rivaled the Butchart Gardens at Victoria, British Columbia. I had only seen pictures of its breathtaking rose garden.

We joined our fellow travelers for a hearty breakfast buffet. Afterward we strolled outside on the walks of the beautiful gardens that cover nearly 27 acres. We marveled at the largest floral flag in the world—the Canadian flag with its center red maple-leaf symbol against white blossoms bordered by a solid array of red blossoms in rectangular side panels. There were paths through 11 teeming garden displays. We admired huge pink blooming roses in one garden plot and a formal garden in another. Walking on, we discovered the painted figures of Snow White and her Seven Dwarfs standing happily, except for Grumpy of course, in front of their little white cottage.

I took a picture of Lib standing in front of a large arbor with many hanging baskets overflowing with blooming fuchsia. Along other paths were larger-than-life topiary figures representing a wedding party. Six gardeners who tend Minter Gardens had fashioned them.

The gardens were outstanding and I would have lingered longer but to paraphrase Robert Frost in "Stopping by Woods on a Snowy Evening," we have miles to go before we sleep.

Then it was on to the Hell's Gate Airtram, about 60 miles north. Paul guided our motorhome into a parking area that was dug into the side of a mountain covered with pine trees. I saw others of our group who had arrived just before us walking across the highway toward the Hell's Gate visitor buildings, a short distance away. I said quietly to Lib that I wasn't sure about going on the tram ride. She wasn't either, she said. That gave me some comfort.

"I took a picture of Lib standing in front of a large arbor with many hanging baskets overflowing with blooming fuchsia."

It would be my first tram ride. When Paul, our son Jeff, and I visited Niagara Falls some years ago, I couldn't watch as the two of them took a tram ride high across the treacherous river at the base of the falls. Miraculously, I thought, they survived. And I put the fright of their daring ride out of my mind, until that day on the RV caravan tour. Soon the Graybeals and we and some other caravaners stood waiting our turn to enter the 25-passenger, rectangular, red tram car with windows enveloping its upper half. By that time, I had learned it would descend *500 feet* down across the Fraser River to a restaurant-and-shop complex carved into the opposite side of the tree-lined, rocky gorge.

It was happening fast—in a few seconds we'd be moving out into air space, high above Hell's Gate, the narrowest point of the Fraser River. The rocky terrain of the gorge at that site had claimed the lives of many construction workers as they built the railroad and highway running through it. I stood in line on that bright June Sunday afternoon looking wide-eyed at the waiting tram paused on its departing platform. Its door open, it stood ready to load its next 25 or so passengers for the descent.

"Boondocking" at Barkerville

I wondered if the cheerful, red-vested operator of the tram knew his cables and safety procedures, if all the equipment and cables were maintained well, and if they had had any tragic accidents. I wondered if any of my newly met fellow travelers felt timorous about it.

Paul stood behind me talking matter-of-factly to others traveling in our RV caravan.

The operator began loading passengers again. I stepped gingerly into the tram. It seemed solid enough on its landing platform. Soon it began moving slowly across the gorge. Its hanging apparatus clung to the cable, our lives depending on it. Ready or not, I looked far below while I stood holding tightly onto the interior handrail. I caught my breath at the great distance below to the turbulent river.

The smooth ride helped to calm me as we glided across, high above the river. My eyes feasted on the views up and down the river gorge—gray, craggy, steep cliffs; gray and white gravel near the water's edge; thin ribbons of railroad tracks on one side of the river and a highway on the other side, both carved into the slope on their side of the river. Above those towered rocky, tree-covered mountains with other ranges behind them as far as I could see, all under a cloud-drifting, bright blue sky. A brochure photograph come true of beautiful British Columbia!

Below us, a suspended walking bridge also spanned the river—people on it looked like specks. Beneath the bridge, the silver-green water of the river swirled and rushed between steep rocky cliffs, creating paisley patterns of white foam. On the side from which we had departed, down at the river's edge, eight fishways had been constructed for salmon to go upriver to spawn.

Exhilarated by the ride and spectacular views, I almost regretted landing so soon on the opposite side of the gorge. I was relieved that we had made it safely, of course, and was glad that I had forced myself to overcome a fear.

We milled around in the restaurant, gift shop, fisheries display, fudge factory, and Christmas shop (later replaced by a "general store") that made up the complex and dared to walk on the suspension bridge that swayed as we and other

"Beneath the bridge, the silver-green water of the river swirled and rushed between steep rocky cliffs, creating paisley patterns of white foam."

people stepped along on it. From it I watched others coming and going on the tram car high above, thinking that I would again risk using it for a trip back across the river.

Trying not to dwell on my fears, I boarded the tram along with Paul and the Graybeals for the return trip, again marveling at the scene below and around me. Soon the tram rested on its station platform and we walked to our motorhomes nearby.

"I enjoyed that more than the gardens," Paul commented.

"I was just glad to get across and back safely," I said.

Once again riding on Highway 1, I realized that the scenic mountains were mostly tree- or brush-covered with some places of bare soil or rocks exposed, not snowcapped. The highway itself was generally paved and smooth. Between Lytton and Cache Creek, the surrounding area was semi-arid with irrigated fields along the Thompson River.

One of our instructions at the orientation meeting in Vancouver was to *always* call the wagonmaster ("Big 50" or sometimes just "50") on the CB before entering a campground. When we tried to raise "50"

"Boondocking" at Barkerville

on the CB before pulling into the Cache Creek RV Park & Campgrounds on that late Sunday afternoon, we got no answer.

We proceeded slowly into the campground and learned that the wagonmaster's rig had had diesel engine trouble. Scott had taken it to a diesel engine service center for repair in Quesnel (silent *s*), a town we would pass through the next day en route to Barkerville.

After a 5:15 P.M. departure meeting at the campground, Karen also went to Quesnel in the Raider. The tailgunners would be doing some wagonmaster duties temporarily. All seemed under control, however. These two couples were professionals, having taken other caravans of RVers on this excursion before.

At the campground was a unique restaurant called the Country Kitchen. The operator did everything except wash dishes—*we* had to do that! In fact, everyone in our group had to bring our own plates, silverware, and glasses; eat the delicious steak or ham dinner that the operator prepared and cooked as we watched; and then take our dirty dishes back to the motorhome to wash. But the price was right—all that for only $13.25 for the two of us!

Mosquitoes buzzed around as we ate on the open-air dining porch. Our group ate heartily and learned more about one another. We laughed and swatted mosquitoes. Needless to say, I got my first bites there.

Back at the motorhome, we washed our dishes. I wrote a letter to Jeff, then walked a short distance to the campground office and paid the correct amount of postage for the campground owner to mail it. After checking the motorhome on the outside, Paul rested on the sofa from the first day's driving and we went to bed early.

I awoke about four o'clock on Monday morning feeling frustrated about not writing in my laptop computer when on the road the first day as I had envisioned doing before we left home. With CB static all the time as we drove and with having to pay close attention to navigation, using my computer was out of the question. I had made handwritten notes when possible in my clothbound book.

I knew I wouldn't be able to use electricity that Monday night at Barkerville because we would be camping without electricity and water hookups. Our wagonmasters discouraged using auxiliary generators between 8 P.M. and 9 A.M. because of the noise that they made, which could disturb the peace of a quiet evening or morning.

I wrestled with the problem of when I would get back to the computer. I didn't want to use the tape recorder because of the hours involved in transcribing my words later, but I sensed that it might be necessary. I wanted to discuss it with Paul, but he was asleep. Instead, I got up and wrote a few pages of handwritten notes, felt better, and went back to sleep.

Thump, thump. Thump, thump.

"That's the kind of service I *didn't* expect," Paul chuckled. At 6:50 A.M. on that same Monday, June 14, at Cache Creek, the tailgunner checked our tires. He used a thumper, a short, thick, round wooden dowel. Somehow he could tell by the sound if a tire was low in pressure.

Paul quietly opened our motorhome door and greeted Don.

"Did I wake you?" Don asked.

"Oh, no," Paul assured him. And Don continued his rounds.

"He must have gotten up in pretty good time—running around thumping everybody's tires. He wants to get to them before they get on the road," said Paul as he opened the front curtains of our motorhome.

The Graybeals were parked on one side of us. On the other was a Class C motorhome (with storage or sleeping area over the cab). Outside at their picnic table, a woman and a man with a prosthetic leg ate breakfast. Their three dogs kept them company.

My breakfast finished, I picked up the video camera, saying, "Before we leave, I want to take a video of where we ate last night. This is our first campground on this Alaskan tour."

Outside, from about 200 feet away, I aimed the video camera toward the restaurant where we had eaten the night before. Through the lens, I was surprised to see the chief cook, but not dishwasher, wave back!

My pictures taken, and seeing the Graybeals ready, we checked in on the CB with Laurie and left Cache Creek shortly before eight

"Boondocking" at Barkerville

o'clock, headed for the overflow parking lot at Barkerville, British Columbia. With no campground available nearby, our wagonmasters had arranged for our caravan rigs to use for our overnight camping a large area designated as an overflow parking lot for tourists that lay adjacent to the visitor's center.

This would be a dry-camping overnight; that is, without water, sewer, and electric hookups or connections. Of course, our RVs were prepared. Each one had a freshwater tank that would furnish water for the sinks, shower, and toilet. They each had a separate black water tank and a gray water tank for waste material and water. And they each had an auxiliary generator to furnish electricity. I assumed that they each also had an LP (liquid propane) tank that supplied the refrigerator, stove, and furnace with fuel. If we were conservative with the use of water, space in the waste tanks, and propane, we could dry camp for a week running. Usually, however, it was more comfortable to dry camp just one or two days at a time unless a separate bath house with showers was nearby.

From Cache Creek, the highway on which we had traveled from Vancouver (Highway 1) turned toward the east to continue on a trans-Canada route. So we took instead Highway 97 north. Small ranches dotted a valley as we drove along.

After driving about two hours, we stopped to stretch at a rest area beside 108 Mile Lake. Alongside was the Heritage Centre with some original log buildings from 108 Mile Ranch and other places. We toured the craft shop and post office, the log buildings that had been relocated, and started back to our motorhomes. Meanwhile, others in our tour group coming along sometime after us had seen the Caravanas Voyagers® decals on our RVs parked there and pulled in also to see what we were seeing.

"Just look at that," I said to Lib as we stood in the parking area. "There's Number One, Number Two, Number Three, Number Four, Number Five, and Number Six!"

Although they were not *parked* in numerical order, the six RVs from our tour group that had stopped at that place were those that had been given the first six numbers assigned by the wagonmasters.

"Was this stop on our itinerary?" asked Mary Jo Cornell.

"No," said Paul, "I just pulled in here for a rest stop."

As we rode on northward, I looked in *The MILEPOST®* to select our next rest stop—lunch. I thought it should be a place where a number of RVs could park, just in case the others wanted to join us. Paul had said several units were spaced out behind us.

"Did I hear someone mention din-din?" asked a CBer.

"We were considering the information center at Williams Lake as a place to pull off and have some din-din," Paul replied on the CB.

I laughed at his using "din-din." It was 11:22 A.M. Riding made me hungry. In sunshine, we pulled into the Travel Infocenter at Williams Lake for lunch. The others except for the Graybeals went past us without stopping.

After lunch, we continued northward. As we went through Quesnel, Laurie's voice came on the CB. "Our leader is waiting for us in Barkerville." She referred happily to the wagonmaster. After Quesnel, we would leave Highway 97 and take a secondary road, Route 26, to Barkerville.

While Paul seemed unperturbed, I felt relieved to know that Scott would direct us into the parking lot at Barkerville. Otherwise, we would have had to find it ourselves. While we never hesitated about finding a campground in the States, I felt uncertain about a different country and a gravel parking lot without marked sites.

After driving by ones and twos from Cache Creek RV Park and Campgrounds through enchantingly beautiful green mountains, past roadside rivers, and above deep views of canyons during that day's 253 miles, we arrived in Barkerville that Monday afternoon.

"Don't get out of your rig unless you're wearing long sleeves and mosquito spray. They're bad out here," advised Karen, referring to the blood-thirsty insects, as we headed into the large gravel parking lot. With a hand transceiver held to her shoulder, she stood ready to direct the next rig to a spot. The overflow lot lay adjacent to a small creek flowing through a dry gulch, sculpted by more rambunctious waters.

"BOONDOCKING" AT BARKERVILLE

Karen's expertise included exceptional communication skills. Both former aerospace engineers, she and Scott, her husband, lived and worked full-time in their RV (for this trip a brand-new 40-foot Allegro® diesel-pusher Class A motorhome), taking tours to Mexico, Alaska, and other places.

She soon had capably directed eight units to park alongside the small stream. She directed three others across the parking lot from the stream to space beside a bank covered with short shrubs. Above the bank lay the paved road off which we had just turned. That road continued directly into nearby Barkerville, dead-ending at the Visitor Reception Centre that was within the length of a football field from our RVs.

Paul and I dressed for mosquito-bite prevention and walked through the parking lot. Soon we caught up with the Graybeals and others in our caravan walking around the town.

A historic place, Barkerville was a restored mining town that had sprung up during a gold rush in 1862. Named for Billy Barker, who discovered gold on nearby Williams Creek, the town eventually was abandoned. Faithful restoration of its buildings and boardwalks from its booming years was begun in 1958 by the provincial government.

Leisurely, we looked and read interpretive signs on over 100 buildings. Only a handful of other tourists vied with us to view the interiors of a doctor's office and residence, a dentist's office, the print shop, the bakery, a miner's cabin, and a variety of other structures. The town's roads remained unpaved to preserve the authenticity of the period. I began to feel a part of the gold rush days.

"Isn't it wonderful to see how people lived back then?" exclaimed Lib. "And isn't it a blessing that we don't have to live that way?"

"We are really blessed," I agreed.

As I walked the town's gray boardwalks, I raised and lowered my umbrella many times when the rain started and stopped (to protect my coiffure, of course). The drops began in earnest as we headed for Wake-Up-Jake's restaurant for the 6:15 dinner reservation for our group. We arrived early, but Jake's owner and staff, dressed in 1860s-style costumes, welcomed us with coffee at tables already set for us. How comforting to hurry out of the damp, cold weather into the warm restaurant. Their decaffeinated coffee tasted delicious. Could it be the real cream they used?

Meanwhile the restaurant people finished serving a large group of loud, boisterous, schoolchildren. Some of us commented to one another about the noise, but when the children left and we heard ourselves talk and laugh, we realized we were loud, too.

"You have a loud one in every group," Laurie said to me. "And sometimes it's me! But it's fun. It livens the group."

Laurie and Don, our tailgunners, lived in Big Arm, Montana. He was a retired state trooper who had been a councilman for five years, and she a retired teacher. They had two daughters and three grandchildren. They ably assisted us with solving mechanical problems and made sure everyone got to the destination each day, which meant that they left every campground last and arrived at the next one last. A congenial couple, Laurie's good cheer and lilting voice added fun to our group, and Don in his seagoing captain's cap looked and talked like the skipper from *Gilligan's Island*.

The Graybeals, Paul, and I sat at a table for four. During dinner, John and Lib, who are both avid and good golfers, explained handicapping in golf to us, among other fun topics.

We watched the women servers in their long sweeping dresses hurry about the dining room. "I should think that one young lady would trip—her dress is so long," observed Lib.

Soon our waitress placed a bowl of steaming hot French onion soup before each of us. A waiter wearing an 1860s three-piece suit brought sourdough bread, hot and fresh and partially sliced, with a knife for us to finish the cut if needed. Julia Child could not have set more delicious French onion soup before me!

Our waitress served each of us a large plate with veal cordon bleu, bright green broccoli florets, wild rice with slivered almonds, and boiled red cabbage garnished with strips of red and green peppers. Our dessert was raspberry crisp with a small dollop of whipped

"Boondocking" at Barkerville

cream served in a long-stemmed sherbet glass. Truly an outstanding dinner in authentic late-1800s surroundings.

Before leaving Jake's, Karen announced to our group that the next departure meeting would be nine o'clock the next morning instead of eight o'clock that night, because of the rain.

We walked hastily to our RVs—glad to get in out of the cold rain. We turned on the furnace. Within the coziness of our motorhome, I actually enjoyed hearing the rain drum soothingly on the roof.

As dry campers, we couldn't use either the television or the microwave oven unless we turned on the generator, which our wagonmasters said was a no-no between 8 P.M. and 9 A.M.

That restriction provided the opportunity a writer dreams of—time in a quiet wooded setting to relax and let thoughts flow. I sat at the dinette table writing by hand in my clothbound journal on that Monday night at eight o'clock as Paul napped on the sofa in front of me, his feet in goose-down booties near the blank television screen. The pages of my journal filled rapidly as I began with a simple prayer of thanksgiving that tumbled into describing that day's travel and sojourn in historic Barkerville.

Early Tuesday morning in the rain, Don the tailgunner knocked on our door. He held an insulated pitcher of hot coffee for us. He remembered my concern at the orientation meeting in Vancouver about not being allowed to run our auxiliary generators early in the morning to use the microwave to make hot water. He also graciously toted another container of hot coffee to the Graybeals; Lib couldn't imagine starting a morning without hot coffee.

He must have made the coffee using the gas burners on the stove in their kitchen. I could have done the same except that I was purposely not using the gas stove in our motorhome. The burners looked so clean that I wanted to keep them that way. It had something to do with my aversion to cleaning them. So ever since our motorhome was new I've never used the gas burners except to turn them on once to be sure they worked.

Instead, we do all our cooking and heating in the microwave/convection oven. Of course, it requires electricity, so when we can-

61

not hook up to electricity at the campground, we turn on the auxiliary generator.

I love that auxiliary generator. Its main purpose in life is to produce current that will in turn supply electricity to the overhead air conditioner, microwave/convection oven, television set, video cassette player, and wall outlets. The generator uses gasoline from the same tank as the motorhome engine. Our generator has an automatic cutoff that stops the flow of gasoline to it when the gas tank gets down to one-quarter full. This gives starting and running the engine first priority when the gasoline supply is low.

As scheduled, we huddled under the awning of the Allegro® for the departure meeting at nine o'clock that Tuesday morning. Rain dripped everywhere. That day's travel would be 276 miles to Prince George, British Columbia. The wagonmasters referred us to page 46 of *The MILEPOST®*, "Highway 26 Log," for specific travel directions and then went over them with us. It was at that meeting that I learned dry camping was also called "boondocking."

Just after the departure meeting, Mary Jo Cornell asked Scott what the letters stood for on a small, long, rectangular plate attached to the outside of their motorhome near the entry door.

"Peace to all who enter," he answered and said it was a mezuzah. Mary Jo said that Christians used a fish to symbolize their beliefs. Scott, at my hesitation to come up with the word used for the piece worn by some Jewish people, recited at length the Old Testament verses from Deuteronomy 6:4-9 including "And ye shall love the Lord your God with all your heart, soul, and mind . . . and shall wear it ["it" refers to those very same words of scripture inscribed on parchment and contained in a small, black leather cube attached with a strap to the forehead and left arm during weekday morning prayers by Orthodox and Conservative Jewish men] as a frontlet on your head and bind it on your wrists."

He said he grew up Orthodox wearing those pieces and the yarmulke, or small skullcap. Now he drives on Saturday, the Jewish Sabbath, and turns on electricity, using the rationale that formerly it

"Boondocking" at Barkerville

was work to drive an animal and light a candle, whereas now it is not work to snap on a switch.

I told him I belonged to the Church of the Brethren and more and more I was coming to realize the importance of resting on Sunday as the Lord so wisely provided.

An hour later, Paul dressed in four layers of clothes and went off in the misty rain with John Graybeal for a Barkerville stroll. They intended to end at a mining exhibition and presentation at 11:00.

I planned to join them later but for the moment coveted that time alone to collect my thoughts. Through our screen door I heard and saw the once-gentle stream now flowing muddy and fast over jutting rocks. The rain had stopped, at least momentarily, but gray clouds continued to hang overhead.

Whenever I started to write and was interrupted, I felt disorganized, frustrated, but I tried to appease myself by thinking that at least I had put *something* on paper. How ideal it would be to have creative time whenever I wanted! No interruptions! But only heaven could provide that!

So, like the nearby water curving, leaping, tumbling, I would go with the flow of life's events. After all, water gave no thought to its interrupted path; it found its way molecule by molecule. I, too, would find my way. I knew the Creator would guide me every bit as much as He did the waters of streams everywhere. I was in His care—interruptions and all.

Later that morning I joined Paul and others of our group at the outside mining exhibition in the rain. Holding my red umbrella, I stood listening to how gold was mined in the early days. From there we walked to the Theatre Royal at the Visitor Reception Centre for a delightful melodrama with actors in period costumes. The packed house included schoolchildren on a class trip.

I had not yet seen inside the small St. Saviour's Anglican Church in Barkerville. So on the way back to the motorhome, I headed there alone. Inside, I marveled at hand-hewn wood pews, the apsidal chancel, and a door at the right of the chancel leading to schoolrooms. Started in 1869, the building was formally opened on September 18,

1870. What intrigued me most was a bronze plaque on the wall of the church. It said:

>Roy Thompson
>Trapper
>Born in Paris, Ont. April 25, 1886
>accidentally drowned
>in Kruger Lake Dec. 12, 1943
>He bade no one a last farewell,
>He said good-bye to none,
>The heavenly gates were opened wide,
>A loving voice said, "Come."

When I returned to the motorhome, Paul told me that as our wagonmasters were leaving the parking lot where our group was camped, Scott apparently turned too short and the right rear wheel went into a deep ditch, burying the hitch for the tow car in about six inches of hard-packed, fine gravel. When I arrived, someone had shoveled enough gravel away to unhook the tow car. Someone had also helped Karen down from the driver's door, now tilted and therefore high off the ground. The regular entry door on the curb side was stuck in the gravel. The wagonmasters insisted they had everything under control and that we should all proceed according to plan.

When we left at their insistence, Scott, Karen, Laurie, and Don waited for a heavy-duty tow truck to pull both the motorhome and tow car from the ditch.

Paul and I departed from the opposite end of the Barkerville parking lot in the rain, hoping that there was enough gravel in the mud surface to give us traction up a small incline. Happily, we reached the asphalt road running parallel to the parking lot and headed away from Barkerville. But first we would pass the end of the parking lot where the tilted Allegro® rested. I asked Paul to stop the windshield wipers long enough for me to videotape the scene as we drove slowly past.

Our brave wagonmasters and faithful tailgunners waved to us as they waited for their version of a St. Bernard to come to the rescue.

"Boondocking" at Barkerville

And so we and the Graybeals went on toward Prince George, British Columbia. Other Caravaners had preceded us and some would follow.

"Well, I would say these first three days have been rather eventful," said Paul as we drove on Route 26 toward Highway 97.

"I would say so, too." We both chuckled. He referred to the wagonmasters' diesel engine failing and their rig falling into a ditch plus all the sights we had seen. So far our nametags labeling the tour as an "Alaskan Adventure" had been truer than anyone expected.

"Well, I guess we're our own wagonmaster and tailgunner now," Paul surmised.

"You mean the Graybeals and us?" I asked.

"All of us, because the tailgunner and wagonmaster are hung up back there," said Paul.

The Graybeals and we traveled together, with us in front and them a reasonable distance behind. As good students, we were obeying the wagonmasters' suggestion from our first meeting in Vancouver not to follow one another closely enough to read the number on the Caravanas Voyagers® logo at the rear of our rigs.

So far the highways had been quite acceptable. In two days we would reach the famous Alaska Highway, which runs 1,523 miles from Dawson Creek, British Columbia, to Fairbanks, Alaska. Built by the U.S. Army during World War II as a military supply route, it connected military posts in Alaska with other highways running to Alberta and Montana and to other points in Alaska. Later, in 1946, the United States turned over to Canada the portion that was on Canadian soil and in 1947 the highway was opened to the public.

I wondered how rough the road actually was, if we would face a mud slide, and how damaging the road would be to our motorhome.

As we rode on, the rain slowed and Paul reduced the windshield wipers to an occasional wipe. Always observant, he commented that you didn't see a lot of commercial signs along the highway. I replied that even on an overcast day the British Columbia scenery was beautiful, just as Karen had said, and not having a lot of signs certainly kept it that way.

· 6 ·

Mile 0 of Alaska Highway

AT HOME, some people who had driven the Alaska Highway by car just shook their heads as if it would be a big mistake for Paul and me to take our motorhome there. Others said the road was not that bad if you went slowly over the rough spots. We would find out the next day when we reached Dawson Creek, start of the Alaska Highway, on the eastern border of British Columbia.

We arrived about five o'clock on Tuesday evening at Southpark RV Park, Prince George, British Columbia, under cloudy skies and in damp weather. That Tuesday evening we attended a departure meeting at the recently rescued coach of the Wagonmaster. Naturally, we all wondered what Scott would say about the morning's "upsetting" experience.

MILE 0 OF ALASKA HIGHWAY

Scott began by telling a true story about a Japanese plane that landed near an airport in water—definitely a case of pilot error. At the hearing, the pilot promptly acknowledged it was all his fault. According to Scott, Japanese custom is that when a person admits his failure, no one says anything more about it—ever. Scott admitted he simply made a misjudgment on where he was and where the ditch was. And we got the message—let the event rest in peace!

Karen outlined the plans for the next day: We should plan to arrive at Dawson Creek by three o'clock. At four o'clock, the mayor would greet us, according to the city's custom of meeting every caravan. The tailgunners should leave the Prince George campground by 8:30 A.M., which meant that the rest of us should leave before that time. At five o'clock in Dawson Creek, we would have our pictures taken at the official start of the Alaska Highway. For that momentous occasion, we should wear our blue Caravanas Voyagers® jackets and bring our cameras. At six o'clock we would have dinner at the Alaska Cafe. On Thursday morning at 9:30 A.M., we would take a city bus tour of Dawson Creek until about noon.

Karen said that a "frontier feeling" would begin at Dawson Creek and grow the farther north we went. That frontier attitude involved helping anyone in need. She also said that up to that point in Prince George, we had seen places connected with the Cariboo gold rush. But from Dawson Creek on up through British Columbia and Yukon Territory to Alaska, we would hear about the Klondike gold rush.

Later in the meeting, when Karen said she and Scott would be pulling out early the next morning to have the Allegro® serviced, Louie Beeler piped up:

"Shall we stake it off for you?" Much good-natured laughter came from the group. I pictured Louie hammering pointed wood stakes into the ground to mark the edges of the campground road. Scott was parked in a level pull-through with no chance of getting into a ditch! Scott grinned and rejoined in equally good humor.

Under sunny skies on Wednesday, June 16, by 7:50 A.M., the Graybeals and we were at the north edge of Prince George driving north on Highway 97 toward Dawson Creek.

67

So far in British Columbia, roads had been good—paved gravel, smooth, two-lane, with a paved shoulder also. Many lodge pole pines grew along our mountainous route in British Columbia, yet we also saw lots of clear-cut timber acreage.

About 10:15, Bijoux Falls captivated us as it tumbled down the pine-covered mountainside. We pulled our two coaches off the road for a closer look. I took pictures of Lib, John, and Paul with the frolicking falls in the background.

As we rode on from Prince George to Dawson Creek that day, we looked for moose and other wild animals.

"See any moose down there in the meadow?" Paul asked as we rode high above a valley with a marshy area.

"Not yet," I said, peering down from my passenger seat in the motorhome. "It seems strange to be up here in a country where you really can hope to catch a glimpse of a moose in the wild."

"I'd like to see one in the wild," said Paul.

Later a thin, tan/brownish, pathetic-looking coyote paused beside the road staring at us, its tail drooped between its legs—an indication that wild animals were in the woods of lodge pole pines that we were passing through.

"Beautiful British Columbia," I found myself thinking and saying again and again. The scenery was so appealing, so picture-taking pretty, most of the time, that I began to take it for granted and even dozed as the miles went by, though it was not yet noon. I'm one of those people—fortunately, says Paul—who can drop off for a brief time during the day and who also usually has no trouble going to sleep at night.

"I'm looking for a moose. Want to see a moose," persisted Paul as I roused.

We passed one of the few houses along our route; the owners were having a yard sale. "There's your opportunity," Paul said to John on the CB, referring to his interest in antiques and flea markets.

"I think we'll pass that one up," John came back, and then quipped, "I think that up here they would make that a *meter* sale!"

We kept going and passed a cemetery just south of Chetwynd. Blankets of blossoms covered many graves—artificial I decided—but fresh bouquets decorated others.

When we stopped at the rest area overlooking the long vista of Pine River Valley, green mountains lay beyond and around it. Far below, in a swampy, tree-logged area, a female moose waded. With her giant snout toward the water, she appeared to be looking for lunch. At last Paul saw his moose!

Dilemma! About 14 miles from Dawson Creek, we moved along in the interior plains with wide fields and no or low mountaintops in view. Very little traffic came toward us.

"Number One to Number Six. If you see me pull over to the side, don't be surprised. The engine is gasping and sputtering going up this hill," Paul said to John on the CB.

John replied it was only a few miles to the campground.

"Unless it gives up entirely, I'm going to keep on going," Paul said.

"When we stopped at the rest area overlooking the long vista of Pine River Valley, green mountains lay beyond and around it. Far below, in a swampy, tree-logged area, a female moose waded."

"Number One to Number Two Voyager. What's our altitude here?" Paul asked of Louie Beeler over the CB. Louie had an altimeter in his RV.

"Two thousand something," Louie replied.

"Well, then it ought not be vapor lock," said Paul, trying to get to the root of the problem. Our motorhome was going on six years old, but Paul had maintained it faithfully and carefully.

"Ah, that must be Dawson Creek," I surmised.

Before us on a plateau setting of tilled fields and green grain sprawled the city of Dawson Creek. From *The MILEPOST®*, I learned that agriculture was important to the economy of that area. Dawson Creek got its name from George Mercer Dawson, whose surveys in 1879 helped develop it as a settlement. It was this same George Dawson for whom Dawson City in the Yukon Territory was named. That city was on our future itinerary.

The railroads at Dawson Creek turned out to be an important channel for supplies and equipment in 1942 when the Alaska Highway was constructed. Now with a population of about 12,000, the city provided all of the accouterments that a tourist would seek—hotels; motels; restaurants; department, grocery, hardware, drug, and specialty stores; two malls; a hospital, library, college, concert hall, skating arena, curling arena, golf course; and an art gallery, plus others. Dawson Creek also contained numerous churches.

"Now, we look for Tubby's," said Paul, referring to Tubby's RV Park, our campground for the next two nights.

We drove onto the dirt surface at Tubby's RV Park, as had others in our caravan, and backed into an unmarked space in front of a young, leafy tree.

Before we knew it, we were seated in our lawn chairs as if for a departure meeting and listening to the representative from the mayor's office of Dawson Creek, Rose Wilson. She welcomed us and told us about the city's history and culture and what to see and then answered questions. She said that Dawson Creek was rationing water already that summer because it had been dry for two years.

MILE 0 OF ALASKA HIGHWAY

As a surprise, two can-can girls came dancing toward our group. Both wore black tops, but one sported a red skirt and the other a green skirt. They joyfully lifted the edges of their voluminous, ruffled skirts to their chins, showing a fancy garter on each leg. Each had long brunette hair, which was tied back and somehow supported matching plumed feathers that cascaded toward their foreheads. What a welcome from Dawson Creek!

By 5:30 P.M., we gathered around Mile 0 Post in Dawson Creek at the intersection of 10th Street and 102nd Avenue for a group photograph. This landmark was simply a white post about 12 feet tall with three flags flying atop that designated the beginning of the Alaska Highway and commemorated its construction.

I wondered if what I read in *The MILEPOST®* would pertain to us. That publication said that although all of the Alaska Highway between Dawson Creek, British Columbia, and Fairbanks, Alaska, was asphalt-surfaced, conditions ranged from poor to excellent. What alerted me most, however, was its caution to watch for and drive slowly where there were frost heaves or risk breaking an axle or trailer hitch.

From the Mile 0 Post in Dawson Creek, our caravan group walked a short distance to the Alaska Cafe dining room. A large, old-fashioned horseless-carriage sign hung from the building at the entrance to the restaurant. Listed as one of the top 500 restaurants in Canada, it was considered a must for tourists beginning the Alaska Highway. We joined others in the several crowded dining rooms and agreed that because of its excellent food and service the Alaska Cafe deserved its listing as a top restaurant.

The next day, Thursday, we boarded a comfortable tour bus for a sightseeing excursion of the area. We stopped at a huge farmers' cooperative, a complex grain storage operation. I was amazed to see modern technology at work—electronic panels of various switches and buttons automatically controlled all aspects of storing and transferring and shipping grain. One control even pulled the grain cars along the adjacent railroad tracks, positioned them to be loaded, and sent them on.

At Pouce Coupe, a small village settled in 1898, we toured the museum with historical displays of a pioneer schoolroom, an old general store, a pioneer kitchen, and other exhibits. "Look, Paul," I said. "Here's an old telephone like we used to have on the farm."

"Yeah," he said. "It's an old magneto wall telephone." As a telephone company retiree, Paul was especially interested in seeing that artifact.

On the way back to the campground in the bus, we passed a bison farm. We saw a long, three-sided building with an open front and slanted roof that was used for protecting the animals from the weather, several metal grain storage bins, and a herd of bison grazing in grassy fields with wire fences enclosing them.

That afternoon, Louie kindly drove Ann and me in their motorhome to the hairdresser's in Dawson Creek.

Later, at the departure meeting, Karen and Scott told us what to expect on our 277-mile drive the next day from Dawson Creek to Fort Nelson. We would be in British Columbia three more days and then go into Yukon Territory. They referred us to the appropriate pages in *The MILEPOST®* and went over the travel directions according to their usual procedure. They told us that we should check the taillights of our vehicles and clean them if they were muddy. They recommended After Bite®, the Itch Eraser, for mosquito bites. We found out later it really worked. It came in a white plastic, lipstick-size tube with a screw top. They said we were in bear country, that there would be bear-proof barrels now in the turnouts, and that bears do not like to be surprised so we should make some noise as we walked a trail. For the fishermen in our group, they would need a license to fish for northern pike in the area.

They said that a "Welcome Visitors" bus would leave the campground at 6 p.m the next evening for a tour of Fort Nelson, so we should all try to arrive prior to that time.

It was during this departure meeting that we drew names of our secret voyagers. During the trip we were to observe the person whose name we drew, then write a poem, create a craft, or buy something that would represent the person. These gifts would be presented at the farewell dinner at Prince George at the end of the tour when the names would be revealed.

Early the next morning, Friday, Paul and I left Tubby's RV Park before the Graybeals in order to take pictures at a stone cairn with an arched sign above it that read: "You are now entering World Famous Alaska Highway." We liked its direct message. This marker was at the tourist information center about a block from the center of the city of Dawson Creek where the official beginning of the Alaska Highway, Mile 0 Post, was located and where our caravaners had had a group photograph previously. The Graybeals wanted to get gasoline at the Husky Esso station before leaving Dawson Creek. We planned to meet at the Husky station and from there proceed together on the Alaska Highway heading northwest.

By 7:30 A.M., Paul and I had taken pictures of one another in front of the cairn. Its colorful flags waved in the breeze. We headed northwest, Dawson Creek being as far east as we would go geographically on the entire trip.

As we drove along the highway, Paul tried to raise John on the CB. When he was unable to do so, we assumed that John's motorhome engine was turned off because he was getting gasoline and therefore so was the CB. Paul drove slowly. As we came in sight of the Husky Esso station, we saw the Pinnacle beside the pumps. Paul slowed down even more to determine where to pull in. Just then the Pinnacle began moving out of the gas pump area toward us.

"That's good timing, Number One," John said on the CB as he pulled away from the gas station just as we moved by.

"Very good," Paul replied. "This is Voyager One moving up the Alaska Highway," he announced to whoever listened.

What a thrill! Although we were still in British Columbia, we were on the Alaska Highway headed toward Alaska! It was 7:42 A.M. on Friday, June 18.

"Number Six to Number One. Ten point ninety-seven on that last run," said John over the CB, giving his miles-per-gallon computation.

ALASKA AT YOUR OWN PACE

"By 7:30 a.m., Paul and I had taken pictures of one another in front of the cairn at the tourist information center that welcomed travelers to the Alaska Highway."

Up to that time on the trip, Paul's and my motorhome's lowest miles per gallon was 6.77 and the highest 9.17.

"You must have been running on the vapors," said Paul.

"Saved enough to play golf when I get home," commented John.

"With a cart," returned Paul.

In that frontier territory, I couldn't help wondering what the wilderness ahead held in store. That same night our campground would have full hookups (water, electricity, and sewer), but the next two nights we would stay at what was called a "wilderness resort." While our itinerary said it had full hookups, I questioned the availability of such amenities in a wilderness.

· 7 ·

Wilderness Camping

LOOKING UP from the computer resting on a pillow on my lap, I was surprised by the scenery. I saw miles and miles of fields of grain, sometimes interspersed with small stands of trees, often jack pines and aspens. I expected dense forests. We had turned onto the Alaska Highway in Dawson Creek and were headed northwest on that partly cloudy Friday morning.

"There's a lot more open land up here than I thought. A lot of it has been cleared, I'm sure," commented Paul.

"That's just what I thought!" So far the area didn't look like a wilderness. But of course, I didn't know what lay ahead.

"Hang onto it! Frost heaves and all that," cautioned Paul about the computer on my lap.

The computer lid flopped back and forth; I held onto the computer itself as we bounced over more and more bumps.

"Sorry about that," Paul grinned, not slowing down.

I began to wonder if I would be able to continue using the laptop computer, because of the roughness of the road. The lid kept closing over my hands on the keyboard. I kept pushing it back. At last, I pushed the lid far enough back without damaging it so that the lid stayed upright.

By that time in our 44-day tour, it was dawning on me that the wagonmasters were not tour guides in the sense of being with us on a bus and telling about various sights as we went along. The wagonmasters arranged for places to stop, guided tours, and resource materials, and they told us at the departure meetings what they thought was important for us to see and know, but they did not take us by the hand and give a commentary over the CB of what we were seeing. We were on our own during the day to learn and ferret out the significance of places and to decide where to stop.

"I'm disappointed that our wagonmasters have not told us more about what to see," I said to Paul.

"That's not the focus of their responsibilities. They can't ride with each RV, but they highlight what they think are major points of interest," he confirmed.

"But, you know, I like it this way," I said. "We can go at our own pace during the day. It's also more adventurous when *we* make decisions about where to stop and what to do and discover interesting and scenic things on our own. It's more *our* trip.

"Another thing I'm learning on this trip is about relating to other people. At home, everybody knows me and I know them. I know what to expect. Here I have to learn to know other people," I added.

"*You* have to make an effort to learn to know people. You can't wait for the other person," Paul said.

"Lib is really good at making new friends. She has a way of making people feel comfortable with her. She has a good sense of humor. People like that," I said, adding, "John has a good sense of humor, too."

"Yes, you're right."

"I think people up here, at least the ones I've talked with, have a set of values that we in the States lost about 20 years ago."

"What do you mean?" asked Paul.

"Well, I talked with three people at Dawson Creek who made me realize they value friendliness and helping others. It must be the frontier spirit that Karen said we would find beginning at Dawson Creek."

About 8:30 A.M., on Friday, June 18, as we were driving up a hill, the engine of our motorhome began missing, acting as if it was not getting enough gasoline. I turned off my computer because of my concern for the problem.

"We'll see whether it gets over that hesitation like it did last time. It did it for about three or four miles last time and then the sputtering stopped," said Paul. That was when we were heading toward Dawson Creek a couple of days earlier.

The engine acted like it would not make it up the hill and so Paul pulled over to a frontage road at Charlie Lake, British Columbia. The Graybeals pulled over as well. It turned out that we were parked there for one and one-half-hours while Paul and Don the tailgunner replaced the distributor rotor and carburetor filter.

Our three RVs continued on the Alaska Highway, and we hoped that the engine problem was solved. But by quarter of eleven, the engine was still gasping as if it wasn't getting enough of whatever it needed to run. Paul pulled into a rest area to take another look at the problem.

The first time we had to stop, John and Lib stayed with us the whole time! This time, I encouraged them to go ahead because the tailgunners were behind us. So they went on, which took some pressure off me and I suppose Paul and Don, too, although men don't seem to care about those niceties. It would have bothered me that the Graybeals were sitting on the side of the road waiting for us when they could have been sightseeing somewhere ahead.

Laurie was going to teach me "Hand and Foot," a card game, while Don and Paul worked on the engine, but before we got to that, Paul decided to remove the in-line filter located between the gas tank and engine.

From my passenger seat window, I saw him blow hard on the old filter. As he did so, silt and dirt came out. Paul himself did not see it, but I did and slid open my window and told him so. Don shuffled underneath the motorhome and replaced the in-line gasoline filter. With the stop taking only about a half-hour, Laurie and I didn't get to the card game.

We returned to the Alaska Highway, climbing hills as they appeared. The engine never missed another beat or gasped for gasoline. Another problem was solved.

That day Paul and I ate lunch on the road without stopping, in order to get to the campground at Fort Nelson in time for the festivities that evening. That was one of the conveniences of motorhome travel, being able to prepare and have your food with you. I fixed a turkey sandwich for Paul and handed him one half at a time. At a construction site, we stopped behind traffic, which allowed Paul to eat pears from a small tin with a fork and then drive on as traffic moved ahead. I fed him peach frozen yogurt for dessert.

As we continued on toward Fort Nelson, I sat at the dinette table enjoying the scenery and eating my lunch—a ham sandwich, half an apple, a piece of chocolate mint fudge that I had bought at Minter Gardens, and about six peanuts. I had learned to count the peanuts; otherwise, the scale numbers went up dramatically!

On that part of the Alaska Highway, there was almost constant conversation on the CB among people other than our tour group. Earlier that day, we had had the airwaves almost to ourselves.

Don and Laurie, as tailgunners, stayed behind us; it was comforting and they were congenial.

We drove slowly through gravel beds of road construction while looking ahead at gorgeous views of valleys with mountains in the distance.

"Paul, did you know Number Six is about a mile ahead?" Laurie asked over the CB.

"No, I wasn't aware they were that near," Paul said.

"They were trying to reach you," Laurie told us.

"Oh, I had the volume turned down somewhat so the madam and I could talk," Paul explained as he reached immediately for the knob on the CB and set the volume to the proper level. We could receive the Petersons' message even with the volume turned down because they were closer to us than the Graybeals.

"I didn't know we had any madams on this trip!" said John who could hear the conversation between Laurie and Paul.

Paul asked John if he had seen any moose. No, but he saw a black, slender animal that Don identified as a mink. It scampered across the road in front of John's motorhome. The Graybeals continued in front and Don and Laurie stayed behind us. In the distance were the majestic Rocky Mountains.

"How about it, Number One, are we in business?" asked Don on the CB.

"You mean have we found the trouble?" asked Paul.

"Yeah," said Don.

"Seems so. I thank everybody who helped, thought about it, prayed about it, and worked on it," said Paul.

Our three RVs arrived on time at the Husky 5th Wheel Truck Stop and RV Park in Fort Nelson, British Columbia, population 3,804. Under sunny skies but with a cool wind blowing, we parked once again on a dirt campground.

At the appointed hour, our chatting and laughing group toured Fort Nelson by bus with the driver pointing out places of interest, including a 41-bed hospital. He took us to the town center where we visited the Fort Nelson Heritage Museum with its displays of pioneer artifacts and wildlife. I stood in awe in front of a mounted, seven-year-old white polar bear towering above me, encased in a glass booth with wood framework. Upright on its hind legs, it was seven feet tall, 700 pounds. A small cub was at its feet.

At our departure meeting that Friday night, June 18, in Fort Nelson, we learned the schedule and events for the next two nights at Muncho Lake. Scott and Karen also presented for our consideration information and costs on optional dinner shows, rafting, tours, and the flight to Barrow that would be available in the coming days.

Back in the motorhome, Paul and I settled in for the night. He stretched out on the sofa, his head propped against a pillow, with the television on but the sound off. Even at home, he liked to lean back in his recliner with the television screen alive and the sound muted.

I began to write in my journal. As I did so, I thought about the good time I was having and how well our group was getting along together. To my surprise, I was beginning to feel more relaxed among these so-called strangers than I felt among some people at home that I had known for years. I suppose it was partly because I knew that our caravaners' time together would be limited, after which we would go our separate ways, and that we had come together for the purpose of having a good time as we saw new sights and enjoyed new activities together.

But it was also from being a part of the congenial interplay of my fellow caravaners at departure meetings, on sightseeing tours, and at special dinners—they were unknowingly modeling for me how to become less "picky" about the *way* in which people acted or talked to me. I was accepting others as they were rather than expecting them to behave in a certain way. That attitude was putting me at ease with them. I looked for the knowledge or humor or truth of what they said instead of at whether I was offended by how they said it.

I realized that at home, too often I took offense when none was intended. At home, too often I assumed the worst in people's comments rather than the best. On the road, I was learning that if someone said they wanted to go rafting and I didn't that was no reflection on me, or if I wanted to paint a sign and they didn't that was no reflection on them.

Already my fellow caravaners were unknowingly teaching me a lesson in human relations. I knew that each of them was well-intentioned while at the same time each of them had a different way of speaking and behaving. I loved their laughter and willingness to respond good-heartedly to one another in what I would have called affronts in my formerly exacting mode at home. In the nonthreatening atmosphere of a caravan tour, I was learning a valuable lesson not only for the remainder of the trip but for the rest of my life.

When we left Fort Nelson on Saturday morning a few minutes before eight o'clock, it was cool and raining. We headed for Muncho

Wilderness Camping

Lake and a wilderness campground where all of its electricity was furnished by a generator.

An hour later the highway turned to a wet mixture of dirt and gravel. Our wipers droned back and forth incessantly. John was ahead of us that day and could pass along to us via the CB information on road conditions.

"Cheer up, Paul. Things could get worse! As a matter of fact, they just did!" said John as we left a dirt and gravel section of construction and glided onto a slippery, slimy section of road. Paul and Don Peterson commented that the mud was better than dust for visibility and for engines.

"I just hit a couple of good bumps, Paul," said John.

We saw a new roadbed on the left off to the side under construction as we traveled the old roadbed of the Alaska Highway.

Thankfully, there was not much traffic as we maneuvered through about 25 miles of construction. A wide muddy road lay ahead in the rain, framed by low banks on either side and scrub pine trees. Huge orange road scrapers and graders continued their work in the muck. We drove through a muddy, rough place that made me feel like the motorhome was being rocked ruthlessly in a cradle. I held on to my seat.

"I never would have believed these roads if I hadn't had the opportunity to come on them," I said to Paul, who gripped the steering wheel and looked intently ahead. Our windshield wipers kept swishing back and forth.

"I see that they've painted the back of your coach recently, John," Paul said over the CB. Instead of a creamy color, it now looked brown. It always frightened me a little when Paul used one hand for holding the microphone of the CB in a situation that seemed to call for both hands on the wheel. Yet I did trust his judgment and driving skill.

We drove through blackish gravel with a shiny look. "Is it slippery?" I asked.

"Oh, yes, it is definitely," said Paul. "I now know the difference between construction and detour," he stated. He likes to examine the meanings of words.

81

"What's the difference?"

"One's worse than the other!" Paul replied and we both laughed.

The gravel highway narrowed and had no shoulder. On the right lay a trench of muddy water.

Getting safely through the construction area, we headed up Steamboat Mountain about 10:30 A.M. in the rain. John commented that compared with the paved terra firma highway we had left behind, this was more terra and less firma! The highway clung to the side of the pine-covered mountain with a drop-off into a valley far below. No hard-surfaced shoulders offered leeway. Roadside signs with arrows indicated sharp curves as we continued up the Alaska Highway. My eyes swept a broad vista of mountains beyond mountains. The magic of the scene seemed to ease the anxiety of the road.

By the time we approached the J & H Wilderness Resort at Muncho Lake, we had seen a caribou going into the brush beside the road, a beaver dam, and two Stone sheep, a kind of mountain sheep indigenous to northern British Columbia.

As we drove along Muncho Lake on our left, stratified rocky slopes edged the highway on our right. The lake lay among pine-covered foothills, some with barren peaks, others snowcapped.

Karen and Scott, wagonmasters, were on the horn to us that afternoon as we drew near. The rain continued as we entered the driveway of the resort about two o'clock and drove slowly downhill toward the shimmering lake. Scott, with his transceiver in hand, walked toward us and directed us over the CB to pull in beside the Graybeals, with our motorhome nose only 15 feet from the water's edge. The beautiful turquoise water reflected arcs of light caused by the steady rain. Its magnificent color reminded me of Lake Louise, in Alberta.

With the motor turned off and the RV in its site, the unexpected beauty of the wilderness lake touched me. I simply sat in the passenger seat gazing at the view. How fortunate we were to stay in such an idyllic place. How thankful I felt to its Creator for our safe arrival, for the peaceful scene with its lake and mountains, for indeed, the

Wilderness Camping

idea of beauty, the ways in which it entered my life, and the ability to enjoy and appreciate it.

Turning away, I set about preparing two scalloped potato casseroles for the potluck supper with our comrades that night at six o'clock in the nearby gazebo. We had signed up for what we wanted to bring; we also were to bring our place settings and any drink we wanted other than coffee.

While the casseroles were baking (one at a time in the microwave/convection oven), I wrote in my cloth journal:

> With rain lightly tapping our roof, Paul lounges, eyes closed, cap still on his head, on the sofa. He drove very well today, negotiating skillfully through wet, muddy, and narrow roads, a lot of them under construction and most of them without shoulders.
>
> The ride was exciting because of the rain, which added uncertainty about slipperiness and earth slides. At the start, our rigs became covered with brown mud. After we passed through the major construction and it continued to rain, the rigs started looking cleaner.
>
> Quiet here, I hear a few birds. Peaceful—healing for the soul.
>
> It's raining, yet the sun has just come out—casting shadows on this table!
>
> I just squashed a big mosquito. We must remember the repellent before we go out.
>
> A speedboat is going down the lake leaving a silver ribbon streaming behind.
>
> Louie and Ann Beeler are walking under umbrellas by the lake shore. They are Number Two in our group from Montana.

Our 24-person tour group held its first potluck dinner in a damp, cold, breezy, screened-in gazebo. The weather, however, failed to dampen our appetites, as was obvious from the way we heaped food on our plates from the sumptuous buffet. Lib said she was surprised how varied and good everything was considering the short stock in our pantries. The Caravanas company furnished apple, cherry, and blueberry pies and coffee.

After we'd eaten the delicious meal, and sat around the tables talking, with some people playing Hand and Foot, Clem Swagerty took it upon himself to give a little speech to our group. He said we had been on the road eight days and we had all gotten to know one another better and were all getting along. Then with his voice that was accustomed to yelling from his years of football coaching, he led us in a rousing cheer for Karen and Scott, our wagonmasters, and Don and Laurie, our tailgunners. Clem had coached football at a college, in the air force, and at Soledad and San Quentin Prisons, California. At his retirement, he was associate warden at San Quentin Prison.

Since it was cold and rainy, Paul and I shortly returned to our RV. The J & H Wilderness Resort had hookups (water, electric, and sewer) but the electricity came from a campground generator that was turned off at 8 P.M. and we didn't know what time it would come on in the morning. So we were housebound with no television!

"Are you planning to stay for the evening?" I asked Paul just for fun as he lounged on the sofa, his cap forward over his brow.

"Well, of course," Paul replied.

"I notice you still have your hat on," I said.

"Yeah, well, it's more comfortable," he said and made no effort to remove it.

It was not yet eight o'clock as I sat once again in the passenger seat of the motorhome looking out at the vast basin of turquoise water called Muncho Lake. A breeze made the lake surface shimmer like quicksilver. Intermittent rain speckled the windshield that I gazed through. Although it was dusk and rainy, the sun almost burst through evening clouds.

A man wearing a baseball cap covered by a hooded parka stood shivering by the shore as his scarfed spouse snapped his picture. Too cold to stay long by the lake, even in mid-June, they soon left. The jetty in front of me jutted into the lake—empty of people but laden with an eight-foot diameter, white satellite dish, an orange trash bar-

Wilderness Camping

rel, a campfire circle with plank seats, three picnic tables with attached benches, and a sign: Please Keep Pets on Leash.

On a sunny evening the area would be popular. But that night only an occasional person visited. Usually a lake draws audiences like the moon draws tides. But while tides always respond, people, with minds of their own, sometimes refuse the call of the lake in favor of a dry, warm recreational vehicle.

As I thought about that Saturday's events, I concluded that the best thing about it was camping in the wilderness so near a beautiful lake. A close second was arriving safely. Third was the excitement of the journey through wet, muddy construction roads and roads with little or no shoulders.

I checked my closet to be sure I had brought along the materials to make two signs for the Signpost Forest coming up at Watson Lake two days away. A craft session was scheduled for the next day at Muncho Lake during which I hoped to work on the signs.

· 8 ·

Signpost Forest, Watson Lake, Yukon Territory

DURING THE NIGHT, snow had capped one of the mountains in the distance. Our motorhome was parked beside Muncho Lake, British Columbia, on a new Sunday morning, June 20. When we arrived the afternoon before, I had not seen any snow on the mountain. Silently, while I slept, the snow had gently blanketed the peaks in the distance. The scene let me know that someone, unseen, far greater than I, kept our world running its course.

The sun shone as Paul and I walked up the hill to the campground restaurant for a group breakfast. I was thinking ahead and telling

Signpost Forest, Watson Lake, Yukon Territory

myself that I wanted to work on the signs in the craft session that afternoon.

Just after we all gathered at scattered tables in the frontier-style restaurant, Karen came to Paul and asked him to say grace. At first, he declined.

"But you're so good at that!" I said.

"Okay. I'll do it, Karen," and he got up to be more in the center of the group.

"I'm sorry I didn't give you more notice," Karen said.

"Heavenly Father," Paul began and the words just poured forth— thanks for our being together, for safe travel, for the hospitality of the campground, and for the food.

On the way back to our RVs from the group breakfast, Mary Jo joined me and was profuse in her appreciation of Paul's grace. She also said that she, Ann, and Louie were getting together at the gazebo at 10:15 for a little church service. She didn't know what they would be doing, but it would be something. We had free time between breakfast and a scheduled boat ride on the lake.

The word spread and almost everyone in the group came and quietly sat around wooden picnic tables on the deck of the gazebo, slightly higher than the lake. The sun shown brightly on us as we talked in soft tones.

Louie's voice rose over the murmurs as he suggested we begin by singing something. Mary Jo said, "Amazing Grace."

Not having a strong song leader or a hymnal among us, we got through it, with memory and determination.

Mary Jo asked Lib to read her scripture passage, and Lib announced what it would be. Whereupon Louie and Ann exclaimed, "That's the very one we had selected!"

Lib read Psalm 104, which fit our surroundings and feelings. I followed with a short essay about friendly living and Mary Jo read a poem called "Family Love." We shared our joys and concerns. Much joy was expressed—Effie, who had sprained her knee on the trip, found herself walking without her cane the day before; Yvonne was glad that Wil was well enough to come on the trip that they had planned for five years; I was glad for the beautiful place. Concerns were expressed for world peace and for comfort for Willis and Yvonne on the death of his sister the day before. With my head bowed, I gave a closing prayer.

Then Paul suggested people give some background of their religious life; the backgrounds revealed were Lutheran, Presbyterian, Catholic, Assembly of God, Church of the Brethren, and Jewish. And there we were, all sitting around the same table, worshiping, sharing, praying!

Afterward we went on a one-hour boat tour of the lake. During the serene ride, our captain and narrator pointed out bald eagles perched high on dead tree limbs, an enormous beaver lodge with its crisscrossed gray sticks above the water, and several bush pontoon planes floating near the shoreline at a dock. He talked about the history, geology, animals, and fish of the lake as well as some of the local lore.

The narrator himself, wearing a captain's cap, a navy blue tee-shirt, blue jeans, and black athletic shoes, said he had lived at Muncho Lake for 15 years, having come from Ottawa. He said it took him two years to slow down and start to live stress-free.

"If you order something, it's usually late coming, and it's generally double the price you were quoted," he said of life in the wilderness. He had learned to take it in stride.

After the boat ride that Sunday, Paul and I walked a few yards from our motorhome to an outside pay telephone, where we called Jeff and Nancy. They said it was 90 degrees in Maryland and that they were well and busy. Jeff asked if we were taking any videos since we were new at that activity and had not had much time to practice with our first video camera before we left on the trip. We assured him we were taking lots of videos, although Paul thought I panned too fast. We told them about our impromptu worship service that morning, about the roads, and that we were having a great time.

On the breezy but sunlit deck of the gazebo that afternoon, Karen did counted cross-stitch during the craft session. She showed us an embellished, counted–cross-stitch piece that she had done. It included small, shiny beads. Skillfully done, it looked elegant and she planned to frame it.

Eunice worked on crocheting covers for canning jar rings that would be coasters. Effie sewed the Alaska Caravanas Voyagers® patch on her Caravanas jacket. Lib smocked a child's dress and showed us a quilted banner she was making. Others had their own projects or watched.

I had heard of people putting up a sign at what was called the Watson Lake Signpost Forest, a famous tourist spot that we would visit the next day. I wanted to make two signs, one for the Graybeals and one for Paul and me, that would show approximately how many miles we were from home at that spot. I also wanted the signs to survive their harsh winters. Using black enamel paint for the letters and numbers, I painted them freehand on an aluminum cookie sheet about 14 by 16 inches that I had bought in the supermarket at home and brought along for that purpose. The signs read

John & Lib Graybeal
Hampstead, MD
June 22, 1993
4,957 miles

and ours:

Paul & Bernice Beard
Westminster, MD
June 22, 1993
4,957 miles

I used the date of June 22 because our printed itinerary listed visiting the signpost jungle on that morning. (It turned out that we actually posted them on June 21.)

Before we disbanded, Laurie Peterson taught ten of us how to play "Hand and Foot," a card game similar to canasta.

Meanwhile, some of the men watched the U.S. Open golf tournament by this configuration—Karen and Scott had a satellite dish on their motorhome. Using an extension cable, someone hooked up the

Graybeals' 12-volt television set to the satellite dish connection and set it on a table outside the Bonises' motorhome. Folding chairs and an appreciative audience completed the scene.

This was followed in due time by the departure meeting at five o'clock, followed by a serving of pie left over from the potluck supper the evening before, followed by the Graybeals, the Beelers, and the Beards having dinner together up the hill at the camp restaurant.

A campfire scheduled for seven o'clock was postponed because the weather had turned cloudy and rainy again. It was to have included poetry readings from the works of Canadian writer Robert Service. I hoped we would do that later. So Paul and I ended the evening with Paul reading *The MILEPOST®* and me writing in my journal.

We said farewell to beautiful Muncho Lake, British Columbia, early Monday morning and headed for Watson Lake, a city of 1,700 located 175 miles northwest and just inside the border of Yukon Territory. Our faithful Alaska Highway led the way with many roadside signs that said Bump. Strangely, drivers could usually not detect those jolts ahead of time. I almost left my seat on one such jar—my seat belt constrained me. After riding the bumpy road for about an hour, we arrived at Liard River Hotsprings Provincial Park.

In swimsuits and sandals, Paul and I walked a long boardwalk, crossing an environmentally preserved wetlands that included orchid species, toward the steaming pools of hot water in a forest setting. At the brim of one, Paul and I paused. This would be our *first* dip in a natural hot spring! Others of our group were already in the pool bobbing up and down and calling out to us to come on in.

Karen had cautioned everyone at the departure meeting the night before to stay in the hot springs only 20 minutes at a time and then stay out 10 minutes. I looked a second time at these new friends to identify them in their swim outfits. Once I was in the pool on their level and enjoying the hot water, they all came into focus. It was great to be a part of that extraordinary hot dip, splashing around, enjoying the hot water, half floating and half walking around, talking and laughing with one another, all of which further developed our friendships.

Signpost Forest, Watson Lake, Yukon Territory

It was unbelievable that ordinary water in the ground would be so warm and enjoyable. Paul and I took videos of one another in the water so that our son Jeff would believe that we actually went into a hot spring.

We were all reluctant to leave, but by almost 11:00 we were back on the Alaska Highway. The hot springs had relaxed me so much that my eyelids felt heavy and I wanted to take a nap. But the road was bumpy, under construction for 118.5 miles, and constantly offered new, charming scenery.

A large sign mounted above a stone cairn announced Welcome to the Yukon—the Magic and the Mystery. The Graybeals, the Foremans, and we pulled over for a photo opportunity and had fun pointing to the sign and standing beneath it smiling at the camera.

By mid-afternoon on that Monday, June 21, under sunny skies with dusty rigs we drove into a dirt campground at Watson Lake, Yukon Territory, called Campground Services, Inc. Riding joyfully in a golf cart, Karen and Laurie came to meet us and showed us where to park in the large campground. Scott then waved us into our specific gravel campsite.

After doing our own thing for a while (some did laundry), we gathered for a departure meeting at five o'clock and first of all got caught up on the day's happenings within the group. A total of five dings marred the windshields of the vehicles in our group that day—a ding meaning that a piece of gravel or stone had been flung up from the road by a passing vehicle onto the windshield causing a starburst or other small break in the glass. We had yet to see a bear. Paul wanted to see more wildlife. When we talked about the hot springs dip, Lib and Mary Jo said it had made them drowsy, too, but Paul and Clem said it made *them* hungry.

Then the wagonmasters gave information about the next day when we would arrive at Whitehorse. There we would wash our rigs. We should get loonies (Canadian dollar coins) at the office to operate the water wand, and we should wear "grubbies" and boots for the operation. At Whitehorse we would attend a dinner show and get acquainted with a Canadian treat known as Nanaimo bars, a two-tone brownie confection that Karen loved. These bars are native to British Columbia and Yukon Territory but generally not known in the United States. They are like double-decker brownies, with the bottom like a fudge brownie with nuts topped with a cream-cheese-and-shredded-coconut layer and crowned with a thin chocolate frosting that is solid like a chocolate bar only thinner. Sweet, delicious, and fattening!

The wagonmasters also gave us an address in Anchorage, about two weeks away, where we could receive mail. That would be the only mail pickup on the trip. Karen let us know that there were nice laundries at Whitehorse and Tok, but not at Moose Creek or Dawson City. She said that the next morning the wagonmasters would leave at 7:30 and the tailgunners at 9:00, as usual meaning that the Caravaners should not leave before 7:30 or after 9:00.

After the departure meeting on her way back to her motorhome, Thel Heathcock accidentally tripped over a tree root that protruded up through the dirt campground. She fell forward, landing on the front of her white sweatshirt and white pants. John immediately rose to the mishap with an ax and summarily cut the root out of the ground in less time than it took the rest of us to think of it. Thel said she was okay, and I knew her wardrobe was ample, since people in our group had been kidding her about buying a new sweatshirt at every opportunity. Yet I was sure I'd be sore and stiff the next few days if I were her.

It poured rain as Paul and I dressed for the canteen show in Watson Lake that night. We had had sunny weather all day with a few drops when I went to the camp store at Campground Services, Inc., but one just never knew what the weather would be—the rain could stop by the time we wanted to go to the show, which was 7 P.M.

A school bus took us from our campground to the area of the Watson Lake Signpost Forest and the canteen show. While riding in the bus, I got my first glimpse of the Signpost Forest. From a distance the signs looked like a mishmash of colors and rectangles with scribbling. The forest stretched for about half a block in several directions with a backdrop of tall pine trees jutting skyward.

Signpost Forest, Watson Lake, Yukon Territory

Disembarking from our bus, which parked on a dirt area near both the Signpost Forest and the canteen show tent, I saw the jungle of signs up close. Posts had been planted in the ground and on these were nailed or screwed handmade printed signs giving the names and other information important to the designer such as age, hometown, miles traveled to that spot, and date. Even license plates from different states appeared among the melange. The forest of signs gave me a sense of the enormous number of people who had walked there ahead of me.

The Graybeals and Paul and I looked for a place among the 18,000 or so signs to post the ones I had made at Muncho Lake. Although our signs were dated for the next day, we wanted to take the opportunity at hand to post them.

We saw that Wil had already found a good place for the appealing wooden one he had made for our whole group. But there was no further room on that post. After marveling at the size and creativity of the varicolored collection that was posted on both sides of long stretches of sign-laden posts so that together they looked like high fences, almost like a maze, we came across a likely place on posts just outside the entrance ramp to the Watson Lake Information Centre.

We didn't realize it at the time, but our spot turned out to be just behind and to the left of the original sign that started the whole thing. Carl Lindley was in Company D, 341st Engineers, U.S. Army in 1942 working on the construction of the Alaska Highway. He first posted the white sign on a red post that gave the distance from that place to his hometown of Danville, Illinois, 2,835 miles. He later autographed the sign in 1992, when he attended the celebration of the 50th anniversary of the Alaska Highway. Also on that occasion, a time capsule was buried nearby with a bronze plaque commemorating the anniversary.

Since Carl's original sign in 1942, visitors from all over the world have been adding their own signs that told how far they were from their homes.

Paul used sheet metal screws to fasten our sign to a post and gave John two such screws to fasten his, which he did. No official

ALASKA AT YOUR OWN PACE

"Since Carl's original sign in 1942, visitors from all over the world have been adding their own signs that told how far they were from their homes."

ceremony, they just did the job. I assisted Paul by holding the aluminum sign in place because it was breezy.

Following this unofficial action, we walked on the dirt grounds to a large brown army-type tent for the canteen show. A summer production, it took its theme from the building of the Alcan highway, not the gold rushes, and therefore its format was similar to a USO show in the 1940s.

Good fun with top-notch performers, it contained a mixture of music, comedy, and long-legged beauty, with audience participation. I laughed until my stomach ached when Clem was invited on stage, underwent being garbed in a Hawaiian grass skirt, and instructed in doing a Hawaiian dance by the star singer of the show. The audience joined in such songs as "It's a Long Way to Tipperary."

Back at the campground, I looked at the map. We had many miles west and north to go before reaching the Top of the World Highway and Alaska. The farm girl in me wondered how many ruts in the road ahead we'd have to straddle.

· 9 ·

Cleaning Up at Whitehorse, Yukon Territory

THE NEXT MORNING, Tuesday, June 22, we left our campground at Watson Lake a little after 7:30 and headed west for Whitehorse. According to the map, the stretch of Alaska Highway on which we would travel that day dipped south into British Columbia and back north into Yukon Territory seven times en route. All praise to the decision makers for improving the highway by removing curves and resurfacing it, but I wondered how such road construction would play out for us.

"Before we left the environs of Watson Lake . . . I wanted to stop at the Signpost Forest to see if our signs were still up and to take some pictures."

Before we left the environs of Watson Lake, however, I wanted to stop at the Signpost Forest to see if our signs were still up and to take some pictures. The Graybeals obliged, and Lib took a snapshot of Paul and me standing beside our two signs and pointing to them.

As we left the Signpost Forest area, Paul drove the motorhome slowly on a frontage road, his eyes scanning the businesses looking for an auto parts store. I got up from the passenger seat, retrieved my blue jacket from the closet toward the rear of the motorhome, and started back along the center aisle toward my seat. Suddenly I saw a red stop sign.

"Whoa, whoa!" I shouted.

Paul hit the brakes, I went forward but stayed on my feet until he realized he was already more than halfway through the intersection and stepped on the gas to continue. That changed my equilibrium a bit too fast and I ended up sitting on the floor and then lying back on it. Not a jolt but rather graceful. Meanwhile, Paul was unaware of what was going on behind him.

I sat up and said: "Look at *me!*"

Paul turned and saw me sitting on the floor. He did a double take.

Cleaning Up at Whitehorse, Yukon Territory

"I was too intent on looking for a NAPA store and missed that sign," he said, apologetically.

"I've had my excitement for the day," I said, stepping back into the passenger seat.

"I'm sorry about that stop," said Paul.

"Well, I was thinking of both seeing our signs still up *and* being dumped on the floor," and I laughed.

During the drive on the Alaska Highway from Watson Lake to Whitehorse, I realized I was enjoying traveling, going to dinner and shows, and sightseeing daily. I realized also that I was enjoying Paul's stress-free attitude about the money we were spending. It was a great feeling to travel when you didn't have someone questioning your spending decisions.

That Tuesday morning, we stopped at a gravel turnout and looked ahead at the beautiful Cassiar Mountains with snow in crevasses decorating its peaks and lush valleys, all under an almost cloudless blue sky. Even though the roads were gravel, curvy, and under construction, and we bounced up and down, the beautiful scenery overwhelmed us.

We went through many wide construction areas with heavy equipment moving dirt. No center line guided us, of course. At one place Paul had to back up because we were about to go on the wrong side of a barrier ahead. Meanwhile, John drove past us and went on ahead, "Sorry about that, Paul, I didn't want to stop," he said over the CB.

We understood completely. At that point, Paul thought we were getting stuck in the deep, damp combination of dirt and gravel as he stepped on the gas to go right and forward. After some hesitation, the wheels took hold and we continued ahead on the dirt highway under construction.

At several construction areas, young women in orange hard-hats gave us instructions on what to expect and do, talking to Paul after he opened his side driver's window. Even as we bounced along in one of the dirt construction areas, we looked out over a deep pine valley to mountains in the distance, with snow spotting their tops and with blue sky in which a few white clouds hung.

After lunch in a rest area, we changed drivers and I drove for almost 150 miles. (On the way across the United States, I had spelled Paul several times in Minnesota, North Dakota, and Montana.) We were about to leave British Columbia and I wanted to have the experience of driving in it. My stint also included driving over the Yukon River Bridge in Yukon Territory, one of only three in the river's 1,980-mile length from that bridge on the Alaska Highway to the Bering Sea.

"This is Bernice driving over the longest bridge on the Alaska Highway," Paul said as he videotaped me from the passenger seat.

Along our route, beautiful Teslin Lake reflected mountains and puffy white clouds. Our paved highway ran beside the lake. Paul said as he videotaped, "This is Bernice driving along in the Yukon and just as happy as a lark and saying, 'Isn't that beautiful! Isn't that wonderful! Isn't that magnificent!' and a lot of other superlatives." (Paul likes to make fun of my exuberance sometimes.) The scenery on the whole day's drive captivated us with its mountains, valleys, lakes, and rivers.

We arrived at the Pioneer RV Park at Whitehorse, the capital of Yukon Territory, about three o'clock. The population of Whitehorse is approximately 22,000. The Yukon River runs past the downtown business section, which lies on the west bank.

The location of Whitehorse made it a hub for transportation, communication, and supplies for its own province as well as the Northwest Territories. The Royal Canadian Mounted Police were headquartered in Whitehorse. Since 1894 they have been responsible for law and order. At first they used dog teams to travel through the Northwest Territories to the Arctic coast. Airplanes and automobiles later replaced the famous dog teams.

The first order of business for our tour group was washing all of our units, now hardly recognizable under layers of dust and mud. Wearing boots and jeans or shorts, we fed loonies into a machine that let us hand-spray water. Our group worked fast to take advantage of the timed water, some caravaners brushing the sides of rigs, while others worked on the front and rear or bent over to scrub the tires.

Cleaning Up at Whitehorse, Yukon Territory

We looked like a group of happy young people doing a car wash to raise funds for a community project.

"Lib, you feed the loonies," John said to Lib, clad in jeans and sandals. And she headed for the slot in the machine that provided water.

"Bernie, would you drive our rig up then, please?" Paul said as he paused in helping the ones ahead wash their rigs. (Bernie is the name Paul usually calls me.) One by one, with the help of many in our group, the RVs pulled away looking fresh and clean.

That job done, Lib went with Paul and me to downtown Whitehorse for groceries. John needed peanuts, peanut butter, and celery. We needed frozen yogurt. We found a Food Fair and hurried back for a steak barbecue and the Sarsaparilla Sisters Show, a musical revue sponsored by the campground.

A full day, but memorable and enjoyable. Memorable because I could visualize our signs at the Signpost Forest at Watson Lake, Paul had accidentally dumped me on the floor of the motorhome as we moved along, and I drove in British Columbia and Yukon Territory and across a Yukon River Bridge. Enjoyable because of the good company Paul, John, Lib, and the others in our group are, the delicious barbecued steak, and the hilarious show put on by the Sarsaparilla Sisters.

Wednesday was a day for group sightseeing and another fun show. A white school bus took us to a dock on the Yukon River. Sunny, bright, and in the low 60s, the weather held for a boat cruise on the river through Miles Canyon, historically known as the last treacherous obstacle for prospectors traveling by boat to Dawson City during the Klondike gold rush. It was at places a narrow canyon, yet turquoise blue water with its swirling whirlpools invited our boat to skim it.

Piloted and narrated by a young woman and an assistant, also a young woman, the boat had an open top deck and an enclosed lower deck. I spent time on both. Paul even sat on the upper deck bow, looking with binoculars and taking videos of the canyon walls; a bald eagle on a high tree limb, a beaver lodge close to the bank; the Robert Lowe Suspension Bridge that we went under; the swirling, swift water itself; and the smiling members of our caravan tour for whom the cruise had been specially arranged.

After the cruise, our bus driver left our group off in downtown Whitehorse for lunch on our own. Libby and I shopped for tee-shirts for our husbands and ourselves to be worn at the Craziest Tee-Shirt contest, a later date on the tour. We got so involved we had to run down the street to meet our bus, which was waiting for us. Everyone cheered as we got on! We were a minute late—1:31 P.M.

The people in our group generally were on-timers. In fact, I heard Clem say that it was like a group of senior citizens he knew—if you were on time, you were late! Hardly ever did we wait to start a departure meeting or a tour.

We toured the SS *Klondike,* a sternwheeler retired in 1955 and resting on land beside Schwatka Lake in Whitehorse. Our young, British-speaking, tour guide from India escorted us around the once-useful cargo-hauling vessel and told of its history. He also pointed out the areas where only first class passengers were allowed—an observation deck with white wicker arm chairs, a dining room that seated 16 persons at a time with white tablecloths and ironstone china rimmed with green rings. We looked into the engine room; we saw the station of the purser who was in charge of the mail.

In sunny, warm temperatures, we lingered outside to take videos and photographs of that white wooden leviathan, almost as long as a football field including its huge red sternwheel. Lib and I posed beside the wheel to show its enormous size. (It did wonders for our images of ourselves by making us look like gaunt fashion models in comparison!)

On we went in the white bus for a tour of the city of Whitehorse. We saw the first church built there, a small building with an A-sloped roof, a small steeple tower, and unpainted wooden board siding.

As we passed the Whitehorse airport Paul was especially interested in the DC3 airplane mounted in such a way that the plane itself was a wind vane. Inside the bus, we chatted, laughed, pointed out sights, and exclaimed about them as we went along. The tour concluded with a video about Whitehorse at the visitors' center.

Cleaning Up at Whitehorse, Yukon Territory

Just before I got back on the bus, I saw a dust-covered bicycle leaning against the portico pillar. It looked like it had a real history. A young man standing beside the bike lifted a water bottle to his mouth. I stopped to chat. I did not ask his name, but he said I could take his picture. He told me that in August of that year he planned to be in Iowa, completing *six* years of travel around the world, including China and Australia, on his bicycle. Mary Jo, who had seen me taking his picture, asked him how he could afford to travel like that all those years. He said he "worked some" on the way.

"Where did you come from before here?" I asked.

"Europe," he replied. What a story he would have to tell!

Back at the campground, we ate dinner in our motorhome and dressed for the Frantic Follies. I wore my blue soft denim pants-and-jacket outfit, low-heeled white pumps, and carried my white handbag with its shoulder strap. Before going to the show, however, we called home. It turned out that the best part of the whole day was talking with Jeff and hearing him say, "Everything's fine!" when I asked if he had heard about his tests of last week. He had been recuperating from an advanced case of testicular cancer.

"Did you talk with your doctor from the hospital?" I asked.

"He called today," Jeff answered.

You can't imagine the relief and thankfulness those two words—"Everything's fine"—gave to Paul and to me!

On to the Frantic Follies. Professional musicians and actors put on a show portraying the history of the Klondike gold rush era. A master of ceremonies who reminded me of Pat Paulsen kept us laughing. Another musician sang an opera selection from *The Marriage of Figaro* by Wolfgang Amadeus Mozart. That same person recited "The Cremation of Sam McGee" by Robert Service. A dramatic poem, the actor did it justice as did two other actors depicting Sam McGee and his pal pushing a dogsled.

We laughed and enjoyed the music, which included some sing-alongs, and audience participation. Don Heathcock from our group was selected from the audience to go on stage and be the fall guy while a belle dressed in an 1890s long, tight-fitting, red-sequined

101

gown sat on his lap and sang to him. "Pooky," she called him, a name that he would hear off and on from that night forward from kidding caravaners.

After the show, we all walked two blocks to a fast-food restaurant. While I licked at a small frozen vanilla yogurt, Paul ate nothing because sweet desserts caused irritation of his intestinal tract. Soon it was time for us to return to the campground. Twelve of us climbed aboard Scott and Karen's 40-foot motorhome, some went with Karen in their Raider tow car, and some with Bob and Rosemary Conway in their 23-foot Tioga® motorhome. Scott and Karen felt that the group could share rides from time to time to nearby places in order to save piles of money for special buses. That money they used to provide additional tours and shows for us.

When we returned to the campground about 9:15 P.M., it was still daylight. With Paul's help, I did two loads of laundry. While there, I talked with Karen, who was also doing laundry. She had a bachelor of science degree in physics from UCLA and had done some work toward a master's degree. Originally interested in oceanography, she became instead a parts engineer first for Rockwell and then for Hughes Aircraft. We had a nice chat before she finished her clothes and left.

It was still daylight when Paul and I carried our folded clothes back to our motorhome at 11:20 P.M. The hairstylist had told me that morning when I called for an appointment that the sun would not go down at all that night, that it would be daylight 24 hours that day. I would not stay up to notice.

Fortunately, the next day, Thursday, was a free one at Whitehorse. I could sleep later than on a travel day. The Graybeals and Wrigleys had a 10:30 A.M. tee off at a nearby golf course. Other campers in our tour group did laundry at the campground, shopped for groceries, and did more sightseeing on their own in Whitehorse.

Using the motorhome for transportation, Paul dropped me off at Strands Hair Salon in the Yukon Inn where I had a 9 A.M. hair appointment. Meanwhile he looked for the correct in-line gasoline filter part. He wanted to have one on hand in case a batch of bad gasoline plugged up the present filter.

Cleaning Up at Whitehorse, Yukon Territory

My hairstylist wore a tan walking outfit, similar in style to a Swiss alpine hiker's, except not quite as short. In her mid-20s, she told me that she had come to Whitehorse four years earlier from Winnipeg and Calgary. Originally a hairstylist, she became a cook for a gold mine. She had panned for gold but found it back-breaking work, especially for only the few flakes of gold that she gleaned.

The beauty salon had no air conditioning but some electric fans because they usually did not need it. When it did get hot, as it did in May that year, about 85 to 90 degrees, they closed the shop.

She did a fine job on my hair. The bill was $16.50 for a shampoo and blow-dry plus G.S.T. (Goods and Services Tax), bringing it to $17.66. I gave her a $3 tip. It was my highest-priced hairdo to date on the trip.

Afterward, Paul and I went to a nearby Extra Foods store. It was the first time I ever bought just one stalk of celery, or even saw them sold individually, and one carrot. I planned to make a chicken casserole for the potluck supper the next evening at Moose Creek.

Paul did not find the in-line filter that he sought, so he would keep looking.

That afternoon, while Paul relaxed on the motorhome bed, I got out the computer and wrote in my journal:

> When I look at the trip calendar and see what lies ahead in Alaska, it seems almost unbelievable—we've already seen and done so much and "the best is yet to come!"
>
> The Alaska Highway, starting at Dawson Creek, has been so unpredictable that I did not even get out my computer. Paul needed my navigational skills, such as they are, and my sight skills—his eyes need confirmation on traffic lights and signs. More than that, my own curiosity would not let me get involved with the computer. I wanted to see whatever was to be seen.
>
> Instead of the computer, I kept my clothbound journal handy and jotted conversations and notes in it. It was handier to use the pencil and journal. Yet when I get home,

it will be a time-saver to have the notes already in the computer. It's a catch-22!

As I think about the worship experience our group held last Sunday at Muncho Lake, I think that we all were just about popping with the gratitude we felt toward God for the pleasures of this trip and other blessings. As Mary Jo Cornell said to me, "I just feel so grateful for everything." We all needed to express it in a group worship.

. . . Sunny and warm when I started this entry, I now hear rain. I had not finished writing those very words when the rain stopped. That's the way it is here. It's really true—if you wait five minutes, the weather changes up here.

I have many mosquito bites. One mosquito flew into the motorhome as I held open the screen door during cleaning this morning. I'll be on the alert until I find it.

And so that Thursday afternoon in Whitehorse, Yukon Territory, I had a great time writing and printing out the yield. In the end, however, I put away all the equipment for now, including the laptop computer. I had found that with sights to see and navigation to help with, shuffling the computer from my lap to the dash was cumbersome. In addition, using the auxiliary generator to furnish electricity for the computer stirred up dust outside when we made rest and lunch stops, something not appreciated by other travelers. So I elected instead to use my orange-colored mechanical pencil and cloth-bound journal.

At five o'clock that day—it was still Thursday, June 24—we had a departure meeting. We learned that we should take one lawn chair per couple to Scott the wagonmaster. He would use the chairs to reserve a campsite for each of our units at Moose Creek, a Yukon Territory government campground, the next day. Since no restaurants or other activities were available in that wilderness setting, we would have a potluck dinner and campfire.

"You'll need your bug spray for the outdoor events," the wagonmasters reminded us.

To prepare for dry camping at Moose Creek, Paul drove the motorhome to the gas pumps on the Whitehorse campground and

Cleaning Up at Whitehorse, Yukon Territory

filled the gasoline tank. Then he drove to the LP gas tank, also on the campground. Most campgrounds provide this commodity. Although our LP gas tank held 21.8 gallons, we never filled it more than 80 percent because the liquefied gas required space to vaporize before leaving the tank. The furnace, refrigerator, water heater, and stovetop range (mine was still a virgin) used LP gas as vapor. Should LP gas reach an appliance as liquid, it would be a fire hazard.

An LP gas detector gave us peace of mind. Ours was mounted on the inside wall of the motorhome behind the swivel chair nearest the entry door. It had a tiny flashing light that indicated it was sniffing for LP gas leaks. Should a leak develop, the detector would automatically shut off the LP gas.

Returning to our campsite at Whitehorse, Paul filled our freshwater tank so that it was two-thirds full. Because water was heavy and its additional weight would reduce gas mileage, he never filled the tank with more than he thought we would need for the next few days. I handed him a plastic gallon container to fill with drinking water from the campground spigot. We would not have a water supply or hookup at Moose Creek the next night.

In the morning before leaving the campground, he would dump, or empty, the "black" and "gray" water holding tanks into the sewer hookup at our campsite. It would not take more than a few minutes. Motorhomes have two separate holding tanks: one for gray water that drains from the sinks in the kitchen and bathroom and shower and the other for black water flushed down the toilet.

To dump, Paul would put on his leather gloves, then retrieve the blue sewer hose from the compartment at the rear of the motorhome. Next he would remove the cap from the concrete opening at the dump site in the ground and place the outlet end of the sewer hose into that opening. He would then connect the inlet end of the sewer hose to the motorhome after removing a safety cap. Paul always drained the black water tank first and then the gray water tank.

When the tanks were drained, he would disconnect the sewer hose from the motorhome and flush the hose with water. He would then reattach the safety cap to the discharge pipe from the holding

105

tanks, return the blue sewer hose to its storage place, and wash down any waste spillage on the concrete apron before recapping the opening. Either Paul or I would later pour a chemical deodorizer and disintegrater into the toilet and flush it into the black water holding tank to help keep it clean and fresh. Dumping is one of those down-to-earth duties that RVers take in stride after the typical initial reluctance.

The Wagonmasters had said we should use our bug repellent at Moose Creek. I wondered just how buggy Moose Creek would be. I did not relish mosquitoes as much as they apparently savored me.

· 10 ·

Campfire at Moose Creek, Yukon Territory

ON FRIDAY MORNING, I sat in the passenger seat of our motorhome ready to leave the campground at Whitehorse, Yukon Territory, for Moose Creek campground, 255 miles northwest. I checked to make sure the bug repellent was under the kitchen sink in that cupboard, but hoped we wouldn't really need it later.

John had pulled their motorhome forward to dump and I saw Lib inside it straightening up their sofa area. The Wrigleys, who were parked between us, prepared to leave also. Numbers Three, Four, Five, and Two had already departed. Big 50 was leaving—Karen had gone ahead in the Raider scouting to see if the Reindeer Farm was open.

Outside, Paul unhooked our water hose from the campground spigot. He stuck his head inside the entry door and asked if I was finished with the electricity. Then he unplugged that heavy, black electric cord from the campground outlet, wound it up, and stored it in the outside rear-end compartment. Soon he sat behind the steering wheel.

"Forty, this is Number Nine. We're ready to leave the park," said Clem over the CB.

"Did you hear Scott? He reminded everyone to turn their lights on," replied Laurie.

"Okay. I got you," Clem confirmed.

Yukon Territory required lights on at all times on the road.

"This is Number One calling 40. Are you there, please?" said Paul on the CB.

"Number 40 is here," said Laurie.

"Okay to move out?" asked Paul.

"Sure is," replied Laurie.

"Number Six going out," said John.

"Number Six," affirmed Don in 40.

And so John and Lib pulled out ahead and we followed them out of Pioneer RV Park toward Moose Creek. We soon gained the Alaska Highway and moved toward the city of Whitehorse, which we bypassed. Shortly thereafter, we left the Alaska Highway and took the Klondike Highway that would take us to Moose Creek for that overnight and eventually to Dawson City and the Top of the World Highway into Alaska. We would rejoin the Alaska Highway at Tok, Alaska. In other words, we would take a loop route in order to visit Dawson City and the Top of the World Highway.

Our wagonmasters had cautioned us not to take the Alaska Highway to Haines Junction, which turned west just outside Whitehorse, but to take the Klondike Loop highway that went north instead.

As we moved along, Paul said it was 40 degrees outside. I was glad we had filled the LP gas tank in case we needed to use the furnace. Old Sol almost, yes did, break through clouds, but only momentarily.

I felt refreshed after a long night's sleep, having gone to bed at nine o'clock. During the night I got up and videotaped how light it was outside at 1:30 A.M. I didn't know how it would look when we showed it back through the television screen.

Hardly half an hour after leaving Whitehorse, we visited the Northern Splendor Reindeer Farm, where reindeer were raised. At the tourist office, a man gave us each a clear plastic cup of grain. We walked behind that building in sunshine toward a wire fence beyond which a herd of reindeer lingered, some gray, some tan with their familiar antlers. Their paddock was a muddy, dark-soiled, wooded field with thousands of hoof prints reminding me of the barnyard on our dairy farm. Through the open spaces in the fence wire, we offered the grain from the palms of our hands. The reindeer came willingly to the fence.

"Through the open spaces in the fence wire, we offered the grain from the palms of our hands. The reindeer came willingly to the fence."
(L-R: Jackie and Paul)

"He doesn't even try to eat my hand," I exclaimed as the reindeer put its snout to my palm and swooshed off the grain with its tongue and big lips.

It was hard for me to identify the Rudolph song with these real reindeer who had no red noses and who seemed like normal domesticated animals, which in fact they were. Yet it was a thrill to actually see and feed one. I took a picture of Jackie Wrigley and Paul feeding them through the fence. A keeper later demonstrated feeding a two-month-old reindeer with a baby bottle.

The owner of the farm told us that there was no difference between a reindeer and a caribou other than that the reindeer was a domesticated animal and the caribou was wild. The animals originally came from Russia by the land bridge thousands of years ago. The owner got into reindeer farming by buying 50 reindeer from a man in Northwest Territory who had about 33,000 of them. His reason for raising them was to provide them to people who wished to get into the reindeer-related industry. That industry included fantasy, tree farms, Christmas productions, and meat.

Leaving the reindeer farm, I drove for an hour. Midmorning, the Graybeals and we stopped at Braeburn Lodge, a place that the Graybeals said was famous for its cinnamon buns. Indeed, we shared one that was seven inches in diameter, the biggest bun I ever tackled! Fortunately, we cut it with a knife, each person cutting what he or she wanted and then eating it with a fork from small plates that came with the bun. Dee-lectable! It was just the beginning of a series of delicious cinnamon buns that we would discover and devour during our Alaskan adventure.

Back on the Klondike Loop, with John in the lead and Paul driving, John said over the CB: "Some of our RVs in the road up here."

"Okay," said Paul.

"Guess they don't need our help. They're waving us on around," John reported.

As we passed, we saw rig Number Eight with Eunice standing by the roadside and the Raider unhooked from the Allegro®. Scott and Karen were standing near the Raider. Another RV of our group, Num-

Campfire at Moose Creek, Yukon Territory

ber Two, the Beelers, was there also. The tailgunner, who had been behind us, pulled in to help Scott and Karen.

"Number One, did you notice any problem back there?" John asked on the CB.

"I thought I saw Lou had a fire extinguisher in his hand," Paul said.

"You know, Scott changed a tire. Maybe a wheel bearing is shot. That's the only thing I can think of that would cause a fire when towing," said John.

"Either that or a rotor dragging. But that's not too likely," returned Paul.

We moved on. Around noon we realized that no one had heard from Clem and Effie since leaving Whitehorse. When the tailgunner tried to reach them on the CB, he got no response. I hoped they had not gone up the Alaska Highway instead of the Klondike Loop.

Paul filled the motorhome's tank with gasoline at Carmacks. He likes to keep the tank at least half full when we're in an area that may not have many gas stations.

Shortly afterward, the Graybeals and we stopped at Five Fingers Rapids turnout for pictures and lunch. It was a spectacular place in the Yukon River where four huge pillars of conglomerate rock (eroded by nature and looking like tiny islands with trees and brush on them) made five channels or fingers through which the river flowed, the narrow spaces creating rapids.

Under sunny skies, we continued north on the Klondike Loop, seeing magnificent mountain scenes with both pine and deciduous trees. Occasionally we saw volcanic ash on roadside banks.

A man in an orange hard-hat stopped us to tell us there was construction ahead and that we should wait for a pilot car to lead us through it. A Caution Loose Gravel sign stood guard. Soon we followed a pilot car (actually a pickup truck) that had Follow Me printed in black on its orange rear truck-bed door. It guided us through a stretch of wetted-down gravel that was a single lane adjacent to a dug-out lane that was being redone from the base up. Crews and huge machines were in various stages of completing that lane.

The pilot car left us as it turned around to go back for another group of vehicles. Our road, while wider than a two-lane highway, remained dry gravel with no center line. As we looked ahead we saw a travel trailer coming steadily toward us.

Then as if by contrast, a big truck with billows of dust behind came barreling toward us, thundered past, leaving us in a mini-dust storm. That part of the Klondike Loop seemed to be a raceway for huge trucks, the race being to determine who could raise the most dust. Paul reached for the CB and said to John, "This gives real meaning to the expression, 'Eat my dust,' huh?"

"Sure does," John affirmed.

To protect our RV from dings from traffic passing us from *behind*, Paul stopped twice to let two cars go past, slowing quickly so the opportunity for throwing stones was minimized. He could only hope that traffic from both directions would go slowly when they passed us.

John reported that a little car gave his new motorhome its first ding.

"Not too bad. Smaller than a dime," he added.

Paul explained to me what caused the dings: "The gravel gets in your tire treads and if it's not real tight, it'll throw it out at a certain speed and throw it up in the air, and the guy behind you gets it. And actually you can throw them up against yourself. But I don't think you can ever get it against your own windshield." So far we had escaped any dings.

On that stretch of the Klondike Loop, the roadbed was raised about three to five feet from the gutters on the sides. Tiny red flags on short wood stakes at the side of the road marked holes or bumps. Very few guardrails prevailed. Similar to ours in the States, those few did stand guard where drop-offs were really hazardous, such as on a long curve high above a canyon or valley below.

Roadside signs alerted us. Usually orange with black letters, the signs were often diamond-shaped and announced the following:

Caution

Loose Gravel

Reduce Speed
Fresh Oil
Bumps (This sign had jagged peaks like a saw blade.)
Be Prepared to Stop
Construction Ahead

"This is 40. Anybody heard from Clem and Effie since we left?" Don asked faintly over the CB at 2:08 P.M.

Neither Paul nor I heard an answer to Don on the CB. (I was still hoping they had made the correct turn onto the Klondike Loop.)

Moose Creek Campground, a provincial one, had no telephone and its 30 campsites could not be reserved. So Scott planned to arrive early and place a lawn chair on each site to hold it for our group. With the Raider problem en route today, I didn't know what to expect at the campground. When we had stopped at Five Finger Rapids for lunch, Scott had sped by in the Allegro®, tooting his horn. I didn't know if he had transferred the lawn chairs to the motorhome, but I did notice that the Raider was *not* being towed behind.

"I wonder where Clem and Effie are," I said to Paul as we neared Moose Creek.

"I don't know," Paul said. "I would not have seen it, if John hadn't said something. I wasn't expecting it so soon," said Paul referring to the turnoff we took onto the Klondike Loop just outside of Whitehorse. I wondered if the Swagertys had taken the road to Haines Junction by mistake.

"I would have gone right on by, too," I said.

The wagonmasters had said that we should slow down after crossing the Moose Creek bridge at Mile Marker 229.2, that the campground would be on the left-hand side shortly thereafter, and to look in the bushes for the sign. It would not be easy to see, they cautioned.

It was almost four o'clock under sunny skies, after 255 miles, when we saw the Moose Creek Campground sign and turned onto the dirt road with its surrounding aspen forest. Ahead, we saw Scott who told us where to find our campsite.

We drove ahead slowly through the Yukon government campground in the wilderness, looking at the individual sites that were

113

almost hidden from one another by the aspen forest. And who should be tucked into their own woodland hideaway but Clem and Effie. What a relief!

Sure enough, our lawn chair marked a site for us and we pulled in. Paul went outside to look over the motorhome and soon came back in. "Boy, there's a million mosquitoes out there! Where's the bug spray?" he exclaimed.

By five o'clock we gathered for a departure meeting, our lawn chairs encircling two heavy, wooden picnic tables, cloth covered and ready for the potluck supper to follow. Scott discussed the next day's travel to Dawson City. He would find out later the fate of their tow car. He said that steam came out of the front of the car and flames came from the motor. They put out the fire, but five miles later, the car started smoking again. Karen had taken it back to Whitehorse for service. If it could be fixed during the three days that we were at Dawson City, Karen would meet us at Tok; otherwise, she would meet us three and one-half weeks later when our tour returned to Whitehorse. The Petersons, true to their tailgunner responsibilities, had gone with Karen to Whitehorse.

Soon we gathered around the picnic tables for another sumptuous potluck meal. Uninvited, the mosquitoes zoomed around, too. Afterward, we sat around, shooing them away and enjoying the campfire that John had built. A veteran in that art, he also adroitly tended the fire, using his ax to split the logs and add them to the blaze at the right time. It seemed strange, however, to enjoy a campfire when it was still daylight.

That campfire gathering turned out to be the one we couldn't have at Muncho Lake because of the cloudy, rainy weather. Rosemary Conway grandly presented large stars cut from cardboard cereal boxes and sprinkled with glitter to Clem Swagerty for his performance in the canteen show at Watson Lake and to Don "Pooky" Heathcock for his debut in the Frantic Follies at Whitehorse. Both had been called from the audience to come on stage and be the fall guy for the leading lady. Both had joined in the shenanigans, doing us all proud, and bringing everyone in the audience a tremendous amount

Campfire at Moose Creek, Yukon Territory

"Soon we gathered around the picnic tables for another sumptuous potluck meal. Uninvited, the mosquitoes zoomed around, too."

of hilarity. It was only fitting for Ro to honor them with a trophy from us all.

At the campfire, Clem enthusiastically told a long but funny story about his travels with one of his football teams when they all bought derby hats for the unbelievably low price of 50 cents each.

The Yukon Territory, Dawson City in particular, where we would go the next day, was home to Canadian writer Robert Service (1874–1958), born in England. In his memory, John recited one of his poems "The Cremation of Sam McGee." All 15 stanzas of eight lines each!

Thel Heathcock introduced us to a group game called "Stir the Mush." Standing up, she used a long stick and moved it around in circles on the ground as if she were stirring a pot of mush. Then she invited others to come and "stir the mush" and she would tell us if that person was doing it right. Many of us took up the challenge but, alas, failed. In the end, the secret was to clear one's throat before beginning to "stir."

Lib stood up and introduced Paul who she said had a turkey story to tell. He did not know she was going to do it, but she had asked me privately if I thought he would be embarrassed and I had said no. He got right into the story. It went like this:

> "It seemed that we were having guests to dinner and the day before, my wife, Bernie, was having trouble thawing a 15-pound frozen turkey. She tried to thaw it in the kitchen sink, but the sink was not big enough to keep the turkey covered with water. So we discussed the matter and decided to try the bathtub. We filled the bathtub with water and put the turkey in it. But the turkey floated to the top. I thought of putting a lawn chair on it, but that was too big. We had a new plastic stepstool, so we got that and put it on top of the turkey, but that didn't work too well because it and the turkey *both* floated. I wracked my brain and I thought that somewhere in our house we had an old heavy iron skillet. So I took that skillet, put the plastic stool over that turkey, and put that heavy iron skillet on top of that stool—and that sucker stayed down!" Paul swung his closed fist downward. "And that's how we thawed out that turkey in time for the next day."

And everyone around the circle just roared.

Scott was also an enthusiast of Robert Service's poetry. Wearing a green-and-white baseball cap, he recited, like John, from memory, "The Spell of the Yukon," and parts of three other poems that had to do with the Yukon. I sensed that the poems expressed Scott's own love for the Yukon, too. Each event that we shared as a group helped us to get to know one another better.

The fickle weather began teasing us with raindrops. Soon our picnic area was quiet and the fire was out as we returned to our traveling homes in the woods. At 8:30 P.M. it was daylight. We had to adjust to going to sleep by the clock rather than by darkness.

Paul's and my campsite, and I imagine the others' also, turned out to be the most beautiful to that date—a spacious hideaway in an aspen forest in the Yukon—memories are made of such things. As I sat at the dinette table looking out, even in the rain, the sun shone on white aspen trunks with their quaking, coin-like, silver-green

Campfire at Moose Creek, Yukon Territory

leaves. They made me think of elegant things, like a fawn or a delicate white-and-green fuchsia plant.

With no television, all was quiet. I reached for my pencil and journal. Paul preferred taking a nap on the sofa to playing a game of cards or dominoes. So while he rested, I wrote, which of course, was something I relished.

I felt miles away from civilization, although I was not. Silence reigned but for the soft brushing of my pencil. How healing. I felt like I could think for miles and miles. How seldom in my life did I have that kind of peace and quiet. It had not been since I was a young girl living on a farm far away from other dwellings and people. I missed that total privacy and peace, which let me be myself.

In my journal, I asked: "What is life about? What is really important? For Paul? For me? Do I really want to know? Is travel an escape from problems?"

Outside the dinette window, two tiny brown-and-white finches fluttered among the blue snapdragon-like blooms of the lupine on the floor of the woods. Quickly, quickly they alit and tugged then flew to another leaf and finally away.

The forest of aspen trees shared a little space with some green spruce trees, their branches accommodating and circumventing the aspen tree trunks.

John had said via CB that we began our fifth week on the road that day, Friday, June 25. Our caravaners and the elements had treated us kindly, and we were truly enjoying the trip of a lifetime.

I realized one thing that made it such a pleasure was my spouse's attitude toward money. "If you want it, get it," he said. During most of our marriage, we had waited and abided by budget restraints before buying something. So his generous attitude was part of the excitement of the Alaskan excursion.

Scott came by, with umbrella and clipboard in hand, to write down our site number. He told us that Karen and the Petersons were back and that Karen was eating supper in their motorhome. The Raider, however, remained at Whitehorse. The garage closed at five that day and would not reopen until Monday, when they would examine the Raider and let Karen or Scott know what needed to be done. In any case, the Raider would stay in Whitehorse until we all returned that way after our circuit of Alaska, in about three and a half weeks. Apparently, it was not necessary for Karen to stay in Whitehorse while repairs were being made, for which we were all glad.

So the day drew to a close with its problems handled as much as possible. We were in a lovely forest with our rigs almost hidden from each other. The rain had stopped. Paul read the outside thermometer from inside.

"It looks like it could be 48 or something like that," he said. "I believe I'm 'oomeroused.' Don't know what I want to do next," he concluded as he stood in the aisle of the motorhome. The term "oomeroused" came from my grandmother who used it when she would stand in one spot not knowing what she wanted to do next. Then he lay down on the sofa, yawned loudly, and turned on his right side. It was 9:05, but still light outside.

At the dinette, I continued writing:

> When we get to Fairbanks, I hope to write and mail lots of cards with a North Pole address. When we fly to Barrow, I hope to mail a few cards from there, if possible. I don't know if they have a post office there.
>
> Much excitement lies ahead. The Top of the World Highway, the Eskimo culture at Barrow, the sight of Mount McKinley, the ocean ferry, and all the sights in between, not to mention the fellowship among our group.

It would not be long before we would tackle the Top of the World Highway—three days. But for that moment I just wanted to enjoy the Elysian woods in which we found ourselves. And I hoped no mosquitoes had snuck inside when we came back from the campfire.

· 11 ·

The Top of the World Highway

"GOOD MORNING," I said to Scott through the screen of the small window above the kitchen sink in our motorhome. It was Saturday, June 26, at Moose Creek Campground, Yukon Territory, a travel day to Dawson City, also in Yukon Territory. And then in two days we would travel that long-awaited and famous, or infamous, Top of the World Highway.

Wearing a red-and-blue cap, Scott stood outside grinning. He said quietly, "We're going to have a pancake breakfast over at Don and Laurie's rig. Bring a plate, silverware, and cup. Between 7:30 and 8:00."

"Okay. Thank you!" I said as Scott walked on, hands in pockets, to the Graybeal site. His low-key manner embodied the "quiet of the morning" spirit implied by his and Karen's restriction on anyone in the group starting a generator before the wagonmasters left the park.

I returned to the dinette table where I had been eating my usual breakfast of cereal and hot water. Paul resumed eating his sweetened corn flakes. "I will go over, but I'll only eat one pancake to be sociable," he said.

The day was bright; sunshine made the aspen leaves glisten. Unlike last night, they were still, not even a quiver. How beautiful it was as shadows and light shimmered across the dinette tabletop onto the sleeves of my yellow sweater.

We covered the 101 miles on the Klondike Loop and arrived at Gold Rush Campground in Dawson City a little after 11:00 on that Saturday. Dawson City lay cuddled up to the Yukon River and the Ogilvie Mountains. It dates from 1896 when gold was discovered in nearby Bonanza Creek. With a population of 1,852, the city is a Canadian national historic site. On June 21 it has 20.9 hours of daylight while on December 21 that decreases to only 3.8 hours. Its present-day gala frontier atmosphere greeted us from places of business like Nancy's Restaurant, Diamond Tooth Gertie's, and the Triple J Hotel.

The campground was dirt, except where recent rains had left large pools of water that a young woman worker was trying to channel away using a shovel. Low, wooden, portable platforms that looked like a boardwalk were provided for us to walk on as we stepped down from the motorhome and gained dry ground.

After hooking up to electricity, Paul and I walked to Front Street, which ran parallel to the Yukon River. After browsing in windows and stores we entered Nancy's Restaurant. I tried delicious salmon chowder and a Nanaimo bar while Paul enjoyed a turkey sandwich.

The Top of the World Highway

At 2 P.M. our group along with other visitors gathered at the information center for a walking tour of the city. A young woman wearing black high-topped shoes, a long black skirt, a high-necked long-sleeved blouse, and a straw hat with a wide black band and matching pouf welcomed us. She told us that the Yukon River flowed past Dawson City into the Bering Sea. By the time it reached Dawson City it was filled with silt, making it a muddy color.

She related the history of Dawson City, describing as she did so the activities and names of the dance hall girls, the role of the Mounted Police, and the gold rush atmosphere. She said that the border of Alaska was about 70 miles away from Dawson City. She suggested places of interest in the city that we might want to visit, including the Robert Service and Jack London cabins. Following her brief tour, we were free to see the city on our own.

While Paul took photographs of the community library, the Robert Service School, and the Triple J Hotel and Restaurant, I walked to the Robert Service cabin.

Tom Byrne, an actor, sat in a rocking chair on the sloping green lawn in front of a small grandstand reading the poetry of Robert Service. All of the seats were taken and it rained intermittently. But I stood for one and one-half-hours holding an umbrella, captivated by the poetry and Mr. Byrne's reading of it. He wore a black suit in the late-1800s style, a white shirt, and a black tie done in a bow with streamers hanging down.

After the reading, I joined the audience in walking up the hill to the log cabin that had been restored by the Canadian Park Service. I signed a register and viewed the inside of the house. I also walked all around the outside perimeter of the house.

On the way back to the campground, I heard what sounded like a crow, familiar to me in Maryland. Sure enough, a big black crow sat on top of a telephone pole, cawing as if it were in a cornfield at home.

That evening, reservations had been made for us at Diamond Tooth Gertie's for dinner and the show that included high-spirited can-can girls. The show girls later graciously posed for photographs with some of the fun-loving, venturesome, outgoing fellows in our group.

Still in daylight at 9:30 P.M., we boarded a coach-like bus for a five-mile ride to Midnight Dome. From that mountain crest we saw Bonanza Valley, the Klondike River flowing into the Yukon River, and beyond the river, the Top of the World Highway looking like a thin, silver necklace draping the side and top of a mountain.

Our guide said that the sun would set at 12:40 A.M. and rise at 2:30 A.M. (He also said that in the winter the temperature got down to *minus* 72 degrees *without* the wind chill factor.) When we returned to the campground by 11:00, it was still daylight, which made it seem like I was lying down for a nap instead of going to bed for the night.

The next day, Sunday, I struggled with what to do about worship. Of all things to do on a Sunday, our group would be touring the gold

"From that mountain crest [Midnight Dome] we saw Bonanza Valley, the Klondike River flowing into the Yukon River, and beyond the river, the Top of the World Highway looking like a thin, silver necklace draping the side and top of a mountain."

rush area and panning for gold! And at the very time I would normally be in church!

I went on the tour, of course. And I panned for gold at GuggieVille—and didn't find much, which salved my conscience. Our guide told us that no prospectors were getting rich overnight, but to those people it was a way of life, a life nobody wanted to give up. We indeed saw a young couple using heavy equipment working their claim. We learned that the oldest prospector there was in his mid-80s.

We saw the Discovery Cairn where the Klondike gold rush began when George Carmack found gold in a tributary of the Klondike River, Bonanza Creek. We learned about the dredging process from a tour at the huge Number 4 Dredge, now in drydock, so to speak. In its active years, it floated on a man-made pond of water as it scooped soil from the land ahead through its system of great buckets, retained the gold, and spewed out dirt trailings behind it as it and its pond of water moved slowly ahead.

"We panned for gold at GuggieVille. Our guide told us that no prospectors were getting rich overnight, but to those people it was a way of life, a life nobody wanted to give up."

That afternoon, at our departure meeting, Karen and Scott primed us for the next day's historic drive on the Top of the World Highway to Alaska. They told us that the road had a high crown; we should not wander too far off it. When we met some trucks that would no doubt come barreling along, we should slow down and stop if we had to. If it rained, the road would be as slippery as ice. We were to drive *very* carefully and slowly—five miles an hour if the conditions demanded it.

The wagonmasters planned to leave the Dawson City campground at 7 A.M. and the tailgunners at 8:30 A.M. They encouraged the rest of us to leave early because there would be a long line of traffic waiting to board the ferry to cross the Yukon River. The Alaskan border opened at 9:00—we might have to wait at the border. Crossing the border without clearing customs resulted in severe fines.

The MILEPOST® told readers that the United States and Canadian customs were open only certain months and hours, that travelers should check with the Royal Canadian Mounted Police or visitor information center in Dawson City before entering the Top of the World Highway to make sure the border crossing would be open.

Our wagonmasters also told us that the next day would be a most important day for using the CBs and to keep idle chatter to a minimum. "Big truck coming" to RVs behind us would be a good use of the CB. There would not be many turnouts for videotaping, so we might want to do that as we moved along. It would be about 186 miles from Dawson City to Tok, Alaska, our destination the next day. They recommended that we go to bed early that Sunday night.

I wanted to drive a section of the Top of the World Highway—partly out of vanity and partly to challenge myself. Since the Graybeals had driven on the Top of the World Highway previously, I asked John for his suggestion. He thought that the best part for me to drive on would be the first part just off the ferry at Dawson City for the first climb up the mountain. That sounded agreeable to Paul and me.

Later that Sunday afternoon, our group cruised on the Yukon River in the direction of the Bering Sea to Pleasure Island. Our wagonmasters had told us that this was a special running of the cruise for

The Top of the World Highway

us. We went ashore at the Pleasure Island Restaurant. There we enjoyed a smoked salmon barbecue in an open-air pavilion with a wood floor and red-and-white checked cloths on the tables. The service was cafeteria style where we could see the salmon being grilled and talk with the friendly women behind the counter tending to the sizzling fillets.

Along with the tasty, fresh Alaska king salmon, we enjoyed a green salad, baked potato, fresh tea biscuits, beverages, and chocolate cake. Shortly after seven o'clock we headed back to Dawson City and our campground to get to bed early.

It was Monday, June 28—the big day! We had been on the road a month, since May 28. Today we would take on the notorious Top of the World Highway and enter awesome Alaska, both first-time events for Paul and me!

The day before, Paul had filled the gasoline tank of the motorhome in preparation for an early morning departure. We planned to leave the campground at 7:20 A.M. with John and Lib in the lead since they had been over the Top of the World Highway once before.

I moved about deliberately, trying to stay calm, as I poured cereal into a bowl and covered it with milk. Paul was still in bed, but I heard him stirring. At the departure meeting, Karen had said that the day's trip made you feel as if you really were driving on the top of the world. It was high and you looked down from a narrow road.

By 7:14 A.M. under cloudy skies, we pulled out of the Gold Rush Campground at Dawson City with Paul behind the wheel. Five minutes later, we waited in line for the free ferry to take us across the Yukon River to the Top of the World Highway that eventually led into Alaska.

We could see some of our group's RVs already loaded onto the small, open-air, red-and-white ferry. The Graybeals were ahead of us in line. A car pulling a trailer separated us. We watched as the Graybeals slowly drove onto the gaping ferry stern. Then the trailer in front of us moved forward and parked beside the Graybeals.

In turn, we descended a dirt slope toward the metal plank of the ferry. The rear end of our motorhome dragged on the dirt bank. A woman in a red hard-hat standing on the ferry signaled to us with her hands to pull up behind the Graybeals. "They're packing us in," Paul commented from behind the steering wheel. The nose of our motorhome was only two *inches* from the rear of the Graybeals' vehicle.

The ferry moved forward. I wrote 7:44 A.M. in my travel log. The Ferry crossed the water smoothly, as if it were skiing on snow. Scott's voice came over the CB. He was already across. The view from the highway was tremendous, he said. The crossing took only four minutes. We docked on the opposite side of the river. Paul drove off the ferry onto, technically, the very beginning of the Top of the World Highway! But of course we were still at river level. Since we had decided that I would drive the first few miles, he maneuvered into a turnoff nearby.

The sun was shining by that time. I got behind the wheel, took a deep breath, thought a short prayer, stepped on the accelerator, and headed the motorhome up the mountainous earthy road with bushes and trees on either side. I had no idea what lay ahead where the road seemed to end and meet the sky.

With both hands on the wheel and my eyes on the dusty, hard-packed gravel road that tracked the ridges of the mountains, I tried to listen to Paul: "You're doing fine. The only difference on this road is that it is not paved and it is higher up than those we are used to."

By then I was thinking, There are no guardrails and no center line on this gravel road. Countless times I had walked and ridden over dirt roads like it back on the farm where I grew up. I could still feel the smooth fine dirt under my bare feet as I walked home from school. When my father drove our car on the meadow road to my grandparents' house, sometimes he would struggle with steering the car as it slid around in the muddy ruts, sometimes he straddled the deep ruts by staying delightfully up on the middle hump and one high shoulder side or the other. Farm life had prepared me well for roads like that Alaskan one.

The Top of the World Highway

On I drove for an hour, not daring to look too much at the scenery below the road. At a large turnout on the left, with the motor running, Paul and I exchanged seats.

As he pulled away from the turnout, I looked over at him. Wearing his tan cap and a short-sleeved shirt, with both hands on the wheel, he leaned forward, eyes ahead. I sensed he had been waiting patiently for that moment. I was glad to give him his turn. Besides, I wanted to look at the exhilarating heights and grand vistas.

"Sharp curve to the right coming up," John said over the CB. As we made what was almost a right-angle turn, I caught my breath, glad to see one of the precious few guardrails separating us from a deep valley below. Contrasting with the seemingly bottomless valleys, canyons, and steep drop-offs, I was seeing *tops* of mountains from *above* them or at their same height. It was like circling in an airplane getting ready to land.

From Dawson City, in our motorhome we had crossed the Yukon River by ferry and were tackling the Top of the World Highway. That same highway, the one that lay before us, would lead sooner or later into our main objective for the trip—Alaska.

· 12 ·

Welcome to Alaska!

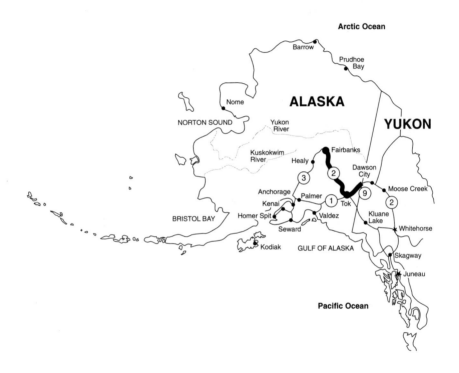

"ARE YOU U.S. CITIZENS?" asked the United States customs agent through my passenger-side window.

"Yes, sir," I replied. Holding a clipboard, he stood erect as if at attention in the army.

"Did you buy anything in Canada that you are taking back with you?" His dark sunglasses made it impossible to see his eyes.

"Yes, some gifts," I answered.

"Is the amount over $400 each?"

"No, sir."

"Do you have any firearms?"

Welcome to Alaska!

"No."

"Do you have any alcohol?"

"No, sir."

"Have a good trip," he said and turned away toward the small building from which he had emerged originally.

Paul pulled forward to a large parking area where the Graybeals had already stopped. A sign welcomed people to Alaska. We had arrived! Called *Alyeska*—the Great Land—by the Aleuts, the 49th state with its beauty, mystique, and adventure lay ahead.

Camera in hand, I hurried out of the coach. After filming a smiling Lib, John, and Paul beside the sign, I knew I wanted to somehow get closer to Alaska. Not caring if anyone thought I was being ridiculous or not, I walked to a nearby road bank, stooped over, and with the soft ends of my fingers, touched the brown soil, dragging my fingertips briefly over it. I brushed a nearby rock with them and gently squeezed blades of grass. I had touched Alaska!

After stops at the gift shop in Boundary and the historic, weathered, brown buildings of the trading post in Chicken, where miners still trade gold for supplies, we continued on our high-level highway.

"We had arrived! Called Alyeska—*the Great Land—by the Aleuts, the 49th state with its beauty, mystique, and adventure lay ahead."*

The Top of the World Highway had connected with the Taylor Highway, where we continued to have "top of the world" views. So much so that when we came to another turnout, we pulled in and both John and Paul climbed atop our motorhome and videotaped the enormous view of the Alaska Range mountaintops and valleys.

Moving on, the CB crackled and sizzled from time to time with messages from John in the lead and Don behind us somewhere.

"Six to One. A couple of nice swales around the curve to the right," John said over the CB to Paul.

"John and Paul climbed atop our motorhome and videotaped the enormous view of the Alaska Range mountaintops and valleys."

"Okay," Paul replied.

Soon the motorhome bounced through those dips, but less so than had we not been alerted by John.

"My co-pilot says we've got a 9 percent grade coming up—heading downward," said Don Peterson to Number Six on the CB a while later. The Petersons had also traveled the road before.

"Got some good ones a quarter mile ahead of you, One. They're very visible," John said. Soon we saw deep potholes ahead to maneuver around.

When not concentrating on the road conditions, I saw the spiked tops of black spruce trees for

Welcome to Alaska!

miles. And then I spied a barren stand of burned-over spruce trees. All of the scenery had a backdrop of a clear blue sky with ever-changing fluffs of white clouds.

"Yipes! Whoa! Yow! Wow! My, oh my! Yikes!" I exclaimed as Paul had to drive dangerously close to the edge of the road at one particular place—so close I could not see any part of the shoulder of the road through my side window when I looked down, only an abrupt, steep drop-off. Several other places were almost as unnerving to me. From my vantage point, looking down at the side of the road in relation to the side of the motorhome gave the optical illusion of being too close to the edge of the highway. That seat location somehow amplifies one's sense of danger and close calls by the driver. I was very thankful that I had confidence in Paul's driving ability.

"Four-wheeler comin' atcha, One," said John.

"All right," Paul replied, in full control.

"Four-wheeler right after the road scraper, One," John cautioned again a little farther along the road.

We descended from the Taylor Highway to link up with the Alaska Highway again. I was surprised to see quivering, leafy aspen trees and dark sand banks beside the road, an indication of the lower elevation.

"Hey, there's light at the end of the tunnel after all!" said John when he saw the Alaska Highway ahead.

Paul guided our vehicle onto the *paved*, two-lane, Alaska Highway. How nice and easy and smooth and fast it seemed.

"Well, we made it, dear!" I said, extending my hand across the carpeted hump between us.

"I would say," Paul affirmed as we laughed and shook hands heartily.

By late afternoon in Tok, our group was once again cleaning up its act at a nearby car wash and filling up with gasoline. At the five o'clock departure meeting, Karen and Scott went over the itinerary and route directions for the next day when we would drive from Tok to Fairbanks as well as details for the group's activities while in Fairbanks.

Karen handed to Paul and me ticket vouchers for our flight to Barrow. We were to be at the airport in Fairbanks 45 minutes ahead of our 9:25 A.M. flight on Wednesday. The return flight time was 9:30 P.M. that same day. Cost of the tickets was $363 each. Karen suggested we wear clothes in layers with a windbreaker, something for the head, and walking shoes.

After dinner and shopping at the Westmark Hotel in Tok, we returned to the comfort of our clean, at least on the outside, motorhome. It had been a long, exciting day. We had made it to Alaska! I wondered what could possibly top that day. Perhaps Barrow?

Traveling "down to earth" on the Alaska Highway brought its own thrills. En route to Fairbanks from Tok the next day, I gasped at the view, "Look over there! Wow!"

The snowcapped Alaska Range stood in the distance across a wide, evergreen valley under a blue, almost cloudless sky. The countryside seemed fresh, clean, green—vigorous. One after another, picturesque views of mountains, rivers, and valleys presented themselves.

That was our first full day in Alaska. One-fifth the area of the continental United States, its great expanse already revealed itself. I wondered how many of its other natural wonders we would see—the two oceans (Arctic and Pacific) and three seas (Beaufort, Chukchi, and Bering) bordering it, three thousand rivers, three million lakes, more than five thousand glaciers, and North America's highest mountain (McKinley). I wondered when and if we would see a dogsled team and meet a real Eskimo.

In the thick of a once-in-a-lifetime opportunity, I couldn't help keying into my laptop computer as we rode along on the Alaska Highway:

Welcome to Alaska!

What am I doing riding along here in Alaska? Am I just waiting, riding as I wait, to get to the next event on our itinerary, like North Pole or Fairbanks, or a bus tour or a cruise or a barbecue?

Or am I relaxing and taking in what I see, letting it become a part of me, realizing this is the time to seize the day. I will not be back this way again, or at least not soon.

It is tempting to "follow the itinerary," to race to the next place, madly taking videos and snapshots, without really getting a feel for where I am. After all, I have only brief moments in the great span of time wherever I go. But if I use my senses—sight, sound, smell, taste, touch—and emotions I will have experienced more fully what the tour offers. The places and people will be in my memory.

This is beautiful territory—Alaska. God has given Paul and me this opportunity to experience it and we want to do just that. Not every spot is beautiful aesthetically, but each place is important. My thankfulness continues.

We had entered the Alaska Highway at its Mile 0 in Dawson Creek, Yukon Territory, 1,520 miles southeast. At Delta Junction en route to Fairbanks that day, the Graybeals and we posed for pictures in front of a large sign that said: "The end of the Alaska Highway; now entering the Richardson Highway." We weren't saying farewell to the Alaska Highway, however, for we would be back on it at a junction farther southeast in a couple of weeks.

After lunch at Rika's Roadhouse at Big Delta State Historical Park, we drove into a nearby parking area for a first close-up view of the controversial Trans-Alaska pipeline. It was simply that: a large silver pipe, 48 inches in diameter, supported by metal posts, serious and industrial-looking. At this point, it had just spanned the Tanana River by way of the Alaska Pipeline Bridge. I would learn more about it at Valdez.

In mid-afternoon, we came upon Jackie and Lyle Wrigley in their motorhome at the side of the road. Over the CB, Paul alerted 40 , who

"At Delta Junction en route to Fairbanks that day, the Graybeals and we posed for pictures in front of a large sign that said: 'The end of the Alaska Highway; now entering the Richardson Highway.'"

was behind us. Paul and John both pulled over to the side of the highway ahead of the Wrigleys' coach and Don stopped behind it.

The Wrigleys had a flat tire on one of the inner dual wheels. They had waited three hours for the tailgunner who had "tailed" us as the last of our group on the road that day in accordance with his duties. The Graybeals and we, of course, had stopped several times for photos and for lunch, unaware of the Wrigleys' plight. When Paul asked Don over the CB if we could help, Don said he could handle it and so we went on.

It was not the North Pole that I imagined because there was no snow in June and it was a town with a population of 1,456, with bustling car and truck traffic and all the amenities of a little city—no elves, no sleds, no flying reindeer. Its history stemmed back only to 1944 when a man homesteaded the land and later sold it to a developer who had hoped to attract a toy manufacturer by naming it North Pole.

It did have a Santa Claus House in the center of its business area. Resembling a charming, rambling Swiss house with white painted

Welcome to Alaska!

walls that displayed Christmas murals and fancy writing on them, it played into my North Pole fantasy. Inside was a fantasyland of holiday and souvenir items, a potpourri of reds and greens, sparkles and bells. Paul bought golf balls with North Pole on them for his "secret voyager." A staffer postmarked "North Pole" on 13 postcards I had written earlier and dropped them in the mail box. (So much for my fantasy.)

Norlite Campground in Fairbanks with its 250 spaces became our home base for the next three nights. Our site was mostly dirt with some patches of grass; the camp road was dirt, too. Pine trees of various sizes curled around the end of the premises. At the office, a cordial staffer said she would arrange for a nail appointment for Lib and a hair appointment for me for Thursday morning.

Soon we all caught the shuttle bus for Alaskaland, the state's only theme park. It was a warm, sunny evening made even hotter as we approached the sizzling grills where we were served delicious salmon and halibut chunks. Not the only ones there, we ate wherever we could find room at one of the many wooden tables in a grove of trees.

Afterward I wandered alone in and out of authentic frontier log cabins and stores. Shopping and visiting museums were not Paul's favorite things to do. Later we and the rest of our group enjoyed a rollicking frontier show and returned to the campground by the shuttle bus.

While the others would tour the city of Fairbanks in the morning, Paul and I had a plane to catch.

· 13 ·

Flight to Barrow

WITH MY ARMS tucked in close to my body yet still touching my seatmates' arms, I sat in a middle seat on the right side of the Boeing 737 airplane. People continued to file into the narrow center aisle of the plane that offered three seats on each side. Large people seemed even larger from my seated perspective as they carried packages and knapsacks down the aisle. The temperature inside the plane was warm—no air conditioning yet. I wanted to take off my long-sleeved jacket. Paul sat in a middle seat in the row in front of me. It was Wednesday, June 30, the day of our flight to Barrow, Alaska.

Flight to Barrow

I looked at my watch—9:26 A.M. The flight had been scheduled to leave a minute earlier. Outside in Fairbanks it was sunny, about 70 degrees, and clear. It looked like a great day to fly and sightsee—unless the weather changed at Barrow.

Jackie Wrigley had lent me a handsome black knit cap, leather gloves, and black fur ear muffs. They were tucked into my purple-and-pink cloth tote bag, along with my 35mm camera and navy Western Maryland College sweatshirt. With the tote bag at my feet, I sat holding an insulated, light-weight coat on my lap. Perched on top of that was my white handbag with shoulder strap, my arms and hands encircling the whole mound.

It had been hard to know what to wear to Barrow. I ended up putting on a short-sleeved knit shirt, my denim pants outfit with its long-sleeved jacket, and my white canvas shoes. In my handbag was the ever-present, tiny, spiral notebook for jotting down the time, date, and subject of pictures that I took. I could put the camera itself in either the tote bag or my handbag. If the weather was really cold, I could add the sweatshirt and coat to what I was already wearing.

Paul, too, dressed in layers. On top of a short-sleeved knit shirt, he wore a long-sleeved, heavy cotton sweater (he's allergic to wool) that zipped up the front, a bright blue weather-repellent, long-sleeved jacket, light-weight trousers, brown leather shoes, and his tan golfer-style cap.

He carried the video camera in its gray canvas case with a shoulder strap. We had decided that he would do the videotaping because of his steady hand and his being the one carrying the bag. I would take pictures with the other camera because I was the one who usually did that.

Earlier, at 8:15 A.M., a taxi had taken us from the campground to the Fairbanks International Airport. Our flight would go first to Prudhoe Bay and then to Barrow, the northernmost organized community on the North American continent, 500 miles as the crow flies from Fairbanks. Unlike Prudhoe Bay, which was land accessible by the Dalton Highway north of Fairbanks, Barrow was accessible only by plane year round or by ship in summer when the ice melted enough to get through.

As we started to taxi down the runway, the flight attendant stood at the front of the plane giving the usual safety instructions. Soon the bump—bump of the paved surface stopped and we climbed into a cushion of air. Coolness flowed through the air ducts of the plane. I prayed for safe travel. When I opened my eyes, I saw the Cheno River below as the airplane climbed.

Both of my seatmates, young men in jeans, one with a tattoo of a heart with two arrows on his right arm, rested with their eyes closed. I looked around. The seats were covered in a plush, maroon material with a tiny, white, dash-like design. Dark red carpet ran the length of the center aisle. Paul wore his yellow night-driving glasses and, being his usual alert observing self, looked at the flight attendants who were talking with front passengers—getting ready to serve us something.

I didn't feel any fear about flying, although I realized its risks. The same was true for motorhoming, too. I wondered what the rest of our tour group were doing and seeing as they toured Fairbanks in a plush modern bus that we had seen at the campground before we left that morning.

The cheerful flight attendants reached me. They served an appetizing continental brunch—croissant, grapes, yogurt, butter, strawberry jam—in clear plastic wrap. About that time, my ears closed from the pressure imbalance; I swallowed, and they opened.

At 10:10 A.M., as I enjoyed the small feast, the captain came on the audio system: "Welcome aboard, ladies and gentlemen." His voice sounded faint, but I made out that we had crossed over the imaginary line of the Arctic Circle about five minutes earlier. I thought he said the temperature at Deadhorse (where we would land near Prudhoe Bay) was 57 degrees and that it was a good day for flying. When I looked out, however, I only saw what looked like fog but must have been clouds. At times I saw meandering rivers and brown land.

As time went on, the young man sitting beside the window on my right told me that he was returning to the oil field after two weeks at home for two weeks at work. He would have an hour's bus ride to his oil company after first attending a meeting at the airport. The young man on my left remained noncommunicative.

By the time the plane descended, I had eaten the brunch, including a gigantic fresh strawberry that was part of Paul's brunch (his doctor advised him not to eat seeds or nuts because of his diverticulosis), and decaffeinated coffee that they brewed for me.

Paul and I got off at Prudhoe Bay/Deadhorse just to see what we could see. The sign on the hangar said: MarkAir Welcomes You to Deadhorse. We had fifteen minutes before the same plane would leave for Barrow.

While Paul visited the men's room, I videotaped inside the airport ticket office area. It was crowded and buzzing with oil field people, mostly young men in jeans and long-sleeved work shirts, coming and going, carrying boxes, some standing in line at the ticket counter with arms folded in front of them. It was definitely an energetic, industrial milieu. As we left, we hurried past the ticket counter and through security again before walking on the brownish paved tarmac and reboarding the Boeing 737 plane.

Inside, only about 20 people remained on the plane for the flight to Barrow. With our former seatmates left at Prudhoe Bay, Paul and I moved over in our rows to the window seats. He sat in front of me videotaping out his window. As the plane taxied down the runway, which was as bumpy as the highways we had driven over so far on the trip both in the United States and in Canada, and lifted into the sky, "Forty minutes to Barrow," came over the loudspeaker.

Outside and below lay the Beaufort Sea. Toward the land, part of its ice packs were broken up, but farther out the frozen white sea itself went on for miles and almost unnoticeably met the blue sky with its low-hanging white clouds.

At times the flat tundra below looked over-saturated, with meandering streams and large and small pools of water everywhere. It was the melting season and with the ground thawing only a foot or so deep, the water could only stand in pools or meander into any indentation, forming overflowing, winding streams. I felt like I wanted to take a huge blotter and sop up the excess liquid.

As the plane flew northwest, the flight attendant offered a treat too tempting to resist. Eating a Haagen-Dazs, cherry–chocolate fudge, frozen-yogurt bar, I looked out the window at the awesome, magnificent Arctic Ocean below. At first I thought it was land, but then I saw very clearly it was water with ice floes. The pieces of ice had broken off from the frozen pack of the ocean under the summer sun. I could see through the melted ice to different shades and shapes of brown at the bottom.

At times I saw flat terrain with no mountains. Rivulets and puddles of melted ice with patches of unmelted white snow made the surface look like the rough hide of a *Tyrannosaurus rex* dinosaur. The patterned brownish-green earth came from contractions of the frozen ground in winter and melted ice in the summer flowing into the resulting cracks, creating countless geometric shapes.

Then we seemed to circle and descend toward Barrow. I saw clouds on my side and blue sky on the other side of the plane. Paul turned his head back toward me and said he thought the pilot was looking for a hole to get through since he appeared to be wandering around. (Paul knew a lot about flying since he had a pilot's license.) We continued to circle above the clouds. Every so often the pilot descended and then pulled up again. Paul leaned back toward me again and said, "I guess it's just socked in too tight." It was 12:11 P.M., June 30. We were about 23 minutes overdue.

The last time the pilot tried to descend, I caught a glimpse both of ice floes in water and some tundra with standing pools of water. I wondered if the pilot would eventually turn back to Prudhoe Bay. The other passengers appeared calm. I, in fact, almost dozed as I closed my eyes because of the very smooth ride and hypnotic droning of the motors.

Paul, more aware than I of the situation, said the pilot was trying one more time. Paul saw him roll out his leading airfoil. "He's got his gear down," Paul said over the back of his seat with his head turned toward me.

Flight to Barrow

We were descending. All I saw were clouds. I told my tape recorder my name and address in case "anybody finds this tape. Thank you."

And then—we bumped down onto the runway! Hallelujah!

Through the window I saw flat, earth-colored tundra and a cloudy, overcast day. The attendant finished her landing speech with "We welcome you to Barrow. And have a pleasant stay here." It was 12:25 P.M. as we taxied up to the terminal. Its sign said: MarkAir Welcomes You to Barrow.

We didn't know what to expect except that we were to be part of a one-day tour of Barrow arranged by the airline (MarkAir Tours). It was to include destination transfers, a guided sightseeing tour of Barrow, a walk along the shore of the Arctic Ocean, and an Eskimo ceremonial program.

We walked down the ramp of the airplane in faith that the airline would indeed provide what it advertised. Being totally unfamiliar with the location and the airline, we had nothing else but faith to go forward with.

On the runway, now that we were underneath the clouds instead of being above them, the air felt raw, like a day in early spring in Maryland, but not as frigid as I had expected. It must have been about 50 degrees. A slight wind blew. I was glad I had put on my tan coat before leaving the plane.

At the terminal building amid a lot of confusion, we saw a cheerful young man with black hair and black mustache telling those who were there to spend the day to go outside to a bus.

Figuring that meant us, we followed his instructions and boarded a white school bus with a wide blue stripe across its sides. Inside it, we found a colorful parka on each of the green vinyl seats and wondered if we should put one on. For the moment, we didn't need them.

Soon, the young man got on the bus, started the engine, and began the tour, making jokes and ad libbing. From behind the steering wheel, he said that he would be our guide that day. Of medium height and weight, he wore a light-colored shirt, dark gray trousers, and a blue, softball-type jacket. A radio transceiver was fastened to his belt.

"I'm gonna show you 'round Barrow, far as the DEW line, and we'll go near the Point of Barrow, and I'm just gonna tell you a whole bunch of names and we're just gonna have a good time, take pictures, and comb the beach about five miles out of Barrow and you'll have an opportunity to take pictures of the ocean. I know once you see the ocean, you just want to start taking pictures, but better if you wait until you get outside. But you can open the windows if you want to while we're cruising along, take pictures. But we're gonna comb the beach pretty soon.

"And then we're gonna come back here, lunch break about 2:30, about two hours, and we'll meet back here at 4:30 and then we'll see a native culture program—Eskimo dancing, native arts and crafts. You'll have an opportunity to get up and dance yourself." Whereupon we all laughed.

He continued, "And you'll have an opportunity to see a blanket toss and native arts and crafts. Are you ready? Any questions?"

As he talked and drove ahead, I saw that the streets had signposts with white print on green just like in any other town in the United States. The names, however, were unfamiliar—Ahkovak, Okpik, Momegana, and Agvik. From my first steps on the ground from the airport terminal to the bus and beginning to ride the bus, I kept expecting that we would turn onto a paved street. It turned out that none of the streets were paved. In summer they were so dusty that the city sprayed them with water. Yet simultaneously, water stood in puddles at places (frozen tundra being the culprit again).

Sidewalks were not defined but an extension of the tundra street, like a very wide country road back home in Carroll County. Telephone and electric poles lined the streets.

The houses were ranch style, rectangular, and wood-framed, some on short stilts and some with additions. Most were of moderate size, one or two storied, and painted blue or light green or tan or dark brown or weathered naturally. Some had board planks and ramps spanning low depressions in the bare ground that led to their entrances. Many had a combination of vehicles—station wagon or pickup truck or all-terrain vehicle—parked beside the home. Various sizes of open boats and canoes were stored near houses, some upside down on posts. Bits and pieces of flat boards, toys, and odds and ends lay scattered on the ground. The houses had no lawns, of course, because of the short summer and long winter, and so the tundra soil was seen everywhere unless a house or other object covered it.

I saw my first little Eskimo girl walking along the tundra street with her coal-black hair and a ruffled skirt showing beneath her fur-trimmed parka and boots. Our guide told us about his people, "Whenever they wave to you—better wave back to them. That way throughout the summer they can appreciate the tourists coming up. 'Cause if you don't wave, they'll say, 'Boy, those tourists.'—Ha! Ha! So whenever you see anybody, wave your hand. And I think it will make your trip much better for you and the people."

The guide showed us the Barrow High School, which contained a swimming pool and gymnasium and cost approximately $76 million to build. Materials and other products coming into Barrow are shipped by cargo air or by cargo sea, thus their cost is much higher than it would be in the Lower 48.

He told us that he was an Inupiat Eskimo, the tribe in Barrow. Of Barrow's 3,500 residents, about 67 percent were Inupiat and 33 percent others. He said, "We get them from Korea, from the Philippines. We got people from Germany, from California. We got people from all over the place up here." He had lived his entire 34 years there.

We passed the new elementary school (with its indoor playground) that cost approximately $40 million. He commented, "If you build a house, you have to have a lot of money on hand to even start one." The price of gasoline was $2.68 a gallon at the only station in Barrow, he told us.

He pointed out the Arctic Slope Regional Corporation's Barrow headquarters. This modern wood building with its oval, extended entry made of large paned-glass won first place in a national architectural-design competition. The building serves as the headquarters for the regional native corporation that was established in accordance with the Alaska Native Land Claims Act of 1971.

He drove along Stevenson Street beside the Arctic Ocean. He kidded, "You can't go any farther north than Barrow, Alaska, unless you go swimming." He added, "There is land about equal (in latitude) to Barrow in Canada and Greenland, but it's not inhabited. So Barrow is the most northern community in the world."

Continuing his good humor, our personable guide pointed to a *signpost*, saying, "There's the Point Barrow National Forest. You see it? It's the red pole with the limbs right in front of us on the right." He laughed softly. No trees grow in Barrow, as I was finding out. He told us that permafrost began at two feet underneath the top soil and went down about 2,000-or-so feet. He told us about underground pits that were dug out and used as freezers by the Inupiats. Ladders were used to climb down into them.

Riding along looking out the bus window at the Arctic Ocean I knew I had to find some time to be alone with it. At that moment, however, we heard the guide say that when the Eskimos capture a

"He [our guide] told us about underground pits that were dug out and used as freezers by the Inupiats. Ladders were used to climb down into them."

whale, they divide it among those who helped; those who do not help do not get a part of the whale. However, since the ones who do get a part often share with their families, a person who did not help may be a part of the family and get some of the whale anyway.

The bus continued past Browerville to the Naval Arctic Research Lab, run by the Ukpeagvik Inupiat Corporation since 1984, and the distant early warning site, where our young friend Fred Teeter had worked.

When we arrived at the DEW site, I saw a large, round, white sphere on a pedestal, looking like a mushroom on a stem, with additional supporting square metal framework on thin poles at the corners. Called a radome, the giant geodesic dome made of hard white plastic housed the main radar antenna, which spun.

An American flag flew from a tall pole nearby. My heart beat faster as I knew it had to be the one I had seen in a photograph that Fred had sent home to his parents in Westminster, Maryland. I hurriedly snatched the green parka that was on my seat and put it over my tan long coat. I added the knit hat from Jackie. I could hardly wait to be outside the bus and see the place where Fred had lived and worked.

We were not invited to go inside the area of the DEW site buildings. Standing near the bus and imagining Fred at that location, I looked at the low silhouette of the complex of several gray-white buildings adjoining each other, at the white radome that was part of the satellite system, and at several windmill-type towers holding satellite dishes facing in different directions. I could picture what it must have been like in the winter with winds blowing snow across the flat tundra there at Point Barrow, the narrow point of land that is truly the northernmost in the United States. The tall utility poles that were part of the complex would have been vitally important to daily work and even survival.

Wearing the red parka that was on his bus seat, Paul stood beside the road with the DEW site in the background. I snapped his picture so that we could show it to Fred when we got home.

I can't fully explain why it was so satisfying to me to see those buildings, especially the radome, and to set foot on the same ground that Fred had in that remote area of the world. It was as if I had completed a pilgrimage, made a connection, that I had never thought possible but one that was meant to be.

Leaving that meaningful site, we headed back toward Barrow. About five miles outside the city of Barrow, our driver parked the bus, saying, "We're gonna go comb the beach right around here for a little while. You might find old bones. Some people find old, old ivory out here. Really old ivory. Especially after a storm they comb the beach. You'll find some seashells and clam shells and some driftwood that comes from Canada, too. So you're welcome to pick up a few and take them back home if you like. 'Okay? We'll get out here for a little while."

I stepped from the bus onto a gray, gritty road and looked for Point Barrow, anxious to get as close to it as possible. I saw it in the distance, almost like a dark line against the horizon. All the others headed for the shoreline. Paul wore the red parka as he videotaped and talked: "The ice floes are dirty and the water is about 25 degrees. The wind's not blowing real hard. Enough to make your fingers cold, very cold."

Meanwhile I walked as quickly as I could in the loose, gray, deep, sandy soil toward the highest mound that I could see. When I gained it, its elevation was disappointingly only about two or three feet. But I stood on top and focused my camera on the narrow strip that was Point Barrow in the distance.

From there I walked about a hundred feet to my left to the Arctic Ocean. Of course, I dipped my fingers into its cold water. They came out wet and cold just like water anywhere, but this place to me wasn't just anywhere.

Then I stood still and looked around. The sky was overcast. My compatriots looked like dots down the beach. The ice floes in the ocean appeared soiled as the sun melted them. Beyond them an uneven ridge of tannish pack ice, formed over many years by pieces of ice driven together by wind and the current, floated about 400 yards from the shore. The visible land *ended* where I stood on the northern edge of North America; from there only frigid water and ice made up the last few hundred miles to the North Pole.

I was alone, really alone. I sensed solitude, for a brief moment the frightening kind. What a desolate, harsh place it would be in winter. Yet I knew that fresh snow and winter white would cover all that I saw and make it beautiful, too. I realized that it was truly an awesome world.

What respect I felt for the Inupiat people who had faced the rigors of the Arctic Circle for thousands of years and survived with good humor and good values.

I looked down and began to pick up small stones and a small piece or two of driftwood and put them in the pockets of my coat under the parka. I wanted enough to share with our RV caravaners and a few folks at home.

Someone called my name. I looked toward the bus. Paul motioned for me to come back to the bus. I had walked farther than I realized and I hurried to join them. Everyone else had boarded. Paul chided, asking me if I hadn't seen the sign that I walked past saying to beware of polar bears. I really hadn't seen it. He had not seen me go off from the group and was frightened for my safety when he realized that I was the figure he saw so far away from the bus. I realized then what a foolish thing I had done in my pursuit of a good photograph and solitude with the ocean.

· 14 ·

Fogged in at Barrow

LEAVING OUR OCEANSIDE STOP, on the way back to Barrow past Browerville, the tour guide said in fun, "You don't see any igloos, do you? We've got real buildings here."

Back in Barrow, he drove on the wide, unpaved main street and parked the bus beside the Top of the World Hotel. It was about 2:30 P.M. With instructions from him on where to eat and what we might do before returning to the bus at 4:25 P.M., we debarked. At his suggestion, we took our borrowed parkas from the bus with us.

Fogged In at Barrow

Paul and I ate lunch in Pepe's, probably the northernmost Mexican restaurant in the world. Its colorful Mexican atmosphere with seating for 234 contrasted with the grayness of the ocean beach.

Afterward we walked up Agvik Street, which we decided was the main street, to Kiogak Street, where we found the National Bank of Alaska in the district court building. While Paul used our debit card to withdraw $800 and exchanged our Canadian money for American, I talked with another cashier and looked around the bank. As we went to leave, a gentleman came out of the enclosed office and gave us each a royal blue corduroy baseball cap with "National Bank of Alaska" embroidered on it in yellow.

Once again on Agvik Street, we saw that some of the commercial buildings had short electric cords on the exterior walls near the ground. A motorist could plug one of these into his or her car to energize the electric heater for the engine's motor block in frigid weather.

Our next stop was Stuaqpak, a store that carried everything from groceries in a large supermarket on the first level to bunk beds,

"Our next stop was Stuaqpak, a store that carried everything from groceries . . . to bunk beds, dining-room tables and chairs, floor lamps, reclining chairs, sofas, coffee tables, end tables, and a myriad of other items."

149

dining-room tables and chairs, floor lamps, reclining chairs, sofas, coffee tables, end tables, and a myriad of other items on the second level.

Walking on the main street back to the hotel, we saw a modern city bus picking up passengers as if it were on a city street of concrete instead of thawing, yet dusty, tundra. The guide had told us that they water down the street each day to reduce the dust.

At the Top of the World Hotel, we visited the gift shop where we bought postcards, tee-shirts, and sweatshirts. I needed something for myself for the Craziest Tee-Shirt contest forthcoming for our RV caravaners group and decided on a tee-shirt I found there.

In the hotel lobby, I used the stamp the hotel offered to ink the indicia "Top of the World" on the postcards I had bought as well as those I had brought along already written. I mailed them from Barrow in the hotel lobby mailbox.

We still had a little time, so Paul and I walked the short distance from the hotel to the beach, which I had trouble thinking of as a beach because I ordinarily associated beaches with hot temperatures. The ice pack resembled piles of dirty snow and ice that a huge snow plow had pushed aside as it cleared a road. The ice pack extended in varying thicknesses and shapes as far as we could see up and down the shore line. Ice floes lay peacefully between it and shore.

About 4:30, our driver and guide welcomed us back aboard the bus, did a headcount, and headed for the community center where the native arts and crafts program would be held. Along the way a man on the bus asked him what the original Eskimo religion was. Church buildings in Barrow included those for Assembly of God, Baptist, Baha'i faith, Catholic, and Presbyterian congregations.

He said that long before the Christian missionaries came, Eskimo people had traditional values such as sharing, giving, and respect. These related naturally to Christianity, which the missionaries established in Inupiat communities. He himself was studying to be a Baptist missionary to the local villages. In addition to his duties as tour guide; arranger of the Eskimo dances, demonstrations, and craft exhibits; co-operator of the Top of the World Hotel; husband; and

FOGGED IN AT BARROW

father of five, he went to school two nights a week at a college held in the local Baptist church.

Answering other questions, he told us that they had 24-hour nighttime from late November until about the middle of January. He said that a lot of people had grown up with the 24-hour nighttime and they were used to it, but to others, it was depressing.

We arrived at the community center where the arts and crafts program was scheduled. Before leaving the bus, our energetic guide said that he was going to join the blanket-toss demonstration outside near the bus.

As I stood on the raised stoop of the center, I watched the famous blanket toss. About 15 Eskimos held the loops at the edge of a squarish sealskin blanket and stretched it taut so that it was like a trampoline. On the blanket, a young girl stood poised for the toss. With her long, black hair tied back, she wore a lavender velvet, long-waisted, ruffle-skirted parka with its hood laid back, gray leggings, and furry mukluks. Then with the people stretching and relaxing the blanket just enough to give the young girl a bounce, they made sounds like they were counting one, two, three, toss. Up into the air she would go, well above their heads, sometimes almost three times the height of the people pulling the blanket. Pedaling and keeping her balance, she came back down and landed on the blanket on her feet. And again, and again. Once she did not get very far up before losing her balance and they all said something like, "O-o-o-h!" After her last successful toss into the air and landing, the blanket tossers let down the blanket gently to the ground, and she walked off it. Fun to do, originally the toss was used by whalers to look for whales across the flat expanse of ice.

Inside the community center, in a large room set up with folding chairs, we met the traditional Eskimo culture of which I had read. Two rows of Eskimos in parkas and mukluks sat on folding chairs facing the audience. On the white wall behind them hung the Alaskan and American flags with a pair of large snowshoes crisscrossed between them.

"Up into the air she would go... sometimes almost three times the height of the people pulling the blanket."

On the floor in front of them lay traditional large tambourine-shaped drums made of sealskin stretched tightly over a wooden frame. Rather than beating on the taut skin, the Eskimos struck the round frame from beneath with a wooden stick. The harder they hit the frame, the more it vibrated, causing a louder sound.

A young man from the Lower 48 began the program by introducing each person sitting in the two rows. As he introduced each person, they remained seated and waved to us in acknowledgment of the introduction.

An Eskimo woman came to the microphone. She had short, curly, black hair and wore tinted glasses. Her rust-and-brown print dress had a long ruffle at the bottom and long sleeves with cuffs. The dress had the usual laid-back hood, a style that we saw everywhere there. She wore purple pants that almost covered her feet, but I think she wore mukluks. She cheerfully and confidently introduced the first number—the "Welcome Dance."

About ten children and youth in fur-trimmed mukluks, leggings, and hooded dresses or tunics of various colors walked forward. In an informal pattern, they began bending their knees and swaying and moving their arms to the rhythm of the drums and a song in Inupiat sung by those who remained seated behind them. The dancers didn't sing but changed their movements according to words.

Each solo, duo, or group dance had movements that indicated a special meaning. Some of the children and youth looked as if they were concentrating very hard to be sure they did their dances right. The adults on the drums gave them encouragement as needed.

Two men in yellow tunics and garb similar to the children's performed a more complicated dance. They were joined by a third man for another number with an increasingly fast beat and dance steps called "The Runner." (In the old days they used to send a runner to another village with a message.) We all clapped heartily.

At one point the woman narrator invited the audience to join them in a dance. Not wanting to miss out on anything, I went to the dance floor along with some other visitors. As the music started, I watched what the Eskimo people were doing and, like them but much more unsure, bounced up and down on my rubber-soled shoes and swayed my body and moved my hands up and down and back and forth to the beat of the drums.

For one song, they invited us to join in the chorus if we wanted to after they sang it the first time through in their native Inupiat language. They all stood up to sing. Two older men in the front row, hollow cheeked and weathered looking, one with graying and the other with white hair, crossed their arms as they sang. Another man put his hands in his front sweatshirt pockets; others clasped theirs together in front of them. The melody came with full force in Inupiat, the older adults singing as if they meant every word and note, as if what they sang was vital to them. Some of the younger ones lowered their heads or seemed unsure of the words.

Not identifying at first the familiar hymn I'd sung many times in church when I was growing up, I soon recognized the English version of the chorus: "God will take care of you . . ." I felt a sudden warmth in my heart. Too enthralled to add my own voice, I took in the singers' sincerity and interpretation. "Through every day, O'er all the way. He will take care of you. God will take care of you." They ended strongly on a high note and sat down. I would carry that memory forever. How I admired these people for practicing their faith in that hostile environment!

However, I noticed one little boy in the back row, true to human nature, yawning as he sat down.

The program continued as they presented a fashion show with a child and a young girl in handsome fur parkas and mukluks made from the brown squirrels, black rabbits, wolverines, wolves, and caribou from their environment. The outfits were very special and not for sale.

Following the dance program, those who were interested shifted to the side of the room where the same woman narrator, with a microphone on a long cord, explained how mukluks were made. As she did so, another Eskimo woman, 81 years old, demonstrated. She worked at a sturdy, unpainted wooden table with a rose-colored cloth. Her silky, purple-flowered, long-sleeved dress had a laid-back hood. She too wore tinted glasses.

Then the narrator sat down at the table and showed us how they made masks to use when dancing in the old days. In the process she showed how she used the *ulu*, a traditional tool of Eskimo women that was a knife with a broad, curved blade joined to a short wooden handle at a right angle to the unsharpened side. She skillfully cut the fur off the skin of the caribou. Then she stretched it over a ceramic mold, trimmed the skin, and sewed it to the mold. She would set the fresh skin aside to dry overnight. The next day she would remove the dried skin from the mold, add fur around it, and complete the mask. No longer used for dancing, the masks have been used just as decorative souvenirs since Barrow became a tourist attraction. Holding up a finished mask, she said that for Halloween you could make a really funny face if you wanted to, and chuckled. The audience laughed also and applauded.

Our tour guide invited us to view a display of Eskimo art and crafts, including little carved seals and owls and baleen, that was set up on tables around the perimeter of an adjoining room.

Fogged In at Barrow

I bought an etching on baleen, one of a series of black, plastic-like, thin plates that form on each side of the palate in whalebone whales. Measuring about three inches wide by fifteen inches long, it showed various symbols including an outline map of Alaska with an arrow pointing to Barrow, Alaska's flag, the silhouette of a whale in the ocean, and a drawing of an Eskimo smiling inside the perimeter of the lush fur hood of a parka and saying, "Home of the Whalers." (Barrow High School team members were called the Whalers.) Holes had been drilled in the top and a tiny wire fastened between them for hanging the work. It turned out to be the artistic creation of the wife of our guide.

When we returned to the large room, a film about the geography and history of Barrow was presented. Fred and Nan Clarifcofer took most of the film's pictures and wrote its narration. Fred was a Presbyterian minister on the North Slope from 1936 to 1945. At the end, the narrator, referring to the Eskimos, said that to his knowledge no other people had had to change from a hunting lifestyle to the jet age in two generations.

Back on the bus, we stopped briefly at the airport. Among the cars and pickup trucks parked in front of the hangar was a black stretch limo, the only one I saw in Barrow. After his errand in the hangar, our guide took the opportunity to pass out commemorative Arctic Circle certificates to each tourist on the MarkAir tour.

Continuing our ride, we talked and laughed as our driver quipped and sang. He pointed out a man who he said was always smiling every time you saw him. He told us the local children were learning the Eskimo language and traditions in school. Answering a question, he said they have a city sewage system with underground pipes.

The tour guide wanted to show us the oldest store, the Cape Smythe Whaling & Trading Co. in Browerville, a community that adjoins Barrow. It was the only one of the original general stores that existed prior to Stuaqpak. We stepped into the store and onto a red-orange tweed, short-napped carpet. Through aisles crowded with merchandise, we squeezed past one another to look at teddy bears and other stuffed toys, racks and piles of parkas and sweatshirts, light bulbs, gloves, canned goods, salt, sunglasses. I bought a black sweatshirt that was embroidered in the Philippines!

Leaving the store, we climbed back into the white bus. En route to the airport again, the guide told us that in the evenings in winter the people of Barrow go out and look for the Northern Lights. They go out at about 9:30 and about 75 percent of the time they see them. He laughed and said that sometimes it's cloudy but even if they didn't get to see the Northern Lights, you got to see Barrow at its best—when it was cold! The day before we came, the temperature had been 65 degrees; it was about 50 degrees that day.

I didn't see television antennas, but I learned that they had cable television. I did see radio antennas on houses, however. The only thing they did not have in Barrow was a movie theater. To see a movie they had to fly to either Fairbanks or Anchorage.

We stopped back at MarkAir. All but six tourists got off the bus and headed into the hangar for their return flight. Paul and I and the other four people remained for a later flight that night at 9:30 P.M. Outside the terminal, I watched as an Eskimo woman with a baby on her back fitted into what looked like the hood of her white sweatshirt leaned forward and backed into the rear seat of a taxi. I later learned that many Eskimo babies are still carried in this "piggy-backed" manner inside their mother's parkas.

Our faithful escort took us back to the Top of the World Hotel where we had free time until he or someone else would again take us in the white bus back to the airport for our late evening return flight to Fairbanks. This gave Paul and me an opportunity to explore on our own. I visited the gift shop in the lobby of the hotel once more.

Then I talked with a young woman at the desk. She was the hotel office manager and was from the Lower 48. She told me the average wage in Barrow was $14 an hour, that the minimum wage was $9 an hour.

Inside the lobby, I watched as our tour guide reorganized some of the display cases. As Paul and I lounged in the hotel lobby, we began talking with another visitor, a schoolteacher from Australia, who was writing postcards to mail from Barrow. Her husband and children did

Fogged In at Barrow

not come to Barrow; she planned to rejoin them in Fairbanks that night. The next day they were to go by train to Anchorage.

I asked Paul if he would go with me one more time to see the Arctic Ocean. It was 8:23 P.M. and still daylight. We walked the few hundred feet and stood on top of the sloping gray sand near the shore. As we looked at the water, seals swam among the ice floes. A boat with motor and enclosed cabin moved past. Two young Eskimo girls in parkas walked on the beach. Located on the beach but facing Stevenson Street was a two-story building painted blue with the sign Inupiat Water Delivery. On its front facade many antlers hung from its balcony and balcony roof. Various items lay around its foundation, the framework of a canoe being one.

The air was windy and chilly and so we turned toward the warmth of the hotel. In front of us a young Eskimo couple rode by on an all-terrain vehicle, laden with plastic bags of groceries. I shouted "Hi!" and the woman sitting behind the driver smiled widely yet shyly, her beautiful white teeth contrasting with short-cut black hair, and waved to me with a black-gloved hand.

Before long, it was time to again board the white bus parked in front of the hotel for the ride back to the Barrow airport. We passed some people playing softball and our driver, a different one from earlier in the day, told us there were three leagues in Barrow—A, B, and C—with several teams in each league. They were sponsored by the city of Barrow. The players provided their own uniforms. "It's pretty exciting," he said.

The bus parked at the airport. Six of us—the Australian schoolteacher, a young woman, and a man and a young boy apparently father and son—entered the airport terminal for MarkAir. It was about 9:15 P.M. and daylight.

Inside in the center of the room and along several walls were rows of modern, orange plastic, shell-shaped seats mounted on metal frames and connected in sets of four. A gentle murmur came from the 8 or 10 people already waiting. Paul went to the ticket counter to confirm our tickets and reservation. Then we waited. The Australian woman and other prospective passengers sat nearby.

The 9:30 departure time came and went. A voice on the loud speaker told us that the plane was delayed and circling because of fog. Then the voice said that the plane was going to make one last attempt to land.

I started to think seriously that the plane might not get through. How exciting that would be, to spend the night! What would happen to us? Paul sat talking in his usual carefully controlled way about the pilot. "He's been circling trying to find a hole through which he can see enough to land. That's what happened when we came in this morning."

And then the female voice said that the plane indeed had to turn back, that the fog was too heavy to risk a landing and the plane was low on fuel. She told us to come to the counter to make other arrangements. Paul went immediately and joined others in line. Meanwhile, the bus driver appeared from somewhere and announced loudly in the room that he would take us all back to the hotel when we were ready. He said to take our time; he would wait for us.

I thought of a lot of things at once. Where would we stay that night? When would we fly out in the morning? Would we get back to Fairbanks in time for the afternoon cruise? What would our caravaners think when we didn't return? On top of it all, I was hungry. Would our bus driver wait long enough for us to get a take-out order from the restaurant upstairs?

· 15 ·

Return to Fairbanks

HAVING JUST LEARNED that our flight out of Barrow that Wednesday night was canceled because of fog, Paul and I naturally wanted an early morning flight on Thursday. We hoped to get back to Fairbanks in time to join our RV caravaners for the 1:00 P.M. *Discovery* cruise. At the MarkAir ticket counter, Paul was told that the earliest flight available was one at 11:20 by Alaska Airlines. That flight might possibly let us make our connection at the campground, if all went as scheduled. Paul arranged for us to switch to Alaska Airlines, which meant paying an additional fee and picking up our new tickets in their building a short distance away the next morning.

The Australian woman wanted to call her husband to let him know what was happening but she needed more change, which Paul gladly supplied.

From the ticket counter, Paul and I went upstairs to Ken's Restaurant and ordered a carry-out supper of two cold turkey sandwiches, French fries, and milk ($18.75, not too unreasonable). We had purposely delayed eating our evening meal because we had assumed we would be fed on the plane.

The bus driver took the six of us back to the hotel but not straightaway. He had heard a rumor that a polar bear was seen outside Barrow along the shore and wanted us to join him in checking it out. He drove to the area where he thought it would be, but it was no longer there. The fact that he seriously looked for the polar bear so that we tourists and he could see it confirmed for me how foolhardy I had been in straying alone earlier that day.

Back at the Top of the World Hotel, Paul and I registered for the night. Ordinarily, the charge would have been $135, but under the circumstances they charged us only $90.

We were assigned to room 116 with an ocean view on the first floor. It was a nice room. It had twin beds and other typical hotel furniture, a bath, a telephone, and a sliding glass door with drapery.

The first thing, Paul tried to call the campground at Fairbanks to let them know our situation. It was 10:30 P.M., but the line was busy. After more attempts and more busy signals, we gave up. We started in on the turkey sandwiches. The room was chilly and I called the desk for more heat. Soon the friendly woman at the desk brought us extra blankets.

By this time, it was almost midnight and still daylight outside. I videotaped through the sliding glass door to show how light it was. We were finding that without darkness to signal bedtime, we had a tendency to just keep on doing things. As I looked outside, I saw the dark soil, sometimes in mounds, stretching down to the water about

Return to Fairbanks

200 feet away and then the water with both the ice pack and sky lost in the fog. It looked very foggy out there.

I went to bed, keeping on my makeup, underclothes, knit shirt, and Western Maryland College long-sleeved sweatshirt and piling on the extra blanket.

We got up at seven or so the next morning. Paul was anxious to confirm our airline tickets, which the hotel desk did for us. I saw a different picture when I looked outside our window at 7:45 that morning. The fog had lifted and it was the beginning of a new day. The water looked blue with ice floes, and the ever-present ice pack looked tannish. The sky was light blue near the horizon with some clouds hanging above.

We subsequently turned in our room key and our borrowed parkas, said our goodbyes to the desk person, and walked toward the airport. Paul walked ahead on the dirt-shoulder "sidewalk" carrying our purchases and my purple tote bag. A water tanker with a white cab and a huge red tank went past me spraying water from its rear delivery system on the opposite side of the dirt street. It moved right along and I got over on my side as far as I could to avoid the splatter. Although it was a cold and windy morning, I heard birds singing.

We walked first to the MarkAir building and upstairs to Ken's Restaurant for breakfast. Inside the restaurant, shoulder-high, wood-paneled dividers partitioned spaces for tables and steel-framed chairs. The dropped ceiling framework with fluorescent lighting supported hanging planters. Framed pictures hung on the walls. I ate delicious French toast with lots of syrup, a scrambled egg, and a slice of orange for garnish. For the two of us our breakfast came to $15.90. We ordered and picked up from the counter, so there was no tip included in the total.

Not knowing just where the Alaska Airlines terminal was, we asked a man across the street who was driving a pickup truck. He actually turned his truck around and came over to where we were to tell us.

The Alaska Airlines waiting room looked freshly decorated with a red-and-black color scheme for the plastic seat shells mounted on black iron framework. The walls were white with fluorescent light fixtures on the ceiling. A waist-high green potted plant stood on the floor beside one end of the white ticket counter. Paul confirmed our reservations and got our tickets, paying an additional $70 for both of us. We waited for the plane.

"When I think about it, if you're looking for glamour, this is not the place to come, but if you're looking for real life, this is it," I said to Paul about Barrow.

"I often wondered what it's like in Barrow, Alaska, where they have mainly a native community, and I often wondered what the temperatures were like, what the people were like, what the town was like, what the buildings in the town were like, what luxuries are here that aren't someplace else, and vice versa. I have a very satisfied feeling about coming here," Paul replied.

After going through a security check, Paul and I headed for the jet airplane, which was white with navy blue trim. Wearing his warm blue jacket and tan cap, Paul carried the white plastic bags of souvenirs and my tote bag. I hung back to videotape him entering the plane, then soon caught up and joined him inside.

Soon after takeoff, I had a last look at Barrow and the Arctic Ocean from the airplane window. I saw puffs of clouds above the village buildings and ice floes on the ocean below. Banks of clouds farther out to sea prevented a further view of the frozen ice.

As we continued to fly toward Fairbanks, the soil looked like a patchwork of green and brown with a myriad of nonsymmetrical white shapes that were ice and snow. Many rivulets and meandering streams wiggled their way across the mountainless tundra.

Lunch on the plane consisted of a baked chicken leg, a bunch of fresh grapes, a ham sandwich with dark brown bread, and a chocolate mint. My Japanese seatmate gave his mint to me. I chose vegetable juice from the beverage cart.

I looked at my watch—12:23 P.M. Out the window I saw that we were high above the clouds. I was glad for the experience of seeing Barrow. Not only did it make me feel like a genuine adventurous traveler, but I saw for myself what would have been hard for me to believe

Return to Fairbanks

otherwise: the people in Barrow *like* living there. I respect them for their fortitude and creativity in adapting to the tundra and its barrenness—no crops of any kind, no cows or other cattle—only polar bears, seals, caribou, whales, and smaller animals. After this visit, I would never be the same. When I got irritated at home, I would think of Barrow—its people's values of kindness, sharing, and Christianity. I would think of our tour guide and bus driver, his good-natured humor, his wide, contagious smile. He was 34 and had five children; the oldest was seven. He and his partner ran the hotel, tours, and he did scrimshaw, too. He studied and worked hard but didn't complain, just made jokes about it.

We knew that our connection with our fellow RV caravaners was questionable, but it continued to remain probable, depending on how quickly we could get a cab at the Fairbanks airport when we landed and how speedily yet safely the driver would go.

We lost no time in getting off the plane and heading for a taxi. It was almost one o'clock. When we told the cab driver our situation, he immediately radioed his dispatcher requesting them to call the campground office and tell them of our pending arrival. He continued driving. I sat on the edge of the back seat of the taxi. I pictured the group not getting the message and leaving without us, maybe passing us as we rode in the taxi. I looked for familiar RVs on the road as we neared the campground. It was already after one o'clock. Our taxi driver drove into the entry of the campground. Then he passed the office. And then he drove into the circle where I saw our caravaners sitting in three RVs ready to pull out, but waiting for us!

We hurried out of the cab. Smiles and cheers all around! Laurie and Don and Karen and Scott came to meet us. Lib gave me a big hug.

After a quick deposit of our packages and excess outer clothing into our motorhome, we joined the others. The Foremans (Number Five), the Beelers (Number Two), and the Heathcocks (Number Seven) with our whole group dispersed among their RVs took off immediately for the sternwheeler cruise.

It was about a half-hour's drive from the campground to where the *Discovery III* was docked. The 160-foot white sternwheeler cruised on the Chena and Tanana Rivers west of Fairbanks for four hours as the captain narrated over a loudspeaker system. The captain had ship-to-shore dialogues with the two famous Iditarod women, Susan Butcher and Mary Shields, on the shore, each at a different location. As the boat slowly cruised or stopped alongside, we listened to their conversations while seeing them. Mary was the first woman to complete the race, and Susan was the first person to win three consecutive Iditarod victories. (The Iditarod is an 1,100-mile dogsled race from Anchorage to Nome, Alaska.) Susan sat on the bank in front of a log cabin with some of the puppies she was raising as potential members of her dogsled team. Mary gave a dog-mushing demonstration.

We saw Athabascan living quarters, including a cache to keep food away from animals, and a large wooden fish wheel used by the Indians. Well anchored in the water, its revolving wheel with attached nets captured passing fish as the current of the river turned the wheel. We cruised past a small airstrip used by bush pilots, those brave people who fly small airplanes over rugged terrain or unin-

"We saw Athabascan living quarters, including a cache to keep food away from animals, and a large wooden fish wheel used by the Indians."

habited areas in order to service places not accessible to or off the route of larger planes.

We went ashore at Old Chena Village, a reconstruction of an authentic Athabascan village along with some remains of early Athabascan Indian dwellings. There we learned about the Athabascan culture, saw a smokehouse, a trapper's cabin, and a cache on stilts to keep food and furs away from animals. Displays and demonstrations of the Athabascan art of bead decorating and fashioning parkas caught my eye. Young women cared for reindeer in a fenced-in area.

I had expected to find Eskimos in Alaska but was surprised to find well-established Indian cultures. And yet I learned that both of these populations were native to Alaska. It is believed that the first people in Alaska came from Asia across the Bering Land Bridge perhaps as early as 30,000 to 10,000 years ago. These early settlers were the ancestors to today's native populations in Alaska—American Indian, Eskimo, and Aleut—which total about 85,698 compared with the total resident population of 550,043 (1990). Most natives are Eskimos who live in Alaska's north and east. The Aleuts, who are closely related to the Eskimo, reside on the Aleutian and Shumagin islands and on the Alaska Peninsula. The American Indian populations include the Athabascan-speaking Indians of Alaska's interior region, which includes Fairbanks, and the Haida, Tlingit, and Tsimshian Indians in the southeast area of Alaska.

I tried to take it all in, but I kept thinking about Barrow. I felt at a loss to describe to my fellow caravaners what Barrow was like and how much I admired the Eskimo people.

That evening I went to the hairdresser at Sears in Fairbanks. The cost for the shampoo and blow-dry was $19.

As I sat on the edge of the bed in the motorhome about 10:00 that night, I continued to think of the Eskimo people, how they must weather the weather whether they want to or not! They truly faced the important challenges in life, like survival.

The next day we were to leave the campground at Fairbanks by 7:30 A.M. and travel 118 miles south to a campground at Healy. At the Healy campground, a shuttle bus would pick us up at 10:45 A.M. Whitewater rafting was on the agenda. We were to be prepared for mosquitoes, wear mittens and a cap for the sun, and apply suntan lotion. Not everybody in our group would be going, for various reasons. After more than our usual deliberation, I agreed to join Paul in going on the calm-water version rather than the more adventurous whitewater one. Since I had never learned to swim, I wasn't sure it was wise to put myself in a watery situation.

I thought of people I knew who had gone whitewater rafting, of the fun they said they had had, and yet of the danger of it. But I would go, albeit on a less risky version. If I survived the rafting, the following day would bring an all-day bus tour to Denali National Park and Mount McKinley, the highest mountain in North America. I wondered if the peak would be as spectacular as its height suggested.

· 16 ·

The Majesty of Mount McKinley

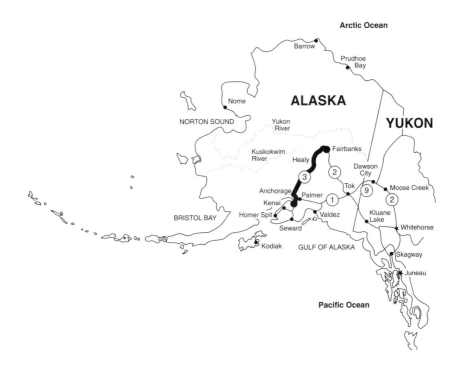

WE LEFT FAIRBANKS under sunny, blue skies early on Friday morning hoping the weather would hold out for our whitewater rafting that day and our bus tour to see Mount McKinley the following day. As we traveled toward Healy, we saw grand vistas of river valleys and low mountains with lots of green trees. The Nenana River, on which we would be rafting, meandered near the highway at times.

Thel sat on a wooden bench outside the McKinley Raft Tours building smiling tentatively, waiting to go calm-water rafting on the Nenana River. She wore the yellow rubber bib overalls and matching parka and rubber boots that the tour people handed out to each of us. When I asked Paul if he had any "last words," he said, "I'm going down the river!" with gusto and continued adjusting the suspenders of his yellow bib overalls.

The porch was a hubbub with our group laughing and putting on gear and helping one another, some of whom had put their overalls on backwards. We would go in two groups—Paul, Thel, and I chose the calm-water rafting while Jackie and Lyle, Mary Jo and Bill, Don, Ann and Louie, Bob and Ro, Effie and Clem, Yvonne and Wil, and Lib chose the more vigorous version.

I asked Lib what her thoughts were at that moment.

"Well, right now, Bernice, I'm not thinking very good thoughts because I saw that water on the way down here and it was ripply. Tell John when you get back that I love him!" she said, bravely laughing in her usual good humor. I admired her courage for choosing the rougher waters of the Nenana River.

"The porch was a hubbub with our group laughing and putting on gear and helping one another, some of whom had put their overalls on backwards." (L-R: the author, Paul, and Thel)

The Majesty of Mount McKinley

We three calm-water people went first after instructions by our youthful crew member. We all wore orange life jackets, of course. The crewman sat on a high seat in the middle of the raft and guided it with the raft's long oars. Thel sat on the side of the raft opposite me holding on to the side ropes with both hands. She didn't let go the whole trip. When I asked her something from the other side of the raft, she hardly moved her head and spoke cautiously. After the ride, she told me laughingly that she was scared stiff. (I was glad to know I wasn't the only one!)

The guide told us the history of the area as we floated down the river. Evergreen and deciduous trees and bushes covered the mountains on both sides. I breathed in the cool, fresh air. The river offered just enough rapids to make it exciting. I even got to the point where I hoped for a few livelier ones. Water splashed on us and we laughed and held on. We could have been Lewis and Clark exploring the West.

By the time we returned to the gear shed, photographs of our expedition were ready. Paul hurried to obtain one. It showed us laughing and having a good time—even Thel was smiling, despite her anxiety.

We removed our yellow gear and waved goodbye to the other caravaners as they boarded a blue bus that would take them to the location of the rafts for the whitewater rafting on the nearby river. The same bus would pick them up where they got out of the river and take them back to the tour office to return their gear. A shuttle bus would return them to our campground at Healy.

Meanwhile Paul, Thel, and I rode another shuttle bus back to the campground. On the way our driver stopped so that we could see our *brave* caravaners coming through the rapids. They quickly waved to us and then regained their hold on the rope of the raft. We waved back. The swirling, fast-moving, white-capped river seemed to go in all directions at places and kept the guide busy maneuvering around rocks and rapids.

When the brave ones got off the shuttle bus at the campground, Effie and Clem pretended to have wobbly knees and walked bent over, grinning. Clem said, "We really had *fun!*" All smiles, Wil and

Yvonne showed us the picture of them in a raft. Eunice, Fred, and John, who had decided not to go, joined in looking at the pictures and hearing all about the rafting.

That evening our group attended a dinner theatre held in a handcrafted log cabin. Salmon and ribs were served family style and followed by an enthusiastic 40-minute wilderness revue set in the early 1900s in a mining-district roadhouse.

Later back in the motorhome, Paul updated the checkbook. I gathered together our laundry and walked in daylight over to the camp store where the laundry facilities were located in the basement. It was a chance to "catch up" and relax a bit from the excitement and rigors of sightseeing. The long days of light gave me more motivation and energy in the evening than if the skies had been twilight or dark.

While the clothes were being washed, I chatted with a man who was doing his laundry and looked around in the store upstairs. In between I shifted the freshly washed clothes to a dryer. I soon finished and returned to the motorhome. The next day would be an all-day bus trip into Denali National Park to see a mountain I had heard about since elementary school—Mount

> **Denali National Park and Preserve**
>
> At the Visitor Access Center of Denali National Park and Preserve, which is near the park entrance, visitors can obtain all kinds of information—lists of campgrounds in the park; maps, brochures, and schedules of events; details on campfire talks, hikes, nature walks, sled dog demonstrations, and wildlife tours; shuttle bus schedules; and suggestions on what to see and do in the park.
>
> While our arrangements had been made by the wagonmasters, we learned that RVers going on their own should allow a minimum of two full days in order to obtain free shuttle bus seat coupons and campground sites within the park. During the summer, the demand for shuttle seats is far greater than the number of available seats, which causes long lines and sometimes two- to three-day waits. Shuttle bus coupons are obtained from the Visitor Access Center. As for camping inside the park, visitors may register up to two days in advance. They may want to

McKinley. I was confused, however, by the name Denali. I thought it was Mount McKinley National Park.

Early Saturday morning, with lunches along, we rode a bus from our campground at Healy to the Visitor Access Center of Denali National Park and Preserve.

From the Visitor Access Center, we boarded a long yellow school bus with maroon vinyl seats that would take us for an eight-hour ride into Denali National Park and Preserve to see Mount McKinley and wildlife along the way. Paul and I sat about halfway back on the driver's side of the bus. John and Lib sat one row in back of us. Ro and Bob Conway had claimed the front seat on the entry side. (Somebody had to sit there!) Others in our group were scattered throughout with the wagonmasters and tailgunners toward the rear where they could keep an eye on their frisky school kids.

I had learned that the park was formerly known as Mount McKinley National Park. The name Denali was the Tanana Indian name for the mountain and was said to mean the "high one." As North America's highest mountain, its peaks reached a reputed 20,320 feet although a

write ahead of time for more information about the park:

Denali National Park and
   Preserve
P.O. Box 9
Denali Park, AK 99755

or hear recorded information by telephoning (907) 683-2686. Or they may contact Alaska Public Lands Information Centers in Anchorage or Fairbanks at the following addresses:

605 West 4th Ave.
Anchorage, AK 99501
Telephone (907) 271-2737 or
   (907) 271-2738 (number for
   hearing impaired)

or

250 Cushman St.
Fairbanks, AK 99701
Telephone (907) 451-7352 or
   (907) 451-7439 (number for
   hearing impaired)

For a free list of maps and other publications, write to

The Alaska Natural History
   Association
P.O. Box 230
Denali Park, AK 99755

recent study by the University of Alaska, Fairbanks, placed the highest peak at "only" 20,304 feet.

Our woman bus driver and guide soon told us that we had about a 30 percent chance of seeing Mount McKinley because cloudy, rainy, summer weather frequently kept its higher regions obscured. At that moment, the sun shone as we headed toward the silent giant.

Our bus traveled first on a paved road. The driver/guide clearly and calmly narrated over the speaker system. She slowed down or stopped the bus when wildlife was spotted either by her or a passenger. When we rode high above the valley floors on roads without guardrails, we came to depend on and respect her expertise.

A large moose loped through the brush near the right side of the bus. Looking out my window on the left side, I saw a honey-colored grizzly bear move nonchalantly behind a bush in the valley beside the park road. Someone else spotted a few caribou on a snowy patch on the hillside. Our bus had been climbing a steep grade and then the road seemed to level off a bit.

I remember when I first saw it. A woman on the bus said, "Is that Mount McKinley?" The driver said that indeed it was, that we were fortunate to be able to see it. We were a long distance from it. I strained my eyes. There it was far off, about 70 air miles—beyond an upland meadow, beyond a range of dark, treeless mountains with crevasses of snow. Not only was it high and fully covered in snow, but it was spread out and sloped rather than one enormous, conical peak as I had expected. I saw *two* snowy peaks, one glistening in sunlight. The whole mass was Mount McKinley! Under the blue sky, immovable, it waited. A few gray clouds floated nearer to us; I hoped they would not interfere with later viewings.

The paved park road ended at Savage River and our yellow bus continued on a dusty, narrow, gravel road barely passable by two buses simultaneously. The Alaska Range was off to our left—Mount McKinley far ahead of us was a part of that group. Melting snow and glaciers from those mountains created many streams and rivers in the valleys along the range. In the bus, we wound downhill, crossed the Sanctuary River, uphill and down, crossing the east fork of the Toklat

The Majesty of Mount McKinley

"The Alaska Range was off to our left—Mount McKinley far ahead of us was a part of that group. Melting snow and glaciers from those mountains created many streams and rivers in the valleys along the range."

River, then uphill to Polychrome Pass, a scary moment at an elevation of 3,500 feet as we negotiated a sharp curve in the road and a steep dropoff. We drove downward and then up again to Highway Pass, the highest point on the park road at 3,980 feet above sea level. Again we descended and crossed Stony Creek only to climb again and reach the Eielson Visitor Center. The mountains at that time of year were mostly barren with valleys of brown-green cover and meandering streams. Wind blew briskly through small bushes.

Along our dusty route, a proud golden eagle sat on top of a tall, pockmarked rock called Marmot Rock. Marmots the size of house cats lived in little caves in the rock. Our guide told us that eagles, wolves, and bears tried to seize the marmots. Indeed, I think it was Clem in our group who saw an eagle divebomb a marmot, something the guide herself had never seen.

During our ride we saw several views of Mount McKinley. We watched a herd of perhaps 15 or 20 caribou in their winter coats foraging in the valley and on a snowy hillside. As we drove, we saw another grizzly, a caribou, four more caribou, and more views of the "high one," looking more enormous each time.

After 66.1 miles from the visitor center, our driver parked the bus near Eielson Visitor Center, our destination in the park. Other tourists milled around the flat-roofed buildings. Inside were rest rooms, a water fountain, book sales, exhibits, and information on the park. The Center building itself offered a spectacular view of Mount McKinley both inside and outside from its observation decks. From inside one of the rooms with large plate glass windows, I looked long and hard through a telescope toward the peaks of Mount McKinley, many miles away. Two climbers, black mites on the snow, appeared to be descending the North Peak. How brave and daring to attempt such a frigid target!

Outside the Eielson Visitor Center, near a picnic area, I looked across the flat, sandy, river area with green-covered slopes on either side, over brown foothills, at the great alabaster mountain beyond. I stood and just looked and looked, my camera tucked into both hands

"The [Eielson Visitor] Center building itself offered a spectacular view of Mount McKinley . . . Two climbers, black mites on the snow, appeared to be descending the North Peak. How brave and daring to attempt such a frigid target!"

The Majesty of Mount McKinley

in front of me. Sunshine warmed me even though a breeze blew against my face. Across the wide, snowless valley, past the snowless foothills, I knew that same wind howled and swirled snow at the climbers on the face of that white mammoth. I hoped they would be successful and safe.

Unlike the lower mountains we had seen en route, all of McKinley was snow covered. In a way its two peaks disappointed me—I wanted to see one crowning jewel. Irregular in shape, the southern peak was slightly higher than the northern peak. I realized its truly great girth. Not only was it high and fully encased in snow, but its shape was spread out like giant dollops of meringue piled high on one of Mr. Benny's locally famous meringue pies.

"Are you ready to eat?" Paul asked. We walked to the parked yellow bus. By that time three other similar-looking yellow buses had arrived.

Following lunch, we began the trip back. Once again we saw lots of caribou on dirty-looking snow on an upland meadow slope. A mother grizzly bear and two cubs appeared to be foraging on a hillside. Inside the bus, we talked and exclaimed as we spied wildlife. "Look, is that another grizzly?" "Oh, yeah. She's got two cubs!"

About halfway back to the Visitor Access Center from which we had started that morning, we made a stop at Toklat Valley Rest Stop. A row of ten portable toilets looked like telephone booths. Back on the bus and the road again, I saw another grizzly moving behind a tree just down the bushy hillside below us. "Boy, he looks big, doesn't he!" I said.

In spite of the constant buzz of chatter and shouts inside the bus, some of our caravaners took a nap on their spouses' shoulders on the way back. I won't mention any names.

We passed two buses coming toward us, once with only inches between us. The guide said that the road was quite safe from mud slides unless it had been raining a lot.

We picked out three bears walking across the valley. And then someone spotted a herd of white Dall sheep at two locations high on the mountainside with its bare rocks jutting out from grassy slopes.

175

I heard John report that there were 13 at one place and seven at the other. The guide said the wolf was a predator of the sheep, which was why the sheep tried to stay up higher on the mountain.

Near the end of the trip, our bus stopped and a woman forest ranger stepped on board. "Did you have a good trip?" she asked. "Yeah, a great trip!" was our ready response. "We saw so *much!* Caribou, Dall Sheep, eagles, marmots, bears, moose," Clem added, his voice carrying the length of the bus.

Back at the campground, I fixed a late supper for us while Paul washed the windshield of the motorhome. Our day was catching up with us and we retired as darkness came on, hoping for sleep after the exciting day.

I awoke on Sunday morning, July 4, with a sore throat and a tired body but determined to be cheerful. I read my Bible and prayed. That day we would drive to Anchorage, 247 miles south of our campground at Healy.

Highway 3 (or the George Parks Highway) to Anchorage went south through the Alaska Range. We stopped at a turnout to admire snowcapped Panorama Mountain, in a picturesque scene across a river valley with lower mountains in front of it. Fireweed bloomed its bright mauve color beside the dirt parking area.

Several other times we pulled into turnouts for the view—one of Mount McKinley, whose peaks were in the clouds that day. How fortunate we were to have seen it the day before!

At one stop, we ate lunch in our motorhomes. At another, Willow, we filled up with gasoline. There, the station operator told Paul that it was the last weekend to catch king salmon in the Willow area and that fishermen were lined up shoulder to shoulder in the creek. We had already seen them from the highway.

As usual we ran into construction, but more unusual was the heavy traffic as streams of vehicles passed us going north. This was about 10 to 15 miles north of Anchorage. All told, it was a beautiful, scenic drive from Healy to Anchorage that day.

With windshield wipers going in a light rain, we approached the Golden Nugget Campground entrance in Anchorage. Paul told Scott on the CB that we and Six were at the entrance to which Scott replied, "Okay. Come on in and go toward the back and I'll see you."

We saw Scott walking on the *paved* street of the campground coming to meet us. Soon our motorhome was hooked up to one of the 125 sites in a campground landscaped with pine trees and the whole enclosed by a fence. Mountains stood watch in the background.

Spying a Denny's restaurant nearby, the Graybeals and we walked there for dinner. I was ready to stay in one place for a few days with some free time. A hairdo was my next objective, besides seeing Anchorage, of course.

· 17 ·

On to Anchorage and Kenai

CHANNEL 2 PREDICTED 52 degrees in Anchorage that Monday with sunset at 11:36 P.M., or 19 hours and 5 minutes of daylight. It was the first of two full days in the city whose skyscraper skyline shown in one of the RV tour brochures had made me introspective about what my vision of Alaska was like before I left home.

A Fun Bus waited at the campground to take our caravaners on a morning tour of Anchorage. A comfortable, late-model coach sported

On to Anchorage and Kenai

a glorious overall design that included brilliant shades of green, red, orange, yellow, and hot pink—fun colors when put side by side. The seats were covered with tan plush fabric with stripes of the same bright colors. As we gathered inside it, we greeted one another, talking and laughing. Some of us wore our blue Caravanas jackets, and of course everybody wore nametags. By this time, fun was a given with the Fun Bus motif egging us on. Only our group was on the bus.

Our congenial male bus driver took us first to the municipal greenhouse where we wandered around marveling at a large variety of beautiful blooming flowers and plants.

From there he drove us around Anchorage, which is in the middle of Alaska's south-central gulf coast. On a low-lying plain, Anchorage is bordered by mountains, dense forests of spruce, birch, and aspen, and by the waters of Cook Inlet's Turnagain Arm and Knit Arm. For its population of approximately 240,000 (half of Alaska's population lives in Anchorage), it has more than 200 churches and temples.

From the bus, our driver showed us the place where the Iditarod sled race began on 4th Avenue (the starting point looked like a busy

"Our congenial male bus driver took us first to the municipal greenhouse where we wandered around marveling at a large variety of beautiful blooming flowers and plants." (L-R: Lib and John)

city intersection to me), going from there 1,100 miles northwestward across Alaska to Nome on the Bering Sea.

We looked out the bus windows as he showed us Earthquake Park, which commemorates where the 1964 (Good Friday) earthquake in Anchorage registered 8.5 on the Richter scale. As evidence we saw sunken trees in an area on one side of a pavement. Over 118 lives were lost along the water's edge because of a tsunami related to the earthquake. Our guide said that Alaska is called the "State of Dangers and Disasters." He told us there were four active volcanos within a 200-mile radius of Anchorage.

We learned that moose and bears come into the city of Anchorage and that moose-and-car collisions kill many people each year, mostly in the winter. We saw the Lake Hood Seaplane Base and pontoon-equipped planes landing on the water.

Our guide passed along local lore also—to be considered a pioneer one must live 30 years or more in Alaska; a sourdough, one year; and a cheechako, less than one year. Sourdoughs, he said, are people who are sour on Alaska but do not have the money to get out.

We debarked from the bus and walked into the Anchorage Museum of History and Art, a handsome building with modern lines. It happened that Mark Russell, political satirist, and "Mr. White Keys," a nightclub owner in Anchorage, were seated at a black baby grand piano in the center of the high-ceilinged lobby taping a show. I walked up a handsome, open stairway where I could look down and see the taping.

I didn't stay long because our wagonmasters had said that we should be sure to see the exhibits on the second floor. They were indeed a feast of displays and dioramas depicting the cultures and history of the Aleuts, Eskimos, and Indians, Alaska's natives. (But I must admit I had been distracted by seeing Mark Russell and did not give my full attention to the well-done exhibits in front of me.)

Outside, along the city streets, planters and hanging baskets overflowed with beautiful, colorful blooming flowers. The streets were lined with street lamps on metal poles. It was a beautiful city in summer.

On to Anchorage and Kenai

By this time, I wanted to find a book about Barrow and so I visited several interesting bookstores without success. I did, however, find a beautiful little book about Denali Park that I bought to give to my "secret voyager" at our farewell dinner.

The Northway Mall in Anchorage could have been my hometown mall. Paul dropped me off on Tuesday morning, July 6, while he took the motorhome to be serviced. Inside the mall, people walked for exercise. Familiar stores greeted me—David's Jewelers, Zales Jewelers, Lamont's, Jo Ann Fabrics, Safeway, Kinney Shoes, Waldenbooks, Arby's, Foot Locker, and more. I spied what I had come for, the Regis hair salon, where I got a shampoo, haircut, and blow-dry for $28. When Paul returned for me, he had had the oil changed in the motorhome and the chassis lubricated and had finally found and bought two in-line gasoline filters.

Always the grocery shopper, I rode with Paul to a Pace warehouse where I again went wild and bought $83 worth of groceries. That led to subsequently stopping at a bank where Paul withdrew $1,000 in cash. At that time in our travels, we hardly ever used credit cards.

That evening with my cupboards once again well stocked, I prepared dinner in the motorhome. Afterward I entered the day's expenses in the trip log and then joined Paul to watch television—first the news, followed by other programs. For once, I was too tired to write in my journal. The long daylight hours and less sleep than normal must have been catching up with me.

The Graybeals, Beelers, and we parked our RVs beside Highway 1 south of Anchorage Wednesday morning. We were en route to Portage Glacier and then to Kenai, a small city located on the beautiful Kenai peninsula.

A stunningly beautiful scene had made us stop. Snuggled up to the highway but on a lower level ran railroad tracks. A body of blue water called Turnagain Arm lay in the valley. All around were forested mountains and in the distance under a blue sky were the bare-top Chugach mountains with snow-laden crevasses. A few white clouds veiled a part of the mountain top. We took pictures—I would later paint the scene from our photograph.

I had learned that Turnagain Arm was at first named Turnagain River by Captain James Cook, who was searching in 1776 for a waterway between the Pacific and the Atlantic Oceans. He thought perhaps he'd found it in the inlet that now bears his name, but—alas—he sailed only into another dead end and had to turn again. The body of water where he did so was renamed Turnagain Arm by a later surveyor.

Farther on, we came upon a unique sight—the bare, brown bed of Turnagain Arm in the Twenty Mile River area where the tide had gone out. When we parked and stepped outside for a closer look, Paul warned, "Don't walk out there."

"Why not?" I asked.

"Don't you see that sign?"

Small pools of water and empty gulches in the sandy soil seemed to invite one to walk there but because of quicksand a sign warned people to stay off the smooth surface.

At Portage Lake, I stood looking at the white cruise boat in the sunny, cool air and thought again of my inability to swim. Soon after boarding, seeing an ample supply of life jackets, I said to Paul, "Am I glad to see those. Now I'll be able to enjoy this ride!"

We all went to the open top deck as the boat headed up Portage Lake toward the glacier. A woman narrator described the passing scenery over a loudspeaker as we cruised. Dark green mountains lined the lake.

As we neared the glacier, the narrator said that it was one-half to three-fourths mile wide and 80 to 90 feet high. What surprised me most about the glacier was its color. Instead of pure white, an awesome "river" of blue-green, sometimes white, sometimes dirty ice and snow curved down like molten lava between two mountain ridges and flowed to the edge of the lake. Black, ragged stripes of moraine, pieces of rock gouged out by the glacier, trimmed it on the middle right and middle left. The moraine contained the same rock as the mountain but appeared darker because it was wet, so the narrator said. The color of the glacier ice reminded me of the glass insulators that are sometimes used on telephone poles.

On to Anchorage and Kenai

Our vessel stopped at the head of the lake near the face of the glacier. At that location, the ice was 60 to 70 years old, the time it took for fallen snow at the top of the mountain to reach the lake. Our guide told us that they get 100 feet of snow a year at the top of the mountain where Portage Glacier starts. Some of our group saw a piece of glacier ice break off and splash into the lake. A flotilla of pieces of ice from previous calvings floated in the water.

Across the lake from the glacier was a huge, steep, rugged mountain of rock. Earlier our vessel had stopped long enough to let off a young photographer.

"You know that fellow that got off the boat a while ago? He's climbing up that mountain," Paul pointed out.

I watched breathlessly as he scrambled up the jagged sides, his gear in a knapsack on his back. He made it, of course.

With a cold wind blowing across the open top deck, most of us rode in the enclosed cabin on the return trip. In addition, it gave us a chance to relax and just enjoy the ride. My eyes kept wanting to shut. When the narrator told of a black bear on the mountainside,

"Our vessel stopped at the head of the lake near the face of the glacier. At that location, the ice was 60 to 70 years old, the time it took for fallen snow at the top of the mountain to reach the lake."

however, most of us got up from our comfortable blue-cushioned chairs and went to that side of the boat to search for it through the large plate glass windows. By the time I looked, it had already disappeared into the woods.

When we returned from the cruise, we saw a movie and toured the exhibits at the visitor center. Then our motorhome was a welcome sight as once again we hurried inside to enjoy its warmth, to eat lunch, and hit the road again. We returned to Seward Highway, Highway 1, and continued south to a junction, S 37.7, where we turned west onto the Sterling Highway, still Highway 1, toward Kenai. We followed the instructions from our wagonmasters that referred to specific pages in *The MILEPOST®*.

During the afternoon's picture-postcard drive, fireweed bloomed along the roadside; the two-lane Sterling highway curved ahead with deciduous and evergreen trees alongside in the valleys and on nearby mountains. In the distance snow lay on the tops and in the crevasses of peaks, all under a blue sky with white and gray clouds drifting about. Who could ask for more!

John said over the CB that he had heard on the 10:00 news the night before that a Denali Park bus slid down a bank in rain and *snow* that day! He did not know the extent of injuries or damage. I thought again how fortunate we were to have had sunny weather when we toured the park on Saturday.

We had been in Alaska nine days already. That day we glided along on a paved highway like those in the Lower 48. Road construction offered short, orange, plastic poles on black plates that lined the shoulders—not concrete barriers as we had in the Lower 48. We saw a young woman driving a large construction roller.

About four o'clock, after traveling 188 scenic miles, we pulled into Overland RV Park, Kenai, Alaska, for a two-night stay. Paul and I walked to the nearby restaurant for dinner and later took the motorhome to a grocery store that had lots of fresh produce. Kenai was a spaciously laid-out town with a population of 6,327.

The next evening at the same Kenai campground, Paul sat in the easy chair in our motorhome about 8:45 relaxing. With the videotape

On to Anchorage and Kenai

recorder focused on him, I asked if he would like to describe what he had done that day. And so he began his saga:

> I took a long walk downtown—there are three banks in this town. I also know that there are four auto parts stores in this town, and I visited two hardware stores, and I've finally been able to purchase at a reasonable price a portable air compressor for pumping up tires on the motorhome. I checked all the tires, I reinflated all the tires using Graybeal's portable pump, which I had access to before I actually got my own. I bought some special paper towels for wiping up oil and cleaning the windshield at the NAPA store. I bought a set of metal valve-cover caps at the NAPA store because I was missing one.
>
> I went to the visitor center and sat through a movie that described the life of Sidney Laurence who did a lot of oil paintings of scenes in Alaska. We had a lovely evening meal with the Graybeals in our motorhome this evening. And now Bernice is trying to use up battery time on this particular battery so we can recharge it and get ready for our sightseeing tour at Homer tomorrow. And that's all I have to say for now."

We switched roles and I sat in the same easy chair.

> We are in Kenai. I was trying to catch up with myself today. I was feeling kind of weak and shaky from being on the go *so much*, and I'm the kind of person who just goes until she drops. So I *dropped* [chuckle], and I slept late this morning, and then I wrote postcards, and I labeled rocks that I had picked up from the shore of the Arctic Ocean in Barrow, Alaska. Then we had lunch, and then I took a nap this afternoon while Paul walked downtown. The Graybeals invited us to go sightseeing with them, but I felt as if I really needed to take the time this afternoon for a good nap. I've been fighting a cold also. So I feel *much* revived now.
>
> We had a good supper. John grilled steaks on his propane grill. Libby fixed buttered potatoes, real potatoes

that she peeled. And I fixed fresh broccoli, opened a can of pears and a can of peaches. We had this monstrous cinnamon roll (about 10 inches in diameter) for dessert, which we didn't finish. John and Lib went over and brought coffee from their rig, which is just next door. So we had a really nice time. Afterward, we talked and I showed them our souvenirs from Barrow. Then we went over to the departure meeting where we got our instructions for traveling the next day. Tomorrow we are looking forward to a six-hour cruise to Gull Island and Seldovia. It's 89 miles from here. It's also near where we will be camping tomorrow night [at Homer]. So we're having a really good time and we've done so many new things that we haven't done in our lives before. It's been a really thrilling adventure for us.

Seven people from our group went salmon fishing that day on the Kenai River—Ann and Louie, Eunice and Fred, Don Heathcock, Don Peterson, and Clem. Six caught at least one fish. Poor Clem was the lone fishless fisherman. (Effie, his wife, rejoiced.) Don Heathcock, however, took pity on him and gave him a hunk of his salmon.

Daylight continued. At 10:30, the sun continued to cast shadows in the RV park. At 11:30, the sun had set but lots of light remained. An orange glow silhouetted the horizon contrasting with the blue sky above. Cars drove by with headlights beaming. Their movement made me think of our caravan tour and of all that we had seen so far, with Barrow a highlight. Yet, just as the cars continued in their travel, I looked forward to the wonders of our itinerary ahead, particularly to seeing Prince William Sound. I hoped that its water and shoreline had regained their pristine state since the infamous 11-million-gallon oil spill by the supertanker *Exxon Valdez* in March 1989. I had looked forward to seeing the sound since first thinking about making the trip to Alaska.

For the moment, however, now that I had labeled the Barrow stones and driftwood, I wondered when and how I would share them with our caravaners.

· 18 ·

Captivating Homer Spit

STERLING HIGHWAY took us through Homer and onto Homer Spit, a long, narrow bar of gravel that juts five miles into Kachemak Bay at the southern end of Kenai Peninsula. Known for its halibut fishing and spectacular scenery, the spit offered a harbor and fish processing as well as a boardwalk of small shops, restaurants, a bakery, a motel, and campgrounds.

Established by Homer Pennock, who landed a party of gold and coal prospectors in the schooner *Excelsior* there in 1896, the city of Homer's population is 3,660. The prospectors didn't find gold, but the settlement grew and a robust fishing industry became the mainstay of the economy. Homer now calls itself "The Halibut Fishing Capital of the World."

Paul guided the motorhome off Sterling Highway at the end of Homer Spit on Friday morning, July 9, and into a dirt and gravel area. We were heading for Land's End RV Park somewhere beyond the buildings on either side of us. Over the CB but out of sight, Scott told us to keep coming and to keep bearing right. We rounded a curve and saw Scott, transceiver to his face, repeating and motioning for us to keep bearing right.

"Very good, thank you," Paul replied on the CB.

Many RVs, some our own caravaners, already populated the campground. A fifth wheel blocked the campground road temporarily and we waited as it backed into a campsite. Then we continued forward and around another curve.

"Pull in—right?" Paul said on the CB, as compared with backing in. Scott concurred.

"Thank you very much," and we drove headfirst onto our site that overlooked beautiful blue water.

"I'd say that's far enough! Whee!" I exclaimed. I'm not usually a backseat driver but it began to look as if we might go down the bank in front of us and onto the narrow, grayish beach.

"This is *beautiful!* Boats out on the water. And this is where we'll be parked for two nights!" We were at the very tip of Homer Spit. I clapped my hands in my excitement.

Ahead of us was Kachemak Bay, but I didn't have time to linger and enjoy it because 18 of our group, including the Graybeals and us, were to be at the office of Rainbow Tours by 10:45 to take a six-hour cruise tour past Gull Island to Seldovia. The office was a 10-minute walk from the campground. We were to take binoculars and cameras, and dress in layers with a jacket and good walking shoes. We would spend two hours in Seldovia where we would eat lunch.

188

Captivating Homer Spit

A great day for a cruise, the sun shone and the water was calm. The *Rainbow Connection* was a white boat with a flying bridge and large, enclosed lounge with wide windows. A young woman with long, blonde, curly hair and glasses was the captain of the boat. As she neared Gull Island, the rock itself almost seemed to move because it was so heavily covered with birds, birds everywhere, almost like bees in a honeycomb. They used the little crevasses of the jagged rock for nesting. We could hear their chatter and squawk. Looking like penguins, most of the birds were the common murres.

During the one-and-one-half-hour ride on Kachemak Bay, sea otters played in the water, making us laugh at their antics. Some were resting on their backs (they sleep and eat while floating on their backs), having wrapped and anchored themselves in kelp to keep from floating away.

Seldovia is one of the oldest settlements in the Cook Inlet area, having been settled by the Russians about 1800. Although Seldovia was on the tip of the Kenai Peninsula, it could be reached only by air, tour boat, or ferry. Because of not being a part of Kenai Peninsula highways, Seldovia had retained much of its old Alaska look and customs.

"Seldovia is one of the oldest settlements in the Cook Inlet area . . . It could be reached only by air, tour boat, or ferry."

Hungry from the boat ride, the Graybeals and we ate lunch almost immediately in one of the three restaurants in the small town. Then a kind gentleman took us on a tram tour of the town with its population of about 400. Impressive to me were houses on stilts beside Seldovia Slough where the tide came in under them. The town contained many lodging places, bed and breakfasts, and a hotel. It also had, among other services and supplies, a beauty shop; a bookstore; a gas station; a market that sold groceries, hardware, pharmacies, souvenirs, and other items; a laundromat; a realty; a post office; taxi service; a newspaper shop; and an ice cream store, in which Lib and I bought ice cream cones to top off our lunch.

We saw the airport on which residents depended. With only a 1,000-foot runway, the airport accommodated 12-passenger airplanes that could also carry freight. Within 15 minutes of takeoff, the passengers would land at the Homer airport, where most Seldovia residents kept their cars.

On a hill overlooking the harbor and the cruise boat on which we had come stood the historic, restored St. Nicholas Russian Orthodox Church, the first church in Seldovia. A medium-sized wooden building with two towers, it was painted white with light blue trim. One of its towers was topped with an octagonal enclosure for its bells. I learned later that there are four other churches in the town (Bible Chapel, Baptist, Catholic, and Lutheran).

All too soon, it was time to board the vessel for our ride back to Homer.

Tired from our afternoon boat excursion, the Graybeals and we decided to eat dinner at the Land's End Resort, which was adjacent to the campground. Afterward, back at the motorhome, while Paul relaxed on the sofa, I brought the trip log up to date and wrote postcards. After a full day, we went to bed about 11:00 although it was still daylight.

On Saturday, July 10, while some of our caravaners fished for halibut, Lib and I sat eating lunch in a boardwalk cafe on Homer Spit. As we looked out at the beautiful blue waters of Kachemak Bay, it was a sunny day and the temperature was well on its way to a record 81 degrees.

With just the two of us at the table, I told her that I felt tired and was fighting a cold. Others in our group on the way back from the Gull Island trip the day before had dozed or were quiet, so I sensed that I wasn't the only one. Also I said I was frustrated about not having a set-aside worship time for our group planned into the travel schedule. The impromptu one at Muncho Lake had shown it was not only possible but doable even with all of our various faiths. I told Lib that one night after that I had actually gotten out of bed and looked at our itinerary for the coming Saturdays and Sundays. All full travel days. No chance for another group serendipity service.

She listened patiently, letting me talk. I mentioned that the long daylight hours might be contributing to the fatigue because of my staying up later than usual. She said that she had to put heavy towels over the curtain rods in their bedroom to make the room darker for sleeping. Then she told me about a close friend who seemed to have boundless energy—Lib thought it came from her daily devotions.

Suddenly I realized that while I read the Bible and prayed before breakfast each morning, my solution for a special *Sunday* worship was to simply get up early enough on that morning before leaving the campground and have my own private worship service. I could use the same worship services that I had prepared for our church camping group to use or other resources that I had brought along. Why hadn't I thought of it sooner! Maybe Paul would join in and we would have a two-member congregation. "Where two or three are gathered together . . ." was all it took. My steps were lighter as Lib and I walked back to the campground.

That evening our whole group of caravaners feasted at the Land's End Resort, a fine restaurant that overlooked the bay. Three women and five men in our group who had gone fishing that day arrived late but triumphantly for dinner—they had each (including Clem) caught their limit of two halibut.

We lingered at the restaurant, having a good time together, and then eventually strolled back to the campground. Later that Saturday night, with my mind at ease about worship services, I sat in the passenger seat of the motorhome looking out at Kachemak Bay. At 11:00, it was light enough to see all the activity and around the Bay. My heart overflowed from the beauty of the scene; I had to write something down:

> How sacred and singular this place is!
>
> How often do we camp headfirst 30 feet from the incoming waves of a blue-green bay, so close I hear the water meeting the shore, and nothing but beach–rounded stones and dark sand—between our motorhome and the tide-driven water?
>
> How often can I look across a wide expanse of glimmering waves to see snow-garnished mountains on the opposite shore?
>
> How often do I see a beach with only a few people walking, stopping, looking, playing—only a few people at a time—not teeming with humankind?
>
> How often do I see small flocks of small birds, white and black, their bodies shining like diamonds as they fly in loose V-formation toward the evening sun?
>
> How often do I see a *lone* boat, its white hull looking golden in the evening rays, met only by one other boat going the opposite direction, only two boats on this large lay of water?
>
> How often do I take time to experience a place, to let myself enjoy its serenity, to let its beauty into my soul, to appreciate the rareness of a place? How often do I even find such a place as this?
>
> And where is this extraordinary scene? In Alaska, in Homer, on Homer Spit, at Land's End.

Under sunny skies and pleasant temperatures, on Sunday our caravan again drove the Sterling Highway, retracing our earlier travel through its magnificent scenery. Another highway, Seward Highway, led us into—what else?—Seward. That city of about 3,000 people was northeast of Homer on the east side of the Kenai Peninsula. After driving 183 miles, we arrived at the City of Seward Public Camping area. This would be a dry camp; that is, without water, electricity, and dumping facilities.

At sea level, Seward faced Resurrection Bay on the east coast of the Kenai Peninsula. The Bay is a year-round ice-free harbor, making Seward an important port for shipping cargo and fishing.

Most of us were parked on sites covered with dry grass, not in the front row this time but up a slight hill with a good view of the bay water and mountains beyond. Behind our campground and the city itself rose the foliage-covered Mount Marathon. An annual Fourth of July foot race to ascend and descend the mountain had taken place since 1915.

The weather in Seward continued sunny and warm; most of us extended our awnings.

For the potluck supper, I prepared a tomato-cheese casserole. We all enjoyed another sumptuous repast from our own RV larders. We amazed ourselves by the variety and deliciousness of what appeared on the potluck tables. In due time, before reconvening for a campfire circle, we gathered up our empty food dishes and place settings from the tables and took them back to our rigs. The wind had picked up and it was cooler than during the afternoon. John nimbly laid a campfire by setting thin sticks of wood in a tepee. Paul leaned over to help when necessary.

With the fire going, we sat around it in a circle in our lawn chairs and talked informally, trying to stay warm. Clem took the lead by telling a funny joke and then a true story about a former prisoner who was currently much appreciated and beloved by everybody who knew him. Meanwhile, Paul was back at our motorhome checking the overdrive transmission fluid and putting water in the chassis batteries, but everyone else was at the campfire.

I left my chair and walked to our motorhome nearby. With Paul's encouragement, soon I carried back to the campfire circle a large, heavy paper plate on which lay the variety of stones and pieces of driftwood I had picked up on the shore of the Arctic Ocean. Each one was carefully labeled: "From Arctic Ocean shore, Barrow, AK 6/30."

I told everyone of my adventure in picking up the stones and driftwood, and said I would like each couple to choose one of the objects. Paul had rejoined our circle by that time and added humorous remarks: "Yeah, she almost got left on the shore of the Arctic Ocean," and "There was a sign there that said beware of polar bears."

Each couple came to me afterward to thank me with much earnestness, and I felt good about their appreciation of the souvenirs. Karen was excited that the piece of driftwood she liked had made the rounds and wasn't selected by anyone else. I had handed the plate to her first, but as wagonmaster she politely let others select before she chose.

Laurie, as tailgunner, picked the smallest piece because "I collect shells," she said.

"That was the only shell I found!" I offered her a stone also since the shell was tiny.

· 19 ·

Up Close to Exit Glacier

A FEW MINUTES before 10:00 on Monday morning, our Trails North bus left the City of Seward campground. Our driver and guide headed toward Exit Glacier about eight miles north. Shortly after passing through Seward, we left the paved road behind as our bus bumped along on dusty gravel. Road construction later on produced even greater bumps and bounces.

When we arrived at the visitor center near the base of Exit Glacier, the driver said that he would park the green bus, which was Number Four, in the parking lot. We would have an hour to walk up the 0.8-mile nature trail to the foot of the glacier and back. We were to be back on the bus by 11:40.

Since the bus ride was hot and I had dressed warmly, I decided to take only my nylon Caravanas jacket. I asked Wil, who was sitting on a bench and did not plan to walk the trail, if I could park my purple tote bag with him. It had my pocketbook in it and about $520 in cash. He said sure, so I left it with him, hoping that it was not too heavy a responsibility. (When I caught up with Yvonne after the trail walk near the bus, she assured me that it was okay.)

The paved trail ahead (the first 0.3 mile were paved for handicapped accessibility) lay between leafy deciduous trees on the left and low evergreens on the right, which somehow survived in the dark, gritty soil. Above the trail in the distance was the icy, blue-

"The paved trail ahead lay between leafy deciduous trees on the left and low evergreens on the right . . . Above the trail in the distance was the icy, blue-green, crinkled face of Exit Glacier. Just to its left was a snowcapped and forested mountain."

Up Close to Exit Glacier

green, crinkled face of Exit Glacier. Just to its left was a snowcapped and forested mountain. Overhead not a cloud hung in the blue sky.

I walked the trail, breathing in the fresh breeze that blew against my face, and liking the feeling of being out in the country with bushes and trees on either side. Near the face of the glacier, a glacier stream flowed forcibly along. I splashed my fingers in the icy cold water.

As I stood at the base of the glacier and saw the 10-foot bank of black sand and rocks that the glacier was pushing ahead of itself, I felt like it was a huge ship pushing its way through waves in the ocean. Looking high above that mound, I saw sooty-looking, blue-green crevices left by melting ice in the face of the humongous glacier. The glacier had receded from its former grandeur but was still awesome in its magnitude and power.

Our bus driver had told us not to get too close to the glacier. In fact there were signs posted not to go within 20 feet of the glacier. A woman had walked under the glacier a few years earlier. It had calved at that moment and she was crushed and killed. Knowing that, I had a healthy respect for the power of the ice. I did not attempt to get near enough to touch the glacier. Besides that, I had actually walked on the Athabascan Glacier (part of the Columbia Ice Field) in 1986 when Paul and I visited Jasper National Park in British Columbia.

Exit Glacier is a part of the Harding Ice Field and got its name from the fact that hikers in the Harding Ice Field could use this particular glacier to exit the ice field. We enjoyed ourselves and lingered at the base of the glacier, taking pictures. Twice more I splashed my hands in the icy, green, silty waters of the several streams running off from under the glacier. It was fun to think I was touching water beside a glacier.

Paul and I had taken the easy trail to the base of the glacier. We could see John and Lib and some of the other caravaners climbing the steep, unpaved trail that wound up nearer to the top of the glacier.

I have some growing concern for global warming. During our trip, we had learned of two glaciers that were receding because of warming temperatures. We learned that yesterday Barrow had a temperature of 71 degrees, the highest ever recorded. When we were in Barrow, it was about 50 degrees and a wind was blowing so that it seemed cooler than that.

Soon Paul and I walked back along the trail and joined the other caravaners on the bus.

As our bus driver and guide entered a woods on a single-lane, gravel road, a sign on a tree said: Van Deusen–Private. He kept on going, however, and soon stopped in a clearing with about a dozen parked buses and some wooden buildings.

It was the home of Whitey and Micki Van Deusen, who owned the tour bus company, Trails North, Inc. As part of the tour, they told us how they came to Alaska, about their Siberian husky dogs, and their log cabin home.

Whitey was Michael Van Deusen, a tall, thin, mustachioed man of Dutch heritage in his forties. His wife, Micki (Patricia Mickens), a dark-haired, brown-eyed, beautiful woman in her late thirties or early forties, was of Indian-Spanish and Irish-English heritage. They met in California, her home state. They decided to go to Alaska to make their fortune. At first they lived in a mining cabin and did some gold mining. Then they were given a log cabin by a woman hoping to sell some land on which the cabin stood. She felt she could sell the land quicker if the cabin was not on it.

So Whitey and Micki disassembled the cabin, a task that was not too hard because of the cabin's dovetail construction. It was just a matter of numbering and lifting the logs off. The couple reassembled the logs on the present site, starting in September and finishing in January. They had to build a kitchen inside and add a bathroom to the rear of the two-story log cabin. They sanded and oiled the logs to preserve them.

Micki and Whitey both told stories about their experiences in Alaska and then showed us through their log cabin, which had every modern convenience including a piano, a television set, and a stereo system for playing audiotapes.

They raised Siberian husky dogs to use as sled dogs and also as a tourist attraction. We had an opportunity to pet some of the dogs and pups.

Micki showed us a dog used in their dogsled team. It was one of a litter that they had bred who had taken his basic training along with his siblings. One day when he didn't come back when called, Micki started to look for him. She heard crying and found the dog had fallen onto a ledge.

Through this incident and an examination by a veterinarian, she discovered that the dog had cataracts and was blind. An operation to correct this condition would have been extremely expensive. Since the blind dog seemed to want to continue his training, they allowed that and eventually placed the dog in the position nearest the sled, a position where a

"They [Micki and Whitey Van Deusen] raised Siberian husky dogs to use as sled dogs and also as a tourist attraction."

dog has to work very, very hard. This particular dog was exceptional and performed very well. One day they noticed blood in his stool and they were told it was because he was working himself too hard. So they put him up in the position just ahead of the one in which he had been where he would not have to pull as hard.

Eventually he seemed to learn all of the lead dog's commands, so one day they put him in as lead dog. He demonstrated that he knew all of the commands: as soon as he heard one, he would immediately obey. So they had a lead dog who was blind! He was a very gentle dog and let us pet him.

We were all impressed with the Van Deusen couple and with their lifestyle. Their two children were temporarily away from home—their daughter, Beth, who was chosen Miss Alaska National Teenager 1991, was at a college in Oregon. Their son, Shawn, was working on a tug boat in the Aleutian Islands.

On the way back to our campground in Seward, the guide showed us the harbor at Resurrection Bay. Two cruise ships were in port at the time, one being the *Golden Odyssey*. He showed us a large coal pile on shore and a conveyor belt that moved the coal out to cargo ships. Once loaded, the ships would take the coal to Korea. He said also that many Japanese ships took fish home from the port at Seward.

After the bus driver left us off at our campground, Paul and I ate lunch in the motorhome. To prepare for the following day's travel, we drove over to town to get gas and a few groceries. From there we found a telephone where I called Jeff and Nancy. We had not been in contact for over a week because they had a vacation week in Missouri. He sounded good, Nancy was fine, and we got caught up on our family news.

At the five o'clock departure meeting, Karen told us that the City of Seward was going to start grading our campground the next morning at six o'clock. We should plan to leave before that time. After our meeting, as some of us lingered, talking about that morning's tour, Scott said that he loved puppies and was sorry he missed seeing the sled dog puppies. Instead of going on the tour with us, he had gone to have his foot and ankle x-rayed. He had tripped over an object causing something in his ankle to give way. The resulting pain caused him to limp. The doctors were not yet sure of the cause of the pain.

That evening, I went alone on a photographic walking jaunt of Seward after inviting Lib to go along. She had other things to do, as did Paul. I walked along slowly toward downtown, which was uphill

Up Close to Exit Glacier

from the campground! I stopped in at the town library, which was warm and inviting. I noticed they had Nancy Drew, the Hardy Boys, and Bobbsey Twins books for young readers. I picked up a few pieces of free literature including a visitor's guide, which helped me find the Iditarod Trail Mile 0 marker.

Today the Iditarod race begins in Anchorage, but originally it started in Seward with a historic race by dogsled to rush diphtheria serum to those stricken with the disease in a gold-mining camp in Nome. A wooden sign marked the spot: Iditarod National Historic Trail, Mile 0, Seward Alaska, 938 miles to Nome.

I took pictures of the sign and continued up Fourth Avenue, meandering in and out of gift shops. I came upon the starting place for the Mount Marathon Fourth of July race and took a video of that spot.

I walked along the residential streets where people lived in ranch-style homes that date back to the early 1900s. A planned community, Seward's streets and lots were laid out neatly in grid form. Many lawns were casual; some had grass that was speckled with white clover. Steep mountains surrounded Seward, some with snowcaps. Back at the campground an hour later, I saw that the blue water of Resurrection Bay moved swiftly with a fast current.

In contrast, I pictured Prince William Sound with calm water and looked forward to seeing it when we reached Valdez in two days.

· 20 ·

On the Road to Palmer

SINCE A GRADING CREW was supposed to arrive at the campground where we were parked at six that Tuesday morning, we had gone to bed early, about 9:30, so that we would get a good night's rest for the early rising. We had to drive north through Anchorage, stay in Palmer that Tuesday night, and go around a highway loop in order to reach Valdez and Prince William Sound on Wednesday.

On the Road to Palmer

The graders did not arrive, so we slept until almost six. Most of our tour group had left the campground before us. The tailgunners were the only remaining rig from our group as we pulled away from the City of Seward Campground.

We passed lakes and creeks in valleys between green mountains. Purplish fireweed, dandelions, and blue blossoms on long stems bloomed along the roadside. Kenai Peninsula was a very beautiful place on God's earth. At mid-morning, the Graybeals and we stopped at the Tidewater Cafe in Portage, Alaska. We enjoyed cinnamon buns and John, Lib, and I had coffee. Paul drank hot water. When the bill came, John looked at it to figure up how much we owed for what we had ordered and he said, "Oh, the hot water's free. I think I'm going to start ordering that!" And we all laughed, including Paul.

Paul said, "Every place on this trip so far has not charged for hot water when I ordered it."

We saw again the barren bed of Turnagain Arm at the Twenty Mile River area when the tide was out. Always, mountains and valleys and water were around the next bend.

Lib had a special mission in Anchorage. She wanted to see the Native Alaskan Regional Hospital gift shop, recommended by a relative who had bought some lovely jewelry there. Our husbands parked the motorhomes and joined Lib and me later in the hospital gift shop. A small area, it contained showcases and shelves of Native American crafts and jewelry. Lib bought a *very* handsome scrimshaw bracelet and lovely dangling earrings that went with it very well. I bought two beaded necklaces, one of which had matching earrings. The name of the Athabascan woman who made them was on the price tag.

Then our dear husbands dropped Lib and me off at a shopping area, D Street and Fifth, I think it was, while they went to get gasoline. We hurried down the street to gift shops to find a stuffed toy resembling a husky puppy to give to Karen and Scott Bonis, our wagonmasters, knowing that Scott loved puppies. After several shops, we found one that we liked and hoped they would, too.

On the way back to our meeting point, I stopped at a photo shop where I had to pay $12 for a 36-slide roll of 200 ASA 35mm film—a horrendous price! But I was almost at the end of my last roll of slide film.

Lib and I were proud of ourselves that we were ahead of schedule and stood waiting on the sidewalk when Paul and John in our respective motorhomes turned the corner and came alongside the pavement. We both hopped in and were underway again.

As we rode along, I fixed for Paul's lunch a sandwich of cooked turkey breast. Knowing that he liked to heat his sandwiches, I asked him to turn on the auxiliary generator so that I could use the microwave oven. He simply reached to the dashboard and pressed the switch to its On position. The auxiliary generator came on. I waited a few seconds until it began generating electricity, then placed the sandwich in the oven and set it for 40 seconds. Sometimes we also used the auxiliary generator to furnish electricity for the overhead air conditioner as we rode along instead of using dash air conditioning, which took some power away from the motor.

When the Graybeals and we reached Palmer, the tailgunners were within CB range and in sight ahead.

"One, this is 40. We're going to have to bear right here," said Don on the CB.

"Where? Oh, the traffic light here. Yeah, yeah, to go to Palmer," returned Paul.

"There seems to be a little bit of a problem here with the intersection," Don said.

"Okay. Thank you," Paul said.

And then Karen came on the CB. She was already at the Homestead RV Park. "Forty and One, this is 50. Come on back."

"Go ahead," said Don.

"You must be close. Are you at the intersection?" Karen asked.

"We're at the intersection of Fox Highway."

"Okay. You're very close. The sign [to the campground] is a little obscured by brush but you come around a hill and there's the entrance to the RV park on the right," Karen's voice came over clearly.

"Okay. Thanks, Karen," Don said.

"Okay, Karen. Thank you," Paul said, too.

We rounded the bend and Paul said, "I think this is it."

"It says RV Park," I said.

At the entrance to the Homestead RV Park stood a reconstructed cache on tall poles. The office was log cabin style and the sites themselves were in a wooded area with a mountain in the background. Edging the dirt campground were more aspen and pine trees.

Laurie came on the CB: "Where do you want us, Karen?" And then she added, "I see Scott."

"Karen, this is Number One," said Paul on the CB. "I'm coming up past the dump station where 40 is parked."

About that time Scott came walking toward us, limping. After telling us where our site was, he asked if we had seen the Cornells. We had not, but Don said they had stopped at a church.

At four o'clock that day, we all got aboard a yellow school bus for a tour of the Matanuska Valley, a visit to a musk ox farm, and dinner out.

Palmer, with a population of about 3,000, is located in the Matanuska Valley. It is the only community in Alaska that developed mostly from an agricultural economy. In 1935, it was thought the valley with its long hours of daylight had great agricultural potential. In an effort to utilize it and to help get people off the dole during the Great Depression, the Federal Emergency Relief Administration had social workers pick 203 families—mostly hardy farmers of Scandinavian descent from Michigan, Wisconsin, and Minnesota—to settle as the Matanuska Valley Colony. Many of the descendants of those early farmers still live in the Valley.

We stopped at the Matanuska Valley Visitors' Information Center and Historical Museum. Outside, as snowcapped mountains stood watch under a blue sky, we strolled leisurely around the landscaped lawn and garden. Brilliant colors stood out against the green background of leaves and grass—blue delphiniums, yellow marigolds, red impatiens, and many other flowers whose names I did not know. A triangular bed lined with tomato plants surrounded petunias and lush cabbages. Everything looked bursting with health.

The garden had been planned as a showcase representing agriculture in the Matanuska Valley. Divided into sections, each part had its own theme—perennials and annuals, everlastings, a rock garden, herbs and edible flowers, commercial vegetables and potatoes, and others.

At the Musk Ox Farm we had a guided lecture tour and learned about the history of the musk ox. Great, brown, shaggy musk oxen grazed in tall grass behind fences. We saw some of the 69 cows, bulls, and yearlings on the farm, the only place in the world where these Ice Age animals are grown domestically. The guide told us how musk oxen are combed and the qiviut is retrieved. The qiviut is the gossamer down that grows under the shaggy outer guard hairs. It takes three hours to comb a cooperative animal, a process that yields a large

"At the Musk Ox Farm . . . we saw some of the 69 cows, bulls, and yearlings on the farm, the only place in the world where these Ice Age animals are grown domestically."

garbage bag full of fiber. The lightweight qiviut is eight times warmer than sheep's wool. The combed qiviut is hand-knit by Eskimos living in isolated villages, aiding their economy.

We dined in a private room at the Chardonnay, a very nice restaurant in Palmer. Individual dinners usually ran from $8.95 to $25.00, according to our campground host, who served as guide. Even though Lou Beeler had a cold and looked tired, he gave the blessing.

I sat beside Clem Swagerty, whose wife, Effie, was on the other side of him. Paul was on my left. We had a pleasant time getting to know each other better. I asked them what they do when they're not on tour and they in turn asked us the same question. They are very active in church and on local boards—Clem is head of the Contra Costa County Parole Board in California as well as a consultant and volunteer on correctional matters in his area. Effie is on committees in her church and does other community volunteer work. They are both active in the University of the Pacific alumni affairs. In addition, they have children and grandchildren. I believe it's seven in all when they get together as a family.

Our meal began with a tossed salad and ranch or Thousand Island dressing. Then it was buffet style for chicken creole; roast beef; steamed rice; new potatoes with the skins on; a medley of broccoli, cauliflower, and carrots in rather large chunks; and delicious rolls. For dessert, we were served spice cake with cream-cheese frosting. We had coffee, iced tea, and iced water to drink.

After lingering at the tables, we all boarded the bus at the invitation of our campground host and returned to the campground.

About 20 minutes later, at 8 P.M., we took our chairs to the departure meeting, which was led this time by Laurie and Don, our tailgunners. It was a practice session for them to see if they wanted to be wagonmasters and to give them experience in giving directions for travel to people on a tour. They did well, especially considering the fact that the directions to our next campground were very complicated.

After the Petersons had finished their part of the departure meeting, Scott read a letter he had written to a magazine directly from his portable computer screen, which was sitting on the picnic table in front of him. At the end of his presentation, Mary Jo asked what that thing was in front of him. He turned it around and said that it was a computer, that it was a wonderful help to them. Mary Jo asked how much it cost. When he said, "About $3,000," her jaw dropped and she said, "Well, no wonder it's so wonderful!" We all had a good laugh. We laughed a lot at the things Mary Jo asked and said, but it was all in good fun.

After the meeting, while I walked around the campground, Paul took the motorhome to the dump station so that we would not be delayed getting away from camp in the morning when a number of people would probably line up to dump.

It was still daylight at 10:08 P.M. that Tuesday night. The temperature had reached 81 degrees during the day. After a full, full day I took a relaxing shower in our motorhome bathroom. I never cease to be grateful for the bathroom convenience when we travel. While Paul showered, I said my nightly thank-you prayers and crawled into our queen-sized bed, between our own sheets with our own pillows. I thought about the many cinnamon buns I had recently eaten and suspected that I was gaining weight. I'm going to have to put a halt to that, I said to myself. And then I thought of the next day's arrival at Valdez and wondered what that port city would look like.

· 21 ·

Prince William Sound

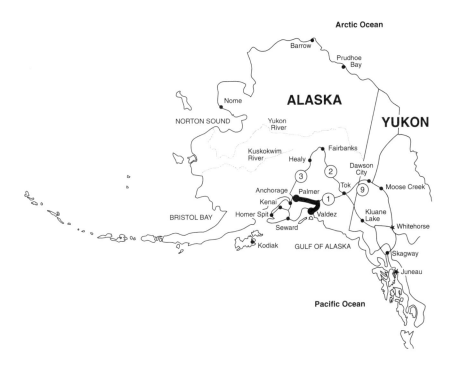

ON THE ROAD in our motorhomes on that sunny but cool Wednesday morning, Lib came on the CB.

"Hey, Bernice, did you hear what the temperature was in Barrow yesterday?"

"No, what was it?" I replied.

"Seventy-nine degrees!" Lib said.

"No. I can't believe it," I said.

We were driving from Palmer to Valdez. According to Karen our wagonmaster, the correct pronunciation of the town's name is Val*deez* not Val*dehz*.

Before leaving Palmer that morning, we stopped at a gas station that sold LP gas and renewed our supply. We also stopped at a grocery store where I had a brief conversation with a young man named Fred who cheerfully pushed my grocery cart to the motorhome.

"Are you a native Alaskan?" I asked.

"No, I moved up here three years ago," he said.

"From where?"

"Reno, Nevada," he answered.

"And why did you move?"

"I wanted a change."

"And do you like it here?"

"Yeah. It's more laid back up here," he told me.

Alas, it could be only a matter of time until the pace of the Lower 48 moved into what we think of as the last frontier. Computer technology and tourism moved in; why not the frenetic pace and competition that seemed to go with them? If that happened, I would regret it because it was comforting to know that Alaska with its massive land area and small population was one of the few places in the United States to escape the time pressures we put on ourselves in the Lower 48.

The Graybeals and we were the last caravaners to leave the campground, which was normal. When we pulled away from the grocery store in Palmer, however, the tailgunner's fifth-wheel and white pickup truck were parked there but they were not in the rig.

"If there's one thing I've learned on this trip, it's to bring plenty of film from home," I shared with Paul. "I've learned that even though I *think* I'm only going to take a certain number of pictures, I end up wanting to take shots that I hadn't anticipated. When I heard Karen say back in Vancouver to have plenty of film, like six or eight rolls, I thought my four rolls would be plenty, but—"

"Your four rolls are all gone," Paul said.

Prince William Sound

"They're all gone, and I've bought eight more so far, and film is more expensive up here in Alaska. So that's a big lesson that I've learned."

Once again during the 278 miles that we traveled that Wednesday, suffering through about five or six miles of road construction with its gravel, dust, bumps, and delays seemed worth the spectacular scenery—snowcapped mountains, river-laden valleys, glaciers, and breathtaking views.

I looked at tall mountains all around us, saw snow melting in streams coming down crevices in the mountainsides, looked across swampy areas for moose, and saw fireweed, a purple wildflower, scattered about. Various shades of green and various types of trees lined the slopes. A railroad bridge arched over one of the creeks. The streams were fast flowing and filled with glacial silt. We were about 18 miles north of Valdez on the Richardson Highway.

The mountainside on my right looked like it was covered with a green velvet blanket that shimmered various colors according to the sunlight and shadows. It was close by and rose up and up, higher than I could see from the motorhome windows.

We crossed a bridge and the water gushed along on either side of us. It seemed to be in a hurry to get downstream. Its path meandered and curved as the water dashed over rocks and had a rollicking good time. At times we saw the silvery Trans-Alaska pipeline headed for its terminal at Valdez.

Paul said over the CB to John that he believed we were entering a genuine canyon.

"I do believe. Keystone Canyon," John came back.

The sides were steep on the green-covered mountains. Water dripped down the rock face and glittered in the sunlight, almost blinding me at times.

We pulled into a turnout at Bridal Veil Falls along the Richardson Highway. With moss-covered rocks alongside, tons of white water hurled down from a great height, narrow at the top and spreading out like a bridal veil as the water tumbled. The Petersons joined the Graybeals and us in admiring the Falls.

Continuing on the canyon road between steep mountainsides covered with small bushes, we came to Horsetail Falls. Once again, we turned in to a gravel parking area alongside Richardson Highway. We stood looking at the whitewater falling down the rocky mountainside; it looked like a horse's tail flinging out behind the animal as it ran. A sign at the end of the parking area said Welcome to Valdez.

Following the wagonmasters' previous instructions and *The MILEPOST®*, we entered Valdez and headed for Bear Paw RV Park. Wearing a white shirt, long black pants, and the ever-changing cap, Scott walked us to our site and directed us to back into it. Paul decided to get out and see what the site looked like before he backed into it. He checked for obstructing tree limbs and rocks and to see the edge of our site, which was also the edge of the campground with only a jumble of rocks separating it and a huge body of water.

That water turned out to be the Valdez Arm of the famous Prince William Sound. We could look across its beautiful water at the snow-capped Chugach mountains and, at the opposite shoreline, see storage tanks for the Trans-Alaska pipeline. With a population of almost 3,700, Valdez was located near the east end of Port Valdez.

The campground itself was close enough to the city's shops and restaurants that we could walk. It offered a laundry and private rest rooms with a hot shower stall, toilet, sink, and a chair.

After hooking up, the Graybeals and we walked a short distance into town for dinner in a restaurant on the main street. Afterward we explored further and found a hair salon where Paul and I made appointments for Friday afternoon, he for a haircut and I for my regular shampoo and blow-dry.

Back at the campground I did three loads of washing at the laundry, which was conveniently just across a broad open area.

I eagerly boarded the cruise boat on Thursday morning for the moment I had been waiting for since we left Maryland—seeing Prince William Sound up close. The *Glacier Spirit*, a Stan Stephens charter boat, would take our caravaners and other passengers on a fabulous eight-hour cruise around Prince William Sound. We would go to Columbia Glacier and enjoy a seafood feast at Growler Island Wilderness Camp. The 189-passenger vessel had 129 aboard.

Soon we floated past our campground. Mountains seemed to surround the deep blue water. Sea otters and seals were having fun in the harbor.

A narrator elaborated on what we saw—a gold miner's cabin, sea otters resting on a green buoy, and American eagles in treetops. Wearing his blue jacket, Paul took time out for a blueberry donut as we cruised the sound.

Facing the cool breeze against my cheeks, I leaned against the rail and looked at the water. So this was the famous Prince William Sound. I had looked forward to seeing the Sound since reading about how its uncontaminated waters had been corrupted by the famous oil spill of the oil tanker *Exxon Valdez*. I had heard on television that it had been a serene, unspoiled, beautiful body of water and wanted to see for myself how it looked since the spill. Happily, I saw no traces of the spill. The water was beautiful as were the snowcapped and white-speckled Chugach mountains all around us.

We cruised on and saw Columbia Glacier coming down to the water between the bases of snow-covered mountains. The water on which we cruised was calm. The boat drew near an ice jam containing moraine. What seemed like acres and acres of ice floes that had broken off from the glacier floated on the water all around us.

Two brown seals reclined on the ice, flapping their tails. Another seal looked nonchalantly our way.

"Checking us out," Don Heathcock said. It was hard to tell whether the seals were sitting or lying, but it was obvious that they enjoyed the sunshine on their ice floes.

We docked at the Growler Island Wilderness Camp, then walked on a long, wooden stairway up a rather steep hillside to the restaurant. The building had large plate glass windows out of which we saw a view of the magnificent Columbia Glacier and the snowcapped mountains around it.

Amid the general hubbub of other tourists besides our gang, we joined in a sumptuous buffet of salmon, halibut, chicken, salads,

ALASKA AT YOUR OWN PACE

"What seemed like acres and acres of ice floes that had broken off from the [Columbia] glacier floated on the water all around us."

broccoli casserole, and rolls and sat eating at wooden, family-style picnic tables.

After lunch, back in the front seat of the enclosed level of the boat, I told John and Lib that I wanted to do a parody on "The Cremation of Sam McGee" by Robert Service for our farewell dinner and presentation of gifts. On the boat that day I had written one verse, which I shared with them, and we talked more about the poem.

Shortly thereafter John and Lib got to laughing. John had composed a verse about Paul checking our overdrive transmission fluid in the motorhome. John continued thinking of verses and I wrote them down. We would edit later.

As the boat returned, the narrator pointed out where the *Exxon Valdez* went aground between an iceberg and a buoy. A full oil tanker with two escort vessels was cruising where the *Exxon Valdez* should have been.

"It's just so beautiful—the color of the water is so beautiful!" I marveled. Like Lake Louise in Canada (we'd visited it during a trip by car before we had the motorhome) on a sunny day, the water of Prince William Sound was blue softened by green.

Prince William Sound

Our narrator pointed out a pilot boat. Two of these followed tankers in to and out of Port Valdez. It seemed strange to me that they followed instead of led the tankers, but that was their instruction.

I kept thinking I didn't want the cruise to end. Everywhere I turned I saw a picture-postcard scene—mountains, lapping water, driftwood ashore, and no houses.

We passed the Alyeska Terminus, the end of the Trans-Alaska pipeline on the hillside. We would go there the next day on a bus tour of the city. And then the fantastic scenic cruise was over. It was 6:21 P.M. when we arrived back at our motorhome from the dock.

Back at camp, I rewrote in clearer handwriting the verses that John and I had composed to date and took them next door to John and Lib. Later he came over and read some more verses he had written. We discussed the overall outline of the poem, what items we needed yet—the Beelers' freezer, the Heathcocks' baby-sitting of the McQuistons' dog, thanks to staff, and more. We had a work in progress. After John left I wrote about six verses for the grand finale of the poem. When you're hot, you're hot!

"Our narrator pointed out a pilot boat. Two of these followed tankers in to and out of Port Valdez."

"Well, we have time to relax a little here this morning," Paul said as he sat down in the easy chair of the motorhome and reached for the remote control of the television. We were dressed, had had breakfast, done the dishes, made the bed, got ready the video and 35mm cameras and accessories, all in preparation for a 9:20 bus tour of the Alyeska Terminus that morning.

Our bus stopped at the gate of the Marine Terminal—Trans-Alaska Pipeline. Flowers bloomed in planters in front of the office. Our woman bus driver gained access for us and drove into the complex of buildings. She described the several berths for loading oil tankers that were at the shoreline. She said the U.S. Environmental Protection Agency had set the standards for environmental protection and environmentalists from across the bay performed checks of the terminal. She gave us statistics on the quantities of oil that the tankers held and the number of personnel required to give the terminal 24-hour coverage, and told us that the 18 storage tanks there could hold 9.18 million barrels of oil, which was the total capacity of

"Our bus stopped at the gate of the Marine Terminal–Trans-Alaska Pipeline [at Valdez]. . . Our woman bus driver gained access for us and drove into the complex of buildings."

Prince William Sound

800 miles of the pipeline, making it possible to drain the pipeline. Each tank was 62 feet high and 250 feet in diameter, and held 510,000 barrels of oil. The pipeline itself had insulation and then an aluminum-based coating around the outside.

We saw the 800-mile marker on the end of the terminus building where the pipeline zigzagged (to allow for expansion and contraction) toward the building and entered it straight on. Variations of temperature in the Valdez area ran from minus 20 to 81 degrees. On our way to Barrow, Paul and I had made a stop at the airport for Prudhoe Bay/Deadhorse, near where the pipeline begins at Prudhoe Bay, and now we saw the end of the pipeline at Valdez. Who would have thought it!

That afternoon, Louie gave Paul and me a ride to a hair salon in Valdez for a cut for Paul and a shampoo and blow-dry for me. We had found the shop on a walk two nights before with John and Lib after supper at Oscar's a few businesses away on the same street.

With the satisfaction of having seen Prince William Sound and a new hairdo, I was ready to leave Valdez the next day. I looked at the itinerary. The next day, Saturday, called for a return to Tok, our last overnight stop in Alaska. The following day we'd re-enter Canada, going first to Kluane Lake, then spending three days in Skagway, two days on the ferry, and a night in Smithers, and ending our tour with the farewell dinner the following evening at Prince George where we had stayed at the beginning of our tour.

· 22 ·

Return to Tok

RAUCOUS RAVENS, sounding like our crows in Maryland, flew from low, bushy trees out over Port Valdez and the rocky breakwater. The back end of the Bonises' motorhome disappeared around the laundry complex, a building with gray siding, rust-colored tin roof, and wide, white boards for the second-floor porch banister. It was foggy about seven o'clock that Saturday morning. To put some humor into the situation, noting the weather, John worked around his motorhome singing, "Oh, What a Beautiful Morning."

We had three travel days ahead—259 miles that day to Tok, 279 miles the next day to Kluane Lake, and 259 miles to Skagway the fol-

Return to Tok

lowing day. Then it would be three days there, two days and nights on the ferry, one travel day of 221 miles to Smithers, and 241 miles to Prince George for our farewell dinner and last night together as a tour group, *and* with John and Lib as traveling companions. I had begun feeling sad about departing from all of them. They were great people and we enjoyed their company.

When we left Bear Paw RV Park at Valdez on that Saturday morning at an early 7:15, it was cloudy and misty and 46 degrees. Just cool enough for me to put on my Western Maryland College, zippered, sweat top. As usual Paul wore a cap, this time the blue one from the bank in Barrow. He didn't need a sweater, he said. I noticed my tennis shoes were looking more tan than white.

As we rode on the Richardson Highway away from Valdez, I reminded myself that enjoying the scenery was why I was there. Goal-oriented, I often found myself thinking about getting to where we were going. The drive on that particular portion of the highway should be spectacularly scenic. It certainly had been on the way down to Valdez, what with the Keystone Canyon, Bridal Veil Falls, and Horsetail Falls.

The evening that we had arrived at Valdez, I was in the laundry room of the campground with Mary Jo Cornell and some of the other women caravaners. With her arms moving from right to left in a dramatic gesture, Mary Jo said, "You know how I had been saying that the mountains were boring, boring, boring? Well, today was different. It was just one change after another. I mean you would go around a curve and there would be a mountain, and then there was a glacier, and then there was a waterfall, and so on and so on!"

I thought of Mary Jo's words as we traveled that Saturday. They were true. To our right was a bare rock face. On the left was a mountain with trees on part of it, rocks showing on the other part. The sky was partly cloudy, partly sunny. Clumps of blooming lavender fireweed were everywhere, sown by the will of the wind. The road curved and then was straight, the views unexpected.

We crossed the Tsaina River Bridge. I looked down into a canyon and saw water with glacier silt in it, greenish, muddy water, flowing energetically downstream. And then we came to an area with old trees and mucky water. Earlier we had passed a small pool of water with a beaver dam in it.

On the left, a waterfall flowed over rocks with purple fireweed lining the banks. And below it another smaller waterfall gushed down at road level. The road ahead on the right had been cut through hard rock. As we drove on, along the roadsides we saw purple fireweed, appearing every so often like a musical theme, with contrasting green foliage giving variations to the passing scenery.

There were humankind's own engineering feats. Electric power lines spanned canyons and tall, tall poles walked up the mountainsides. Yellow, white, and orange aerial-cable marker balls were attached to individual high wires strung across the canyon to make them visible to low-flying aircraft.

The road (Richardson Highway) went downhill, uphill, and around curves. Many lofty places had guardrails, thank goodness. Bridges carried us across streams such as Stuart Creek. There were blueberry bushes and aspen, black spruce, and alder trees beside the road.

Something else that kept it interesting as we rode along was looking for moose or caribou or even a bear. Lib had seen a moose when we passed that way before, and I looked for one as we traveled that Saturday. Moose like to eat in marshy areas because the plants under water are nutritious and tasty to them.

Earlier Louie and Ann had passed us and were ahead beyond our sight. At mid-morning when we turned off of Richardson Highway, which had been full of substantial frost heaves, onto Glenn Highway toward Tok, Paul wondered what that road would be like.

He said over the CB to Louie, "Number Two, is it any better up ahead, is the road any better up ahead?"

Louie replied, "It's a little better, but not all that great, but a little better."

Paul returned, "Were you able to keep your freezer in place?" The Beelers had bought a small freezer in which to keep the salmon and halibut that they had caught on several fishing expeditions.

"I've got Ann sitting on it!" Louie said.

And Paul said, "Okay. I'm not going to make any comment about that!"

At Glenallen, we left the Richardson Highway and took the Glenn Highway, also called the Tok Cutoff.

Riding along on that Saturday morning, I realized that we had seen very few houses and no people about them. That was true during the week when we drove down to Valdez. We saw a few people at roadside cafes and gas stations. At that point in my observations, I saw a man driving a sport-utility vehicle moving along a side road, but he was the first that I had seen that day and even for most of the time in Alaska. It was, after all, a mostly unpopulated state except for Anchorage, which contained half of the population of Alaska, or about 250,000 people.

John continued to work on the farewell parody. When we stopped a little earlier that morning to take a video of the Trans-Alaska pipeline, he got out of his RV with his yellow-lined pad in hand, grinning. He said that while Lib was sleeping that morning en route, he had begun to think of a few more verses. He read them to Paul and me. They were hilarious!

"There's a lodge up here about 10 or 12 miles or so, left-hand side," John said over the CB.

"Okay. Are you saying you want to stop in there?" Paul asked.

"Yeah, if it's the one I think. We need a little break here and might want to take on a little nourishment."

"Sounds good to me."

A little farther up the road, we passed a tiny, deserted log cabin with a rusty tin roof surrounded by a rather dense forest, mainly spruce trees but also some deciduous ones that I couldn't identify.

"I got news for you folks back there. The road's not gettin' any better," Louie's voice came over the CB.

"I thought you were smoothing it out as you were going along," Paul said.

"Gracious, these really are some bumps!" I said as I almost left my seat. At the same time I noticed that it was partly cloudy and the sun was trying to come through.

With microphone in one hand and the other on the steering wheel, Paul said on the CB to Louie: "The thing that amazes me is that where you don't think there are any, all of a sudden there are."

"I've been marking 'em for ya. Can't you see it?" Louie asked good-naturedly.

"No, I've gotta have better skid marks than that! It's good your fish are frozen because they would be like Swiss steak bouncing around in there if they weren't."

"Even the fish in the freezer are getting seasick," Louie said.

"You couldn't take a nap on this road," I said to Paul.

"Not too well. I haven't bottomed out yet on this road but I betcha I've come very close to it."

On the CB, John said, "I believe this is the worst section of the road we've been on for frost heaves."

"Yeah, you're right! As far as frost heaves go, John, you're better off being in the mountains. For the most part, you don't have nearly as many as you do in this flat tundra," Paul replied.

"That's for sure," John said.

At 11:03 we made our first stop at Chistochina Lodge, a ranch-style, brown, wooden building with a large statue of a brown bear on the roof. Antlers hung on the entrance roof and on the side of the log building. We had decided that it would be a brief rest stop and that we'd have lunch in about an hour down the road. With pantries on board, John could get his nourishment from a snack as he drove.

On the road again, Paul commented to John on the CB, "I'm glad I had all my wheel bearings repacked before I left home. I think that probably was a good idea."

"How often do you do that?"

"I think the book calls for every ten or twelve thousand. Chevrolet garages say that's more frequent than they think is necessary but, yeah, ten or twelve thousand."

Return to Tok

We continued on Glenn Highway toward Tok. The road was paved but heavily frost-heaved. Spruce and deciduous trees grew on either side. Ahead was a mountain, bluish white in the distance, misted over. The sun was still trying to come out. We crossed Indian River, and later passed a private home without landscaping as we know it but with a satellite dish toward the front.

Along the roadsides, white wildflowers, purple fireweed, and a very fine, light-green grass greeted us. A breeze blew through bushes and the tops of spruce trees.

We came upon another construction site. "Looks like they're working here, even on Saturday," I said to Paul. A flag person, a woman, was on duty and there was a man operating a huge earth mover. The dirt looked rich. A line of traffic waited ahead of us.

After making our way through that and another road construction site, the Graybeals and we pulled into Duffy's Roadhouse for lunch. It was a few minutes after noon and we were at mile 62.7 on the Glenn Highway.

The flat-roofed, dark brown, wooden building sat at the back of a huge dirt parking lot with pine trees at the edges. Inside, Duffy's Roadhouse was reminiscent of the 1940s period. There were stools at the counter and three booths. The floor was slanted beneath our booth table, which also caused the tabletop to be tilted.

A young man with adolescent complexion and changing voice came with order pad in hand to wait on us. He asked if we would like coffee to drink. Lib and John said yes.

I asked if he had diet cola and he said, "Yes, from a machine over there."

"Well, then, I'll just have water with some ice in it," I said.

"Oh, I can get it for you," replied the young man.

We sat trying to read the menu sign on the wall, which was behind John and Lib, and decide what to order. Noticing our struggle, the waiter said, "Would you like to see a regular menu?"

He disappeared quickly and soon came back with four leather- or vinyl-covered menus from which we ordered—except Libby, who by that time had decided she would have the patty melt listed on the wall board.

Country and country-rock music played in the background. The food was excellent and the young man was very polite and quick. I asked him if he was Mr. Duffy's son. He said no, Mr. Duffy had sold the place to a Mr. Ellis 18 years earlier. Mr. Ellis was the young man's neighbor. The young man had been in Alaska since he was 12, when he came up from Utah with his parents. He said that Mr. Ellis had been trying to sell the cafe for 18 years. It had a small building for gifts and then a main building for the separated bar and cafe.

Eating our delicious lunches, we reminisced happily about our previous days' experiences and had a new one at the same time. The cafe was a place where we felt like we were going back in time and we liked it. The people were real-life people and the young man was quite earnest in his service and replies to us.

That afternoon I rode in the passenger seat with the video camera on my lap and my hand through the strap ready to take a video of a moose should we be fortunate enough to see one.

Although the road was mainly asphalt, we continued to bounce along, having to slow down frequently for the rough road, frost heaves, and sometimes loose gravel.

I realized that I had not actually driven the motorhome in the state of Alaska. I checked back in our motorhome travel log. The last time I had driven was the first 30 miles on the Top of the World Highway. That section was still in Yukon Territory. Perhaps the next morning as we started out for Kluane Lake, I could drive. On most trips, Paul usually drove most of the time because he enjoyed it. On this trip, because of the tricky roads and the scenery I wanted to see, I was glad that he was behind the wheel. However, I liked the driving challenge also, and so we discussed when I would drive next.

When we turned into the Tok RV Village, with its familiar gray stone road, we looked ahead to the green grass and short evergreen trees that were planted between sites. Tall pine trees lined the border

Return to Tok

of the campground area itself. Scott signaled for us to go ahead. Karen, in a plaid shirt and white pants, her red hair shining in the sun, carried a piece of paper and pointed to our pull-through site. We were back in Tok, Alaska. We had not seen any moose, bears, or Dall sheep on the Tok Cutoff road.

· 23 ·

Tok to Kluane Lake, Yukon Territory

WITH THE FERRY RIDE coming up in less than a week, the wagonmasters chose the departure meeting at Tok late that Saturday afternoon to prepare us. Before we boarded the ferry at Skagway, we should get gasoline in our RVs and dump. We would have a cabin on the ferry with linens and turkish towels furnished. We would have access to our RVs only when the ship was in port or when a break was announced. Therefore, we should have with us a bag for clothes, a coat, books or hobbies, postcards to write, and

Tok to Kluane Lake, Yukon Territory

an umbrella. We should pack our bags and be ready to go when we left the campground at Skagway. Once the rigs were on the ferry, we should turn off the propane, pull the side mirrors in close if possible, and lock the rig. We shouldn't open the refrigerators in our RVs the entire time on board because the propane would be off. We would be on our own for food; there would be a nice big dining room on the ferry as well as lounges indoors and out. A group tour was planned at Ketchikan and tours were available at Juneau. Guided tours in a town were each about 45 minutes long. The ferry people would let us know in the morning about them. The ferry waited for *no one*.

The next morning, Sunday, I drove away from the campground, headed for Kluane Lake. It was sunny and early, only 7:30, yet I needed only short sleeves. In the lead, I asked John by verse over the CB, "At what speed/would you like to proceed?" and chuckled.

After a brief pause, he came back, also in verse, "Fifty-five would be fine/Unless the road gets out of line." More chuckling.

And so I accelerated to 55, put the RV in cruise control, and drove away from Tok on the Alaska Highway. Paul picked up the video camera and aimed it at me and said, "This is Bernice driving in Alaska. We have just left the Tok campground and we are now cruising at 80 miles an hour down this highway heading toward the night's rendezvous. She looks very confident this morning and the scenery goes whizzing by at 80 miles an hour. This woman has driven a little bit of everywhere in the world, but she's left John and Libby in the dust. They're trying their best to catch up. That's all for now. Bye."

I drove on the Alaska Highway from Tok to Northway Junction. I soon had to begin slowing down for bumps, loose gravel, little red flags stuck at the roadside indicating uneven pavement, a 45-mph sign, and common sense to protect our vehicle and ourselves. I'm glad I drove—it was a significant part of my Alaskan experience. What a pleasure our Lower 48 roads would be without frost heaves!

About an hour later, at Northway, Paul took over. It turned out that after my stint the road became much worse, the worst road we had on the entire trip—potholes, frost heaves, patched places, loose gravel places, and just bumps, often not identifiable until we rode, or should I say bounced over them. It was literally like riding a bucking bronco—we seemed to go every which way unpredictably!

It was too bumpy to write in my cloth journal, my little tape recorder wouldn't work, and it was far too dusty to use my laptop computer. So I rested and silently prayed for safe travel.

We had had lunch when we came upon a line of six or seven RVs and some pickup trucks stopped ahead in our lane. A tow truck was getting a hold of something at the left side of the road. Some people got out of their vehicles and went across the road to look although we stayed in place.

Laurie said on the CB, "I can see the boom and the light flashing, but that's about it."

After a time, the traffic started to move ahead on the paved road with its center line but no white lines to mark the shoulders. As we got nearer the accident scene, a man directed traffic. An orange triangle had been set on the shoulder of our right lane as a warning to slow down. A police car with lights blinking blocked the left lane. Off the shoulder of the left lane in a small pond leaned a partially submerged white pickup truck with an attached white fifth-wheel. It sobered us and we hoped that no one was hurt. We learned later that the driver had taken his eyes off the road momentarily. The road had almost no shoulder at that place. Once the fifth-wheel started over the bank, there was no way to regain the road surface.

By the time we reached Kluane Lake, we had "bottomed out" three or four times.

"That's hard on a frame when you do that. Do it often enough, you crack the frame, or if you do it hard enough one time, you crack the frame," Paul said.

At the Cottonwood RV Park beside Kluane Lake, we drove to our site, passing the RV of the Cornells. Early birds, they had already parked and Mary Jo lounged in front in a lawn chair as Thel walked toward her.

Tok to Kluane Lake, Yukon Territory

"Ah. This ought to be wonderful!" I said as we pulled into a site that overlooked the jade blue water of Kluane Lake.

"Oh, how beautiful!" I said as I looked across the lake toward mountains with a blue sky overhead. And then I opened the refrigerator door to begin making a meat loaf for the potluck supper that Sunday evening. What chaos I saw!

During the bumpy ride, the lid of an instant coffee jar had somehow unscrewed itself, spilling the grounds throughout the refrigerator, even into the shelves on the door and inside the egg carton underneath the eggs. It was one big mess! So instead of going to the campfire after the potluck supper that evening, I gave the refrigerator a *thorough* cleaning, taking everything out and washing absolutely everything. Paul assisted me in some of the removal and putting back. But then I had the cleanest refrigerator around.

Karen and Scott had hinted earlier in the trip that they would choose two "worthy" candidates to be initiated into the Royal Order of the Machete. The ceremony was to take place between the departure meeting and our potluck supper on that Sunday evening. Don Peterson and Paul were selected as the initiates and were told so a day or two ahead of time at a departure meeting.

Dressed in Mexican garb, Scott and Karen stood before our caravaners. In front of them was a large, gray, flat log. Scott described their attire and then asked Karen to escort the two candidates beyond earshot. We waved goodbye to them. Scott began to read: "In this solemn ceremony we have selected two worthy candidates." Tongue in check, he told the history of the Royal Order of the Machete. The candidates must attempt to strike with the machete between two lines made with duct tape on the gray log. We the audience were to help them stay within the lines by saying, "More to the right" or "More to the left."

It was time to bring in the candidates. Karen had them by the arm walking between them as the three walked toward us.

Paul, Karen, and Don stood in front of the log for a brief ceremony. Scott said that Paul and Don must demonstrate their familiarity with the machete. They must strike the log five times, one right after the other, between the duct-taped lines. Scott had them practice, one at a time, on their knees in front of the gray log, raising the machetes high above their heads.

Then they sat in lawn chairs provided so they could be blindfolded by Karen. They had to strike the logs with the machetes while blindfolded and stay within the lines in order to be worthy of the order. Scott read the oath for the Royal Order of the Machete which they repeated after him word for word. Since it was a solemn ceremony and they were on holy ground, they had to purify their feet, Scott said. They must take off their socks and shoes. Still blindfolded, Don and Paul did so. Karen quietly placed each pair of socks on the log in front of each candidate between the lines where they were supposed to strike with the machete.

Then Scott had Don kneel in back of the log as Scott placed the machete exactly in the center between the duct tape lines in front of him. Scott told him to strike five times in rapid succession hitting the log between the lines. As Don struck the log, we called out encouraging remarks. Don, of course, cut his socks into pieces without knowing it. He was helped back to his chair still blindfolded.

Paul was next. Scott prepared him as he had Don. Paul went right at it and soon was back in his chair with the help of Karen, his socks in shreds. Scott then asked Karen to stand them up and turn them around, still blindfolded, to face Scott, so their backs were to the gray log and their battered socks. Scott asked Karen to remove the blindfolds. Scott asked us, the audience: "Do the candidates meet the test?"

We all shouted, "Yes!"

Scott then pronounced that they were members of the Royal Order of the Machete and solemnly handed each a certificate. They turned around to put on their socks and shoes and saw that they had chopped their socks into pieces. Grinning, Paul pointed his finger playfully at Scott. Don said he had a hole in his anyway. They both put on their shoes without socks amid much laughter, applause, and chatter.

In the spirit of the moment, Clem led rousing cheers for Don, Paul, and the wagonmasters. Our potluck supper followed. The picnic tables were loaded with hot dogs, hamburgers, the meat loaf, salads, and desserts. On his own, Clem brought out from his motorhome an organ-grinder monkey, the old-time kind that you wind up and it plays music. All in all, we had a great time. We did hear a report of two grizzly bears headed our way. But they were about three miles away, so we were not too concerned. We sat around in our lawn chairs and enjoyed the beautiful lake and the balmy evening.

I knew I wanted to stay there more than one day, but our itinerary called for moving on to Skagway the next day. I wondered where that name came from—it sounded humorous, like "scalawag."

· 24 ·

Kluane Lake to Skagway

BEFORE WE LEFT on Monday morning, I scrambled down the bank in front of the motorhome to touch the water in the longest, largest lake in Yukon Territory, Kluane Lake. Waves lapped at the shore where I stood on the pebbly beach, small waves with white foam. Purple blossoms that I had come to know as fireweed brightened the bank. I looked up and saw that Paul was behind the steering wheel of our RV and John and Lib were both in

KLUANE LAKE TO SKAGWAY

their motorhome seats. "Goodbye, Lake," I said and scrambled back up the bank.

"Boy, how much better the scenery looks when the road is nice," I said to Paul after leaving Cottonwood Park and driving along Kluane Lake on the Alaska Highway, which led to Whitehorse. From there we would take Klondike Highway 2 to Skagway. According to *The MILEPOST®*, Skagway (originally *Skaguay*) means "home of the north wind," in the Tlingit dialect. I had a notion that the north wind could be quite a rascal and so I figured my fun image of scalawag was not too far off target.

The scene as we circled the end of Kluane Lake was beautiful with morning sun shining on the light jade-green water to our left and casting shadows from trees across the road ahead. Snow-topped mountains stood behind rocky, green-patched ones. This road was much, much better than that between Tok and Kluane Lake the day before.

"If there's one thing I've learned on this trip, it's the importance of vehicle maintenance," I said to Paul.

"Yeah. There's a couple of things I could have done before we left—replace the in-line gasoline filter and the carburetor filter. But there was no way to know about the rotor cap," Paul replied.

At mid-morning, I remembered something I had found in the refrigerator when I cleaned it the night before. "I just finished the chocolate-mint fudge I got at Minter Gardens!" I said to Paul, who never ate fudge.

"You mean it was fit to eat?"

"Yeah—good!"

At Whitehorse, Yukon Territory, our caravaners did different things. We got gasoline, the wagonmasters picked up their tow car, another had an oil change, and another had the front end of the motorhome checked for a vibration. Leaving Whitehorse, we passed the airplane on a pedestal that served as a weather vane at the airport and we saw again the very modern information center building.

With John in the lead, we stopped at Emerald Lake. The scene was breathtaking—an absolutely beautiful and enormous emerald-and-blue body of water curved gracefully in the valley below. I had never seen such a clean-looking lake. Its waters reflected the blue-green rays of the sun because of the white sediment that was on the bottom of the shallow lake. (Later, at home, I did an oil painting of the memorable scene.)

We stopped for lunch at Frontierland then headed toward Skagway on the Klondike Highway. The paved, two-lane road ran high above a canyon.

As we began the steep descent into Skagway, Paul said over the CB, "Going into low gear, John. Might be a little slow but that way I can stay off the brake."

The Graybeals were ahead since they had come that way before. The tailgunners were somewhere behind us.

The highway descended around a curve and onto a straight stretch. Tall, thin poles at the side of the highway told road clearing crews in winter's snow where the edge was. A beautiful lake lay on our right. We passed rocky mountainsides at a narrow place as we

"With John in the lead, we stopped at Emerald Lake. The scene was breathtaking—an absolutely beautiful and enormous emerald-and-blue body of water curved gracefully in the valley below."

continued the descent. A sign said that a truck escape ramp was ahead as we wound in between mountains. We passed the ramp going up our side of the mountain, glad we didn't need it. We traveled around numerous curves, crossed a small bridge, and rounded another curve, still descending.

"The last time we were over this one it was so foggy you almost had to have a pilot car. It was getting late in the evening and we had twice as many rigs as we've got now and everybody was having quite a time seeing," Don said over the CB.

Paul told Don that he would hate to ride his brakes all the way down. "I'm in low. I haven't touched my brakes for two miles," Paul added.

I saw our road ahead from across a deep valley; it wound around the side of a tree-lined mountain. As we continued going down the side of the mountain, we talked over the CB with the Graybeals ahead and the Petersons behind us. Mary Jo also joined the conversation.

We stopped at the United States customs station with its small office located at the side of the road against the mountain. A man in a blue uniform came out with papers in hand. He asked where we were from, how many people were in the vehicle, if we had any pets or firearms, and if we had bought anything in Canada.

We continued our descent toward Skagway. I looked across the deep valley and saw railroad tracks built against the side of the mountain with bulwarks underneath to support them.

John said that he had spotted the top of a cruise ship docked in Skagway. I was glad we were getting close. Our road continued paved with two lanes, a yellow double line in the center, and a white line at the shoulder. We neared the same level as the river flowing beside the road.

As we entered picturesque Skagway, Karen came on the CB and told us where to get gasoline before going to the campground. Skagway looked both historic and modern with old-time yellow limousines, paved streets, street lamps, and people walking everywhere.

After filling the motorhome with gasoline, we drove to Pullen Creek Park Campground. It had packed-down dirt roads and gray gravel sites surrounded by dried grassy areas. Scott stood in the middle of the road gesturing where we were to turn in to our site. Then he tipped his hand to his hat. The Graybeals and we were side by side again. Scott told us that the hookups were at the front. Paul said that he could change the angle of the motorhome to accommodate that. I was afraid I was getting completely spoiled by the royal treatment of advance reservations and wagonmasters on hand to signal us into the very site in which we were to camp each night.

Skagway lay in the valley between mountains at the north end of Taiya Inlet on the Lynn Canal. It was about three blocks wide and a mile long and had a population of 712, excluding tourists. That afternoon Lib, John, and I walked a short distance to the historic district, which was actually the main street for business, shopping, and tourist attractions. It was a busy place, and we weaved in and out among lots of people on the board sidewalks. A motorcycle, vans, and the historic-looking stretch tour cars moved along the street. While

"Skagway . . . was about three blocks wide and a mile long and had a population of 712, excluding tourists."

Kluane Lake to Skagway

getting acquainted with the town, I made a hair appointment for the next day at 1:30 P.M.

Paul and I were in the motorhome and I was about to prepare supper when the manager of the park came to our door with a mobile phone, saying our son was on the telephone. Since we could not hear him very well from the motorhome, we walked across the road to the small building where the manager had his office. He left us alone inside the building while we talked with Jeff. We held the receiver so that both of us could hear what Jeff said. He wanted to let us know about developments at his work. We had a good conversation.

Then we came back to the motorhome and I fixed frozen dinners. Too tired by that time to further explore Skagway, we stayed "home." I began organizing the poem for the farewell dinner. John had written several more hilarious verses.

For the first time in weeks, it got dark at a reasonable time—about 10:00 or 10:30. We watched some of the videos we had taken of the trip, making it after 11:00 before we went to bed.

Skagway was a noisy place, beginning early in the morning. Airplanes droned in and out of the local airfield, helicopters chopped the air, two cruise ships in the harbor blew their whistles, a steam locomotive blew its whistle as it rattled past every so often, and the ravens were rather vocal.

On Tuesday morning, Paul and I walked to the Skagway Marine Ferry Terminal adjacent to our campground. The huge cruise ships, the *Star Princess* and the *Crown Princess*, floated in their berths. The cruise business appeared well and thriving in Skagway.

Then we walked leisurely uptown, where we had a good time exploring both sides of Broadway, the main street and historic district. We had lunch in the Golden North Hotel cafe, a very quiet place with tablecloths and good food.

After lunch, Paul went back to the motorhome, and I did a little more shopping before my hair appointment. The hairstylist did a good job of shampooing and blow-drying my hair for $20. When I returned to the motorhome, Paul was taking a nap. I got out the computer, but it was not working. When Paul roused, he tried to help. In the end we decided that it needed a new battery but that we would discuss it with Jeff.

Meanwhile I would use my cloth journal and tape recorder for notes about the trip. The day before, after we arrived at the campground in Skagway, John had generously given me a new battery for my tape recorder. After installing it, I discovered that the controls of the recorder had been somehow set to "pause," which of course meant that it would not record in that particular mode. Another lesson learned! As for the computer, I put it away for the moment and we prepared for a group tour of the city of Skagway late that Tuesday afternoon.

Period-dressed tour guides in 1937 sightseeing cars took our group on a tour of Skagway. Our limousine was bright yellow; the other one was bright red. Ours was made by the White Company and the red one was made by the Kenworth Company. It was a delightful tour, made particularly so by our personable guides. It included seeing the cemetery where the infamous con man Soapy Smith was buried. Near the end of the tour, one of our guides, a male, laughingly asked, "You know what Alaskan women say about Alaskan men?" We said no, we didn't know. He grinned good-humoredly as he said, "The odds are good but the goods are odd!" Personally, I saw no odd ones.

This was followed by a historical presentation in the Arctic Brotherhood Hall during which we were all made honorary members of the Arctic Brotherhood and were given a business card to prove it. As bearers of these cards we were to "spread the good word about Skagway, Alaska in general, and the Arctic Brotherhood in particular." But the important thing about the brotherhood, we were told, was that Warren G. Harding was an honorary member! (He was the 29th president of the United States, you know.)

Following this program, we had a little time to do some more shopping before going to Eagles Hall, where we were given mock poker chips to play roulette or blackjack or other games. I joined a game (I didn't know what it was called) and won a couple of times but

KLUANE LAKE TO SKAGWAY

then purposely put all my chips on one number and lost them all. I had about $2,500 at the time in so-called winnings, but it was all play money.

Then we saw *The Days of '98 Show* with Soapy Smith © (1973 through 1997 Gold Rush Productions Inc.). It recreated the story of Alaska's most notorious con man, Jefferson Randolph "Soapy" Smith of the Klondike gold rush days. The scenery and acting were excellent. The music was good, although some of the actors were a little weak in their singing. But it was all done in good fun and with *a lot* of professionalism. The hall was hot, however. At the end of the show, it was announced that one of our group, Don Heathcock, had won the prize for the most winnings in the pseudo-gambling part of the evening. He won $63,000; of course, it was all just play. His prize was a tape of the music in the show that we saw.

After the show our antique cars awaited us. We shook hands with each member of the cast, discovering a man from near Baltimore among them. He had been in Alaska 25 years.

We stepped into the old cars and our chauffeur-guide took us back to the campground. He was very sociable and we all had a good time. It was a very pleasant evening with good food, good company, and good entertainment.

The next morning, Wednesday, our group met at a restaurant uptown for sourdough pancakes. Afterward, Lib and I shopped and shopped and shopped. I watched her enter a store, look over the merchandise in the showcase or hanging up and comment enthusiastically on the beauty of a specific ring or the beautiful colors in a scarf.

Over the years, I had trained myself not to fall in love with something for myself until I saw whether I could afford to buy it. If I could afford it, then I would decide whether I liked it enough to actually buy it. It seemed an efficient way to shop—both for my pocketbook and for my feelings. It didn't always work, however, because sometimes if I really liked a dress, I went ahead and bought it even when it stretched the budget limits. Now that I thought about it, my mother-in-law, who spent her money wisely, had this philosophy: You never go wrong if you buy something of quality that you really like.

239

Paul thought the same way. I was the one who had imposed the budget restraints on what I bought for myself.

I asked Lib a question: Did she look first at the object itself to see if she liked it or at the price? She giggled and said that she looked first to see if it was something that she really liked. I must confess that I had been so used to looking first at the price that I hardly knew what I liked without seeing the price!

I began trying to pick out what I really liked. It was hard at first, but I began to catch on. By the end of the day, I had selected a solid brass letter opener with a scrimshaw handle as a surprise for Paul, a crystal seal with mirror stand for my small crystal collection, and a pair of handcrafted, sterling-silver earrings for myself. I couldn't resist, however, buying Paul and me matching red Alaska sweatshirts that were on sale and on which the front embossing was slightly askew. Old habits do die hard!

Since that day, I've given Lib credit for teaching me how to shop. It's a lot more fun to shop when I look for what I *like* first; it doesn't cost any more money, and the purchase is more satisfying! I can still catch the sales, but when I buy something on sale, it's what I like.

Skagway itself had been a fun place—to shop and otherwise. I wondered how the process would all work the next day when we were scheduled to board the Alaska Marine Highway ferry.

· 25 ·

On Alaska's Marine Highway Ferry

THE FERRY WAS LATE in arriving at the dock—it was supposed to *leave* Skagway at 11:00 and it was already a half-hour beyond that time. Many of us from the caravans stood at the guardrail of the dock at Skagway in the sunshine waiting, chatting, occasionally laughing. We had lined up our rigs to board the ferry before 10:00 that morning. In Lane Six of the large ferry terminal parking lot from the front to the end of the line were the RVs of the McQuistons, Beelers, Conways, Heathcocks, Foremans, and Cornells. Lane Seven contained those of the Bonises, Beards, Graybeals, Swagertys, Wrigleys, and Petersons—12 in all.

A white luxury cruise ship nestled in the harbor beyond the ferry terminal building to the right. Looking toward the terminal building itself, I saw the covered walkway that we walk-on passengers would use to reach the ferry and, beside that, the sloped ramp that our drivers would descend to reach the gangplank and the bowels or car deck of the ferry.

At last, a ferry headed toward us. With a white top and dark blue bottom, it was the MV *Malaspina*, and it was an hour and 45 minutes late. I learned later that unusually low tides were the culprit. With low tides the ferry did not sit high enough in the water to allow a safe amount of slope for the ramp. The ferry moved slowly but steadily toward the dock as we watched and waited.

Eventually, its huge door opened near the water level, and RVs disembarked from the ferry and drove slowly up the ramp, passing us at the guardrail and going toward the parking area. One RV *backed*

"At last, a ferry headed toward us. With a white top and dark blue bottom, it was the MV Malaspina, and it was an hour and 45 minutes late. I learned later that unusually low tides were the culprit."

down the narrow ramp from the ferry's car deck opening, turned in a small area, and headed up the steep ramp toward us. My heart beat faster when that RV came up the ramp successfully.

Since Paul would be driving our motorhome onto the ferry, I went inside the terminal building to join other walk-on passengers. In the crowd of people, the women from our caravan stood waiting amid the conglomeration of luggage and other passengers. All the seats were taken. Lib pointed her finger and counted to be sure we were all present. Commotion and hubbub filled the room.

Yvonne waited with us—Wil was going to drive their RV onto the ferry. She had done most of the driving so far and seemed to relish it. Other couples in our group shared driving responsibilities. While the husbands in some rigs did all the driving, I suspected that all the people on the tour could drive their RVs if necessary.

At someone's signal, those of us in the waiting room followed one another down the walkway beside the terminal building and into the same huge opening that our RVs and other vehicles were entering. Carrying our bags, we walked upstairs to a small, crowded reception area. Karen was first in line at the purser's office to confirm our cabin assignments. The ferry was full. We felt in good hands, with Karen and Scott paving the way for us in ways that we were hardly aware of. Meanwhile, Paul, Wil, John, and the other drivers parked the RVs on the car deck and joined us as soon as they could find us.

Paul and I went to number 128, an inside cabin without windows. In mid-ship, it gave a very smooth ride. I barely noticed that I was on a moving boat. The cabin, though closet sized, offered all the amenities such as a wastebasket, a small sink enclosed in a wood-sided open booth, a toilet, and a shower. On the right-hand wall were two bunk beds. After stowing our gear, Paul went up on deck and I took a 20-minute nap on the lower bunk. Refreshed, I went up to the next deck to view an orientation film about what we would see on the trip.

We arrived downstream from Skagway at Haines about 4 P.M. and stopped only long enough to unload and load passengers. Had the ferry not been four hours behind schedule, it would have stayed there longer. Because the town of Haines was four miles inland from the dock, our wagonmasters had not planned for our group to tour it. By 4:15 we were underway again.

That Thursday afternoon, I checked at the purser's counter to see if I could use a typewriter or computer to type out our "Farewell to Alaska" parody for our caravaners' farewell dinner at Prince George on Sunday night. Unable to obtain that or copier opportunities, I hoped that sometime between then and when we landed, I could go to the dining room where there were tables and write off that great verse, which was now about five pages long. Perhaps at some port or even at a campground office, I could get copies made, but I didn't want to let it all go until the very last minute.

That evening, Paul and I joined some of the other caravaners to go through the cafeteria line in the large dining room and shared a table with them.

Optional tours would ordinarily have been available for the ferry's stop at Juneau, but because of being behind schedule and arriving about 9:30 that night, that option was moot.

Later that night, when hardly anyone was in the dining room, I went to a secluded area of it and accomplished my task of hand writing the verses. I had learned that we would be able to go ashore the next day at Petersburg and I hoped to find a place that would make copies.

On Friday morning, Paul and I left the ferry to see Petersburg, Alaska, where the *Malaspina* was docked. We had one hour to disembark, see the town, and return to the ferry. We both wore our blue nylon Caravanas jackets for easy identification by other caravaners and townspeople and took our boarding passes along so that we could get back on the ferry.

In sunshine, we walked the paved sidewalk past pretty homes made charming by their Scandinavian influence. We came to the business district that served a population of 3,620. I had copies made of the handwritten parody. They would be available for our fellow caravaners at the upcoming farewell dinner.

ON ALASKA'S MARINE HIGHWAY FERRY

The Clauson Memorial Museum that we wanted to see didn't open until noon and we needed to be back on the ferry before then. We walked past the two-storied Petersburg General Hospital and Long-Term Care facility nearby and noted a National Bank of Alaska building at a corner of the main street. The small boat harbor was crowded with lots of sailboats and motorboats. Some houses near the water were set on pilings, looking picturesque. On land but near the water was a replica of a Viking ship, *Valhalla*.

As we neared the ferry, a uniformed person from the vessel checked people's tickets. Ahead of us, Bill and Mary Jo talked with the ticket checker.

Later that Friday afternoon, the ferry stopped at Wrangell, Alaska, long enough for people to buy garnets from boys selling them at the dock. A former mayor had deeded land that contained a garnet ledge to the Southeast Council of the Boy Scouts of America. The bequest said that the land be used for scouting purposes and that the children of Wrangell could take garnets in reasonable amounts. The

"Later that Friday afternoon, the ferry stopped at Wrangell, Alaska, long enough for people to buy garnets from boys selling them at the dock."

children dig up the garnets themselves. Several caravaners went ashore and brought back some of the beautiful semiprecious gems.

I explored the ferry at different times throughout the trip. I went to the upper solarium deck at the stern and saw where the passengers slept who did not have cabins. Under a roof but with the entire entry open, the area was crowded with chaise lounges. Some were laid back flat; others were being used as chairs for reading. All were covered with sleeping bags. Outside on the open deck, a tent had been pitched. These solarium passengers could, of course, use the other lounges on the ferry.

As we moved through the famed Inside Passage, I saw the magnificent ever-changing views of mountains, some snowcapped; glaciers; and small picturesque communities, all across beautiful blue water. We were on the return part of our tour, and so while the scenery was breathtaking, it was no longer new to me. Yet I wanted to see as much of it as possible before the opportunity floated away except in my memory.

Off and on during the days and evenings, we watched for whales. As I walked on the outer promenade deck on Friday evening, I passed the lounge. Sitting inside, Paul, Don, Ro and Bob, and Fred watched for whales through the large plate glass windows. It was about 9 P.M. and still daylight.

I walked forward to the bow where a narrator talked but I was not close enough to hear. Instead I looked out across the great expanse of calm, shimmering, blue water toward the horizon. The sun had set but it was still light enough to read. Its glow continued to reflect on some of the clouds that floated above the peaked mountains in the distance. It was like seeing light at the end of a tunnel—a message of hope.

By 9:30, it was dark and the lights of Ketchikan twinkled on shore. Although the ferry stopped there, again we did not go ashore because it was nighttime. The ferry's next stop, and our place of departure from it, would be Prince Rupert early on Saturday morning.

By 6:39 A.M., on Saturday, July 24, those caravaners with cabins near ours stood waiting with their luggage in our cabin hallway, ready to go to the car deck. Ahead of me I saw the Beelers, Foremans, Wrigleys, McQuistons, and Paul.

Soon we and seemingly hundreds of others walked downstairs to the car deck where cars and RVs were parked with just enough walking room between them. Both Paul and I got into our motorhome this time. A crew of men with flashlights and orange vests directed the unloading of vehicles.

The Graybeals, who were in a line of vehicles on our right nearest the huge exit opening, were directed to pull out, then the Raider (wagonmaster's tow car), another car, and some more vehicles also parked on our right. Then a crewman directed Paul and looked carefully to make sure we did not get too near the wall to our left. We passed the crucial contact points and had the open gape of the ferry and daylight ahead.

"Thank you very much," Paul said to the crewman.

"You're welcome. Have a good trip now," the crewman replied. Since vehicles were leaving from several parked lanes on the car deck, Paul paused to let a converted bus exit ahead of us. Then it was our turn to drive across the level metal plank onto a single lane with yellow concrete barriers on either side that was actually a pier over the water, something like going between the rails of a car wash, for about 100 feet or so and onto the parking lot at Prince Rupert.

We waited in line to go through customs. RVs, cars, and other people waited to get *on* the ferry that we had just left.

We cleared customs without any problems and found our way slowly through Prince Rupert. The Graybeals had stopped ahead about a mile. We passed Scott and Karen who were hooking up the Raider to the Allegro® on the right shoulder of the road.

"Number Six, this is Number One. I've just passed Scott and Karen," said Paul on the CB.

When we saw the familiar Pinnacle on the side of the road ahead, Paul said, "Number Six, this is Number One."

"Gotcha," said John. As we drove past, the Graybeals pulled in behind us.

Later, all of us caravaners stopped at the Ksan Indian Village and Museum, located near Hazelton, British Columbia. Our pretty tour guide welcomed us as she stood beside a totem pole. She told us about the totem poles and the history of the surrounding area. On totem poles, she said, the most dominant or most significant commemorations are at the bottom and the least are at the top. We toured the buildings and admired the blankets and other crafts on display.

As we headed toward Smithers, it was hard to believe that our time together was coming to a close. Our plates had been filled and we had enjoyed every morsel, but we were about to leave our traveling friends. I was glad the wagonmasters had planned fun activities for that evening and the next.

· 26 ·

Farewell Dinner

THAT SATURDAY EVENING at the Riverside Park at Smithers, British Columbia, we gathered for the Craziest Tee-Shirt contest. The attractive campground had a gravel road edged with wood poles laid horizontally. It was landscaped with green grass, green shrubs, and pine trees. Pretty blooming flowers in pots lined the edge of the lawn at the office building.

In the center of our lawn-chair circle was a red wooden picnic table. We laughed and giggled as we gathered, some of us self-conscious as we held our jackets or coats closed until the time for showing our zany tee-shirts. Eunice surprised us by dressing Pepper, their dog, in a tee-shirt. Pepper looked right at home in it as she sat politely beside Eunice's chair.

One by one we paraded around the picnic table showing our creativity in crazy tee-shirts. As an example, Bob Conway wore a *sleeveless* white tee-shirt with the American flag on the back and hand printed on the front: "The right to bare arms."

Eunice, who loved to fish, wore a long tee-shirt that sported the image of a large fishhook on the front with the words "A Happy Hooker."

Paul wore a white tee-shirt with a huge, colorful eagle on the front. He said to the group that while he was usually a pigeon, that night he was a big bird—an eagle. To prove it, he strutted around the table holding out the front of the shirt for all to see the picture of the eagle and then got up on the table with his arms in the air as if he were about to fly.

Under my coat was a long white tee-shirt that said "Arctic Sun Tanning Club, Barrow, Alaska." It had a picture of an Eskimo in full winter garb and sunglasses on a chaise lounge reading and relaxing on an ice floe beside a polar bear with the sun shining high above.

After all was said and the tee-shirts shown, Effie won hands down. When she lowered her blue Caravanas jacket enough for us to see the *back* of her pink tee-shirt, we all just howled and cheered and applauded. It said, "I may be married to him, but I'm not responsible for him." Along the way, Clem had spoken out or led us with his exuberant voice, sometimes when and in ways we least expected. I suppose Effie, in her charming, patient way, never quite knew what he would do next, which is why the tee-shirt hit the nail on the head.

It was a unanimous decision. Karen presented Effie with a mug that was decorated with scenes and the name Alaska. "A little token and remembrance from Alaska," she said.

Not to be outdone, Clem stood up and said if it hadn't been for him, she wouldn't have been able to win the prize! We all just roared with laughter.

Farewell Dinner

During our last departure meeting that evening, Paul copied into our notebook the directions for our final leg of the Alaskan tour the next day. It would be from Smithers to the Southpark RV Park at Prince George, 244 miles away. Our farewell dinner would be at the Prince George Golf and Curling Club at 6 P.M. We would meet at 5:45 at the campground and travel in several RVs the five miles to the Club. We were to bring our "secret voyager" gifts, which did not have to be wrapped. While the women could wear dresses, ties were not required for the men. It would be Beef Nite at the Prince George Golf and Curling Club and prime rib would be our entree.

Karen thanked us all. The sun was casting long shadows on our group as we slowly folded our chairs and returned to our vehicles.

By early afternoon the next day, Sunday, we entered the same campground where we had stayed on the third night of our 44-day tour of Alaska, Southpark RV Park at Prince George, British Columbia. We had completed the circuit. It was time for our last group occasion.

That evening dresses, skirts, dressy pants suits, ties (some bolos), jackets, and special shirts came out of our RV wardrobes. Everyone sported a new look for our final time together at the Prince George Golf and Curling Club on the Yellowhead Highway 16 West. We laughed at how dressed up we were.

Lib wore a smart looking, light gray bouclé, three-piece dress and black pumps with dangling earrings and a small black purse. I brought out the summery flowered dress I had brought along, added white pumps, my white handbag, and a white sweater on my arm. John wore a short-sleeved shirt and tie, brown pants, and carried a rose-colored jacket on his arm. Paul wore a shirt and tie, gray pants, and gold jacket. Many in our group carried cameras and bags with gifts.

Paul and I rode with Don and Thel in their Southwind motorhome. Then, on that beautiful sunny evening, we stood for a group picture on a grassy slope above a round floral logo outside the clubhouse.

"Everyone sported a new look for our final time together at the Prince George Golf and Curling Club on the Yellowhead Highway 16 West. We laughed at how dressed up we were."
(Front row L-R: Eunice McQuiston, Yvonne Foreman, Laurie Peterson, Mary Jo Cornell, Don Heathcock, Thel Heathcock, Ann Beeler, the author, Jackie Wrigley, Lib Graybeal, Ro Conway, Karen Bonis, Scott Bonis. Back row L-R: Fred McQuiston, Wil Foreman, Don Peterson, Bill Cornell, Louie Beeler, Paul Beard, Lyle Wrigley, John Graybeal, Clem Swagerty, Effie Swagerty, Bob Conway)

Inside, we gathered around the perimeter of a large U-shaped, white-clothed table on a private side of the large dining area. Husbands and wives sat next to one another. On one side of the table sat Yvonne and Wil Foreman, Bob and Ro Conway, Thel and Don Heathcock, Bill and Mary Jo Cornell, and Lyle Wrigley; around the corner at the end of the U-shaped arrangement sat Jackie Wrigley, Don and Laurie Peterson, Scott and Karen Bonis, and Lou and Ann Beeler; then completing the other side of the U-shape were Effie and Clem Swagerty, John and Lib Graybeal, myself and Paul, and Fred and Eunice McQuiston.

I think it was Louie who offered the blessing for the meal. Following the delicious and well-served prime rib dinner, many voyagers snapped pictures of other couples, one last memento.

FAREWELL DINNER

We began the gift exchanges to our "secret voyagers." When she presented her gift to Thel, Ro said, "We were together and admiring these, and I bought one for her. Afterward she bought three to take home!" We all laughed. As she looked at the package, Thel said, "Want me to read the poem she wrote?" Sure, we all said.

> Now the time has come to tell
> My secret voyager's name is Thel.
> With all apologies to Robert Service
> You'll all agree that she's deserving.
> Now that our trip is at its end,
> I feel I've made a brand new friend.

Much applause and approval followed the reading. Thel unwrapped the package and showed a colorful matruska, a nest of Russian dolls.

One by one we identified our secret voyagers. Thel's was Yvonne, Yvonne's was Eunice, Eunice's was Lib. Lib's was me. She handed to me a wrapped package that turned out to be a hardcover edition of *The Spell of the Yukon* by Robert Service, by that time something very meaningful to me. Inside she had written a lovely inscription.

Using her given name Euphemia, I gave to Effie a colorful booklet of Denali National Park, knowing that, as an artist herself, she liked art and beautiful pictures.

Laurie gave Mary Jo dangling earrings with a pheasant design, with much admiring and oohs and ahs from the women present. Mary Jo gave Jackie a large, square scarf with an Alaskan design and a poem:

> Picking out a gift for Jackie was not easy.
> Buying sweatshirts for her daughters made her queasy.
> But she looks so great in those shades of blue,
> Maybe this Alaskan scarf will match her earrings, too.
> She's ready to laugh, quick as a wink;
> It's fun to know her, that's what I think.

Applause burst forth as Jackie held up the colorful scarf.

Jackie, in turn, presented a special mug to Karen, one that Karen had admired in Pouce Coupe. As the presentations were made and the gifts were opened, we quipped and joked and laughed. Karen gave Ro something that would help her remember the fun times in Alaska, a book, *Coming into the Country*.

Paul gave Lyle some golf balls with North Pole inscribed on them amid much laughter about playing golf while waiting to have a flat tire fixed on his motorhome. Paul also said that rumor had it that Lyle was so proficient that he only used one ball a year and this would keep him in stock for several years.

Lyle said, "I do have a tendency to lose balls."

Lyle, in turn, got up from his seat and stood behind Don Heathcock, who wore a white dress shirt. "I was so afraid that he wasn't going to accomplish what he set out to do that I thought I'd better get him this." He handed a wrapped package to Don, who subsequently opened one after another of increasingly smaller packages. Finally he came to a small double button pin for his cap. I couldn't see what it said but Don had been collecting them all along the way and his goal was to cover his entire cap with them.

As Clem presented his secret voyager gift to Bob Conway, he said, "I got a lot of flack from Bob and others about not catching any salmon. So I went out and scooped up some hot air and canned it." As a gag gift, he gave Bob a can of Alaskan hot air. The real gift, however, was a handsome miniature totem pole. After acknowledgments and compliments, Bob pointed to the totem pole and said, "Now this fellow on the bottom is the strongest," (referring to what the guide had said at the Ksan Indian Village) as he looked at Clem. Clem quickly responded, "Yeah, that's you," to which Bob chuckled.

In turn, Bob read a verse composed by Ro, whom he dubbed "Roberta Service," which was a combination of her given name and a reference to the poetry of Robert Service, as he gave to Wil a special calendar: "When you turn each page and change the month and June arrives in '94, / Look back remembering the good times once more." More acknowledgments and clapping.

Farewell Dinner

Perhaps the most poignant moment came when Wil got up and walked slowly and deliberately across the open end of the U-shaped table toward Paul. He stood in front of Paul and said with great effort, "Before I left home, I had a stroke. You all know I had a stroke. And I lost all my memory and I can't even remember your last name, fella. You appear to remember me, I remember you . . ." and he struggled for the right words. "You had a good . . . good thing about you," and he smiled at Paul. "And so I said well, I said I'm gonna give him what he really likes . . . and so . . .," Wil himself wrestled with unwrapping the gift as he leaned over the table, "so I bought you that."

He handed a miniature, black stone bear to Paul, looking closely at Paul's face to see if he liked it. Amid applause, Paul stood up and thanked him very, very much and held up the black stone bear for all to admire.

Wil said, "I can't remember your name but I remember your face."

"Paul," Paul said. Wil repeated it and then turned like the gentleman he was and walked back to his seat. Lib quipped that Paul had been looking for that black bear the whole trip.

Dressed in a western-style shirt and sporting a shiny, silver belt buckle, Lou stood up and said of his secret voyager, "Here's something for early in the morning when your wife's still sleeping in bed." (Lib is not a "morning" person.)

Lib laughed and lowered her head to the table as Lou handed John a squarish package. "A big golf ball," John guessed as he unwrapped the gift. Soon he held up a coffee mug. "I'll fix my coffee, walk outdoors, and you can sleep," he said to Lib.

Then John walked around the open end of the U-table and stood behind Bill Cornell as he presented his gift and said, "This guy at some time will travel down enough paths that he will get the 'view from the end of the road.' "

When Bill opened the package, he found a book by Tom Bodett called *The End of the Road*. Bill quipped, "We'll keep the light on for you!" and everyone howled.

After the secret voyagers had all been identified and presented gifts, John presented the 17-verse ballad that he and I had written.

255

He acknowledged thanks to Robert Service and his "Cremation of Sam McGee," upon whose rhyme scheme the verses were based. Much laughter had punctuated his rendition of the original poem when he gave it from memory at the Moose Creek Campground campfire.

In a humorous vein, the ballad told of 10 RVs meeting with the wagonmasters and tailgunners in Vancouver. Everybody was included in a stanza. It concluded with the following verse of appreciation to our leaders:

> How can we thank you folks of high rank
> for sharing yourselves with us?
> With a hearty cheer led by Clem right here
> and a gift wrapped with great fuss.
> So lead away, Cheerleader, today,
> this is your time to shine.
> We'll join with you in a cheer or two
> for friends who've been so fine!

Having referred to it in the poem, John invited Clem to lead us in a cheer—it would not have been a satisfying get-together without one from him. So with his usual gusto, swinging his arms and shouting the words, he led cheers for Scott, Karen, Don, and Laurie, and then one for the people who served our meal.

Following the hearty college-type cheers with many rah, rah, rahs, John suggested giving Clem a big hand by pretending to clap but not letting his hands meet as he swung them back and forth. More laughter and applause.

Continuing the fun, John presented playful gifts to the tailgunners and wagonmasters—a "Mr. Fixit" mug with a hammer through part of it for Don, a pair of ptarmigan oven mitts for Laurie because she liked those birds, and the cuddly husky pup for Scott and Karen. Before sitting down, John handed each caravaner couple a handwritten copy of the group ballad.

On behalf of everyone, Jackie presented the wagonmasters and the tailgunners with cards with everyone's signature and gratuity checks of appreciation for a great trip.

Farewell Dinner

John asked for a hand for the women standing on the other side of the room who had waited on us and who would be clearing the tables. Turning to another subject, he said, "Lib and I are leaving early tomorrow morning. Don, I suggest you not even bother to go to bed tonight. The last thing, when I get unhooked and ready to pull out, Lib's going to jump out of the motorhome and whack on all your tires and we'll take off. But, seriously, we've enjoyed the trip. We may not see some of you in the morning. As Lib was telling some of you over here, if you ever get through Maryland north or south, we do have a full hookup in the driveway, so you're welcome to park. So come see us." And he walked around handing out cards with his home address and phone number.

Like jack-in-the-boxes, a representative from each couple stood up and invited everyone to visit whenever they were in the area. Eunice went around the table giving a bookmark and magnet to every couple.

Louie stood up. "Some of you will be coming close to our place as you go and each and every one of you are invited to visit us. And we've enjoyed this trip immensely. A lot of you folks have done this over and over again, maybe not quite like this here the last few days, but this has been our first experience, and I tell you we just are so grateful and so happy to make friends with each and every one of you. It's a clan is what it is. It's going to be hard to split the road tomorrow with some going south and us going more east. But you're invited to our place any time. And we don't have quite the scenery that Alaska does, but it's second." He sat down to hearty applause.

Before I was ready for the time together to be over, Scott stood up. He wore one of his multitudinous hats, this time a flowered, Irish-style cap. When he asked for the number of hats he had worn during the trip, nobody had the correct answer, which was 103. John came closest by calculating the number of days times an estimate of the number of hats worn each day. But since the answer had to be right on the nose, nobody won. And anyway, we had had such a good time on the tour and at the dinner that evening that everybody took it in stride.

Then Scott warmly but seriously said, "I think that I'd like to end this little gathering of ours with a toast from Old Mexico, one which we like very much." He held up his water glass and spoke in Spanish. Then he interpreted: "I wish to you from all my heart—health, love, long life forever."

"Here, here!" and we drank the toast with our water glasses.

I didn't want it to end. I looked around, realizing I had made new friends. We had the common bond of having seen Alaska together and had done so with congeniality and consideration of one another. In the beginning, I questioned how 24 people would get along for 44 days. Now, having experienced it, I felt lifted up, positive, and grateful for the trusting attitudes of my fellow travelers.

Our laughter still rang in my ears—laughter at nervously meeting one another at Burnaby, finding our way, joshing over the CB, listening at departure meetings, sharing group meals. The wondrous sights that we saw lay forever in my psyche—glaciers, sea otters, early mining towns, Mount McKinley, large and small lakes, and Prince William Sound.

I was glad that the general health of all of us had held out although Scott was still limping. (I would learn that later he had surgery in which a steel pin was inserted in his ankle and he was then pain free.) At that moment, though, I was fighting what I thought was a cold.

Here is the poem that John and I wrote, in its entirety.

Farewell to Alaska

(With thanks to Robert Service and his "Cremation of Sam McGee")

Ten RVs roamed so far from home
to meet in that Vancouver city,
To greet each other and then discover
they were looking for fun, not pity.
We met Karen and Scott, wagonmasters hot,
and tailgunners Laurie and Don,
For a caravan tour of twenty-four,
it was on to the great Yukon.

FAREWELL DINNER

We tried every way to lead them astray,
but they stuck with their plan to the end.
Here in Prince George, once more we did gorge,
now on our own we must fend.
Our journey's complete, with leaders so neat,
Scott and Karen, we bid you farewell.
No turbo tonight, nor the Raider out of sight,
we solemnly swear not to tell.

They were put to the test to follow the rest,
to be there just when needed.
The few who were troubled would surely have doubled
if Don's sound advice were not heeded.
He thumped on the tires while some still aspired
to get more minutes of sleep,
But you couldn't be mad with the smiles Laurie had,
so as tailgunners we think we'll keep.

On to Barkerville just to share the thrill
of no hookups to be had this night.
A town we would leave, wearing memories on our sleeve,
of a motorhome leaning far right!
But off we did run to the Gold town for fun
and dinner at Wake-Up-Jake's.
History we didn't know, we learned from a show
and about a dredge that made its own lake.

While at Muncho Lake, we got ready to partake
of that famous event–potluck.
If one should look, how our ladies can cook,
with husbands most ready to cluck.
Many towns look the same, but Watson Lake's the name
of that town with the forest of signs.
Wil did the task without being asked
and produced a fine one from pines.

Carried by the Force, we entered Whitehorse
to spend a couple of days.
We took a boat tour, Wrigleys golfed some more,
we had fun in so many ways.
To the Follies we went, 'twas money well spent
to see Don wrapped in a tassel,
But the look Thel gave said he'd better behave,
or there surely would be a big hassle.

Though from Cuomo land, we let them stand
Number Three among the group,
You could always depend Bob and Ro would not end
traveling on the wrong road loop.
When you speak of Mary Jo, it's ho! ho! ho!
for she's leading the group at a gallop.
It's "why, oh why?" for information I cry
while Bill's patience is taking a wallop.

Lib said "no way," but Bernice said "okay,"
to drive the Top of the World.
"After 20 miles of bliss, I've enough of this,
and I don't want Paul's hair to be curled."
In the deep Yukon we listened to John
quote verses from Robert Service.
But Lib did shop at every stop
and that's what made him nervous.

Some shopped in a loft, while others played golf
in that city known as Fairbanks.
Lyle and Jackie yelled, "Fore!" while the shoppers yelled "more"
as they returned to join their ranks.
John shot many a par, but there were skeptics afar
of that scorecard turned in that night.
Lyle 'fessed up at once, John looked like a dunce,
and the scorecard soon became right.

FAREWELL DINNER

If you're looking for Paul, you may have to fall
on your hands and knees on the ground.
He only looks mean under his machine
to make sure all his gears go 'round.
I do not know how long in the snow
the Beelers have lived in Montana.
"Move that chair out of sight, set that freezer in tight,
we've got to be ready for mañana."

Eunice and Fred brought an extra small bed
for their loyal pet named Pepper.
At their request, Don and Thel said "yes,"
and during fishing trips kept her.
The call went out to fishermen about
to go look for that Salmon King,
And six did claim that fish of fame,
but one, alas, caught nothing.

Though from south of the border, it would take a special order
to beat the couple in unit five.
When Scott needed a chauffeur, Yvonne said she'd be a gopher,
and kept us all safe and alive.
If running a race, Wil couldn't keep pace,
but Yvonne kept them both on time.
Although he looked shy, he had a gleam in his eye
when he pulled off that humorous line.

One day we cruised, and looked and mused,
at awesome Prince William Sound.
Sea otters played, harbor seals laid,
and icebergs floated around.
We looked for whales, saw boats with sails,
and breathed in many beauties.
We cruised along on water strong
and too soon returned to Valdez.

We tossed about with many a shout
on the road to Kluane Lake.
We finally got there with many a scare
and enjoyed Effie's great cake.
When first we met, plans were set
for the following day.
Then blindfolded each one, candidates Paul and Don,
at their own socks hacked away.

When we got to Skagway for a three-day stay,
extra sleep was not to be had.
If it wasn't a plane, it was some damn train,
blowin' and tootin' and being so bad.
A new day was born with ships blowing their horn
at just a few minutes past eight,
As if to say, "We'll ruin your stay,
if you had any desire to sleep late."

We met strong Clem, organ grinder pro tem,
and prayed for Effie his wife,
who sprained her knee beside the sea
and leaned on a cane in her strife.
This work of rhyme, its meter sublime,
was done to say to you,
Thanks for the fun on this trip now done
and your topnotch leadership true.

How can we thank you folks of high rank
for sharing yourselves with us?
With a hearty cheer led by Clem right here
and a gift wrapped with great fuss.
So lead away, Cheerleader, today,
this is your time to shine.
We'll join with you in a cheer or two
for friends who've been so fine!

· 27 ·

Reaching the Lower 48

THE AIR WAS CRISP and the sky was clear that Monday morning at Southpark RV Park in Prince George, British Columbia. The 44-day Alaskan tour had ended the night before; our 12 rigs were on their own. That morning all the others would break camp and return to their home bases. When I awoke, I felt weak, on the verge of a cold and sore throat, and had a fever of 100.1 degrees. Unquestionably, I couldn't let my health interfere with the leave-taking of our newly found friends. I wouldn't breathe, sneeze, or cough on anybody, in case whatever I had was contagious.

Someone laughed outside. I hurried out carrying the video camera and joined Paul, who was grinning. True to her word, Lib was laughing and thumping on the tires of Don Peterson's fifth-wheel. She wore a deep purple sweatsuit and carried a wood rod made for the purpose at hand. Her task completed, she chuckled and talked with Don and Laurie through the window of their RV.

"Bye, guys," I heard her say as she turned away.

She and I visited briefly and then hugged one another. I stepped quickly into our motorhome and returned, handing her a white paper bag with a cinnamon bun inside it. The bun was one of the huge ones I had bought and frozen at Homer Spit—I knew she and John enjoyed them. Besides, I had to lose weight. Lib walked quickly to their Pinnacle. John waved to Paul and me just before following her inside.

"Have a safe one," he called back to us.

"Thank you, John, you too," Paul replied. And they disappeared into their vehicle. Paul and I stood outside our motorhome and we smiled and waved as the Graybeals pulled away from their site, headed out of the campground and for their home in Maryland. They would be traveling alone the rest of the way, as would we.

As others on our tour unhooked from water and electricity and prepared to leave the campground on their homeward journeys, Paul and I joined in hugging goodbyes and wishing everyone a safe trip. Scott and Karen, true to their early-bird routine, had already gone.

Wil, in white shorts and short-sleeved knit shirt, checked the oil in their motorhome engine.

"That was so nice of him last night when he gave you the secret voyager present," I said to Paul as we watched from across the campground road.

"He couldn't remember my name," Paul said tenderly.

"He remembered your face and that you were kind."

Like parents seeing their families off after a holiday gathering, we waved goodbye to each of our new friends as they, one RV at a time, pulled out of their sites and headed home. Then we stood alone

Reaching the Lower 48

among the empty spaces of our Alaskan voyagers. It was quiet. The recent goodbyes echoed in my ears. It was hard to believe that the time had come to part company. I sighed inside and sensed their absence but also detected a deep joy for having had 44 days with these people. Yet that day's needs began to surface.

Feeling the cool morning air, I darted back inside the motorhome because of my fever. I wondered how one would find a doctor if needed in that province of British Columbia. I wondered if Paul and I would actually visit the people and places we had planned to see before leaving home. We'd been away two months already.

We had stayed behind at Prince George in order to pick up a new battery for my laptop computer that was being sent by Federal Express. The motorhome needed a new fuel pump and both it and the auxiliary generator needed a change of oil and filter. So we signed up for two more nights at Southpark.

Later that Monday afternoon, we picked up the computer battery, got groceries, and went to see where we could have the RV serviced. Back at the campground, Paul installed the battery into the laptop computer, but the computer needed some configurations that only an expert like Jeff could do. It would remain unusable until later.

On Tuesday, the necessary work was completed on our vehicle and generator.

By Wednesday, both Paul and I needed to see a doctor. But where? He had a sore throat and I had severe congestion in my head and throat. We decided to take our chances on finding medical attention at our next campground. At 8:41 A.M. under overcast skies, we left Southpark and headed for Cache Creek, 286 miles away. It was a misty, rainy trip and still overcast when we arrived at Cache Creek RV Park & Campgrounds, British Columbia, at 3:11 P.M. The campground office told us where we could find a doctor.

By 4:41 P.M. we had arrived by motorhome at the Ashcroft Medical Clinic, Ashcroft, British Columbia. Soon a very kind, cordial, young doctor examined both of us. He prescribed doxycycline for my sinusitis and penicillin for Paul's sore throat. We had the prescriptions filled at the local People's drug store. On the way back to the campground we stopped for dinner at the Wander-Inn restaurant where I took my first capsule. I continued to run a slight fever and my head felt very congested. And it was time for a hairdo.

That evening I fixed commercially frozen dinners in the microwave and tallied the trip log, and we both turned in early.

The following morning, Thursday, July 29, we continued homeward. We wanted to visit family members and friends in British Columbia, Oregon, California, Colorado, Kansas, and Indiana. We hoped to have the motorhome worked on in Oregon, Iowa, and Indiana. The age of our vehicle was beginning to show. The automatic steps, for example, were not working. We used a blue plastic stool as a substitute. Many times Paul gallantly placed that stool on the ground for me to step down on or step up on. I felt like Elizabeth I walking on Sir Walter Raleigh's cape.

But first, the hairdo. We left Cache Creek early on that Thursday and by noon arrived at Parkcanada Recreational Vehicle Inn, Delta, British Columbia. We registered, then went immediately to a nearby mall where a hairstylist soon transformed my straggling brown locks.

At the campground telephone, Paul called his first cousin to confirm his visit the next day. I knew I wasn't well enough to go.

On Friday, July 30, even though my temperature had come down to normal, I coughed incessantly. Paul took a taxi from the campground to the ferry that took him across the Strait of Georgia to Vancouver Island. Barbara Beard Howell and her husband, Douglas, graciously met him and showed him parts of the island and their home in Sidney.

Paul videotaped much of what he saw. Through those pictures, I thrilled at the prolific works of fine art by Barbara that were showcased throughout their handsome home—sculptures of owls, a woodcock, and various animals done in both clay and porcelain; lamp bases and vases; woven baskets; framed wool weavings; embroidered pictures done by sewing machine; and oil paintings. Outside, flowers bloomed radiantly amid rocks and in pots on the deck—camel-

Reaching the Lower 48

lias, Easter lilies, Canterbury bells, and others. What a feast of art and beauty I had missed!

Leaving Delta, British Columbia, on Saturday morning, we soon arrived at the Heritage Duty-Free Store on the U.S.–Canadian border. Here we exchanged what Canadian money we had left and bought a few duty-free gifts. From the store, we joined a line of traffic moving toward the customs booth. Soon we cleared that requirement and continued south to the American Heritage Campground, Olympia, Washington. It still seemed strange to us to be alone after our 44 days in the RV caravan.

We awoke that night to the sound of running water. High campground water pressure had caused a pipe connection to leak and water had poured into the hot air duct running just beneath the length of our carpeted motorhome floor. Paul immediately turned off the water at the outside campground faucet. Then he removed the registers from the metal duct that usually carried warm air from the furnace but now was half-full of water. Using two battery-suction bulbs and dippers, we worked several hours sucking and dipping all of the water from the duct into buckets.

We learned from the experience to use a pressure regulator at the connecting faucet located on the side of the motorhome. To be on the safe side from that time forward, Paul turned off the campground water on the outside of the coach just before he got into bed at night. He simply leaned out the bedroom window, reached down, and turned the spigot handle to Off.

By mid-afternoon of the next day, Sunday, we had parked at Jantzen Beach RV Park, Hayden Island, Oregon. A beautifully landscaped area with spacious sites, it became a restorative spot for the motorhome, the computer, and us.

While there, we had a vibration in the motorhome's overdrive unit repaired, Jeff led me by telephone through the necessary steps to get the laptop computer working again, and I got a haircut and shampoo, bought (with Paul's input) new runners for the motorhome

267

aisle, and finished taking the sinusitis medicine. While Paul still had some penicillin to take, we both felt much better.

As we left Hayden Island on Wednesday, August 4, going south on I-5, I typed into the computer:

> It's hard to believe that our tour group said farewell a week and a half ago! Most of them must be back home by now. We are only in Oregon. At this rate it may be Labor Day before we get home!

By Thursday, we were in Drain, Oregon, at the company that made the steps for our motorhome. A young man cheerfully and expeditiously repaired them so that they once again moved in and out automatically. Alas, I had to give up my knight, Sir Paul, with his gallant courtesy!

On Friday, we left I-5 to go a few miles east to Myrtle Creek, Oregon, to visit Harold and Louise Bock for the second time in two years. The Bocks and Paul had met during World War II when Harold and Paul were both doing U.S. Forest Service work at a Civilian Public Service camp at Mount Hood, Oregon. I wanted to see both them

"The Bocks and Paul had met during World War II when Harold and Paul were both doing U.S. Forest Service work at a Civilian Public Service camp at Mount Hood, Oregon."

and their backyard again. Like the showcase garden for the Matanuska Valley at Palmer, Alaska, their yard exuded blooming flowers (lobelias, petunias, snapdragons, geraniums, roses, irises, lilies); dogwood trees; peach trees; apple trees (Granny Smiths, Priscillas); nut trees (filberts, Barcelonas); raspberries, blueberries, and Marionberries; grape vines (raisin, yellow, orange, Concord); a fig tree; yarrow herb; rhubarb; a vegetable garden with California miner's beans; a wisteria vine; and a woodpile because they burned wood in winter.

Affable, silver-haired Harold and soft-spoken, gracious Louise prepared lunch for us and generously gave us some of their backyard harvest to take along. Lunch was a special treat: fresh salmon, green beans that I helped to pick from their garden, fresh red potatoes, good brown bread with Louise's Marionberry jelly, butter, and ice cream with fresh peaches and blueberries from their backyard.

It was the middle of the afternoon when we left the Bocks and Myrtle Creek and regained I-5 headed toward Crescent City, California. At the border, an agricultural inspector carefully looked for gypsy moth eggs in all the outside compartments and underneath the motorhome. We passed the examination. Paul asked him about the road ahead to Crescent City, U.S. 199. "You can only go about 20 miles an hour—hairpin curves—a beautiful river."

He was right about the curves and river. But we also gazed in awe at magnificent, sky-touching, leafy trees and California redwoods—some gray-barked ones among those gigantic *living* monuments. At their bases grew green ferns in that lush, forested area lining the two-lane Redwood Highway just below the Oregon border. We stopped in the Amelia Earhart Memorial Grove for a picture showing a great tree standing so tall I could not possibly fit it all into the view through my lens. The gigantic nature of these trees reminded me of magnificent Mount McKinley that had so recently captivated me.

On that Friday evening, as we entered a campground near Crescent City and looked for the office, I said to Paul, "I wonder where our wagonmasters are," and then answered myself, "We are

"We stopped in the Amelia Earhart Memorial Grove for a picture showing a great tree standing so tall I could not possibly fit it all into the view through my lens."

our wagonmasters." Paul grinned as his eyes searched for a place to park beside the office.

My sinusitis had been cured and Paul's sore throat had healed. We had had two delightful visits with family and friends with equally pleasurable ones anticipated. On two previous trips, it was necessary to return home suddenly without completing our itineraries because of the deaths of Paul's parents, first his father and later his mother. In each instance, we were at the farthest point of our trip and drove continuously, even through the night, to arrive home in time for the visitations and services. We wouldn't have wanted it any other way, of course. And so I couldn't help wondering whether something would happen—even though we had passed our farthest terminus and were well into our homeward journey—to cause us to head straight home or if we would indeed be able to complete our trip in the leisurely fashion we had planned.

· 28 ·

Homeward Journey

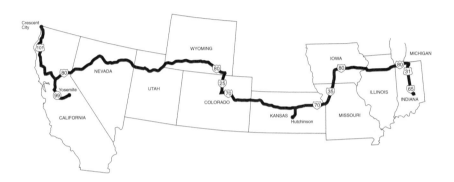

CALIFORNIA COUSINS whom we had never visited before came next on our homeward journey. After that would come other relatives and a friend as we traveled across the continent toward Maryland. We also had motorhome service calls to make in Iowa and Indiana. I wondered if we would actually get to do it all. It seemed too good to be true that in addition to our fabulous Alaskan tour, we would also visit people whom we had wanted to see for a long time.

As we left Crescent City on Saturday morning, August 7, we paused at the rock-hewn Battery Point on the Pacific Ocean to photograph the lighthouse with its round white tower and white residence in mist and light rain. How rocky the coast of the Pacific Ocean was in comparison to the gray sandy shore of the Arctic Ocean. And I saw only blue water out to the horizon, no ice floes or ice pack with miles of ice beyond.

Later that morning, off of Elk Prairie Parkway, we spotted a herd of about fifteen Roosevelt elk, members of the deer family. Seeing them took me back to Denali National Park and Preserve where we had seen several herds of caribou (the wild, North American version of the Old World reindeer) moving along the snowy slopes of the mountains. And we had fed domesticated reindeer on a farm through a fence in the Yukon. As we drove past, I watched as the elk grazed unconcernedly in their lush green pasture in California.

By Saturday evening we had left scenic U.S. 101 and were on Route 20 in a campground at Nice, California. We parked facing Clear Lake. The next morning, unlike the quiet, peaceful Kachemak Bay at the end of Homer Spit, a power boat with a water skier and a jet skier zoomed around our end of the enormous lake.

After we left Nice on that Sunday morning, we stopped near Glenhaven for devotions on a hillside above the same Clear Lake; from this vantage point we enjoyed a beautiful peaceful scene with mountains around part of the lake. I thought of the worship service at Muncho Lake that Mary Jo had initiated and how we caravaners had participated in it as we sat around picnic tables on the patio in the now-distant British Columbia.

Later that afternoon, as we drove into a campground at Manteca, California, off of Route 99, and searched for our campsite, I said,

"After we left Nice on that Sunday morning, we stopped near Glenhaven for devotions on a hillside above the . . . Clear Lake."

Homeward Journey

"There's a Conquest like Mary Jo and Bill's!" But when I looked closer, I saw that the license plate was from California instead of Connecticut.

By Monday afternoon, August 9, we had traveled from northwestern California to the central part of the state, Modesto, about 500 miles. It was now our turn to visit my cousin, Grant Ecker; his wife, Patty; their family, Muffie, Coree, Diana, and Bo; and their Dalmatian, Molly. Although Muffie was at work, the others met and hosted us at lunch in a nearby restaurant in Waterford, after which we followed them to their 50-acre almond ranch.

Patty showed me through their processing and packing operations, which were in a huge, warehouse-style building. Outside, as I looked at the rows and rows of leafy almond trees, she explained that the almonds were harvested by shaking the trees, then letting the almonds dry on the ground, after which a machine swept them into rows and another machine picked them up and took them to the processing plant. The almonds went to Germany, Japan, and the United States. All were inspected by the United States Department of Agriculture before shipment.

A collector and restorer of old cars, Grant took Paul and me for an open-air, top-down ride in a '51 Plymouth convertible, a beauty that was cream colored with white sidewalls. Grant also took us on a tour of their ranch-style house, which they built themselves in two phases. After a full afternoon of visiting and getting caught up on family news, we left these attractive and hospitable relatives about six o'clock. Their pioneering spirit reminded me of those people who had gone to Alaska and had made a home and living for themselves.

It was nine o'clock and pitch dark that evening when we registered at the Yosemite Mariposa Fairgrounds for a campsite for two nights. I couldn't help thinking that had we been in Alaska, we could have seen quite well at that hour.

The following day, Tuesday, we headed for the mountainside home of my husband's, Paul *William* Beard, first cousin, Paul *Webster*

"We headed for the mountainside home of my husband's, Paul William Beard, first cousin, Paul Webster Beard, and his wife, Marcia, who lived only about 30 miles from Yosemite National Park."

Beard, and his wife, Marcia, who lived only about 30 miles from Yosemite National Park.

Once we were in the mountainous area, Paul Webster Beard met and escorted us in his four-wheeler to a place to park our motorhome on a sandy area off the narrow road among pines, cedars, and scrub trees.

We rode with him about a hundred yards to "Beard's Boneyard," as he had named their acreage. The name came from the hundreds of animal bones that he had collected and used to show students when he had taught school. We toured the house and surrounding buildings and land with Paul Webster.

A naturalist, among other talents, he showed us his extensive and handsome collection of mounted butterflies acquired gradually over 25 years. In his retirement, he guided groups through the State Mineral Museum at Mariposa and gave talks on butterflies, rocks, and natural history. After a fascinating visit that included lunch and warm conversation, we went back to our motorhome. Later that evening, Paul Webster and Marcia came into Mariposa so that we could all have dinner together and he could show us the town. More great relatives!

Homeward Journey

On Wednesday, August 11, we were about to leave the fascinating state of California and head east. We had traveled five days there, enjoying its vistas of redwoods, pines, rivers, lakes, dry areas, canyons, narrow roads, mountains, canals, and highways with median strips of bushes of flowers. The lush blooms made me think of the plentiful purple fireweed that grew wild along the roadsides in Alaska.

As we ate lunch at a rest stop along I-80, I asked Paul, "Are you anxious to get home?" I personally wanted to linger awhile; it seemed unusual that so far it had been unnecessary to hurry home. I was thankful that our families were well and healthy.

Besides, I liked being in California. I liked reminding myself I was in California, perhaps because it was on the opposite side of the country from Maryland. It was like a dream come true to just *be* there. If I *lived* in California I would want to travel to Maryland. It was a psychological thing—wanting to be where I was not. Part of it was the fun of being away from routines, work, and normal stresses of my life in Maryland. It was fun thinking of ourselves being so far from home.

"In some respects there are things I should be at home taking care of. As far as break-neck speed to get there, no, I'm not interested in killing myself to get there," Paul replied as he put his sandwich in the microwave oven to heat it. Then he reached for the video to take a picture of me eating my last meal in California. I wore a short-sleeved, blue, knit shirt that I had bought in Skagway that mentioned climbing the Chilkoot Trail nearby.

At our last rest stop in California, in my own little ceremony, I deliberately stepped onto the dry, pale tan dirt of the parking area with my tennis shoes and, looking down, videotaped them. They were on California soil at 4,500 feet elevation.

From that rest area, we continued on I-80 into Tahoe National Forest and passed Donner Lake. Although we were once again driving in the mountains as we had in Alaska, there were no frost heaves to worry about on the highway.

"There it is," said Paul of the Nevada sign.

"Farewell, California, farewell," I said. "I hope to get back again someday." It was another farewell. I felt once again the absence of our Alaskan tour friends.

Continuing on I-80, we entered Nevada. We soon arrived at the Reno Hilton Camperland. Much to my surprise, it was adjacent to and run by the Reno Hilton hotel and was a very nice campground.

After hooking up the motorhome, we walked into the hotel lobby. Seeing a hair salon, I went inside. I said that I did not have an appointment and asked if someone could shampoo and style my hair. After I waited a short while, a stylist who said he had also done the hair of some famous actors worked on mine. The fee was $25.

That accomplished, Paul and I went upstairs to the casino-restaurant level and ate at an elaborate buffet. Afterward we strolled around the casino looking at the huge numbers of machines, people, chandeliers, and the monitors above the gaming tables. It was all very modern compared to the old-time casinos on our Alaskan tour. Back in the motorhome, I did the daily tally in the trip log and we both relaxed by watching television. Overhead, we heard lots of airplanes, very low, very loud, and very fast.

The next morning, Thursday, before leaving the city of Reno we went to an RV service center where we had the oil and oil filter of the motorhome changed. Then we proceeded to I-80 heading out of Reno. Paul drove through very barren but rolling mountains. The Truckee River flowed through the valley beside the highway with a few green, stunted-looking trees growing beside the river.

Paul took videotape pictures of the salt flats and dry desert grass on either side of I-80 during one of my two stints behind the wheel that day. In the distance were low, flat mountains. The desert landscape around us contrasted sharply with the green mountains and blue lakes of Alaska and with beautiful British Columbia. The people who pioneered over that desert wasteland had to be just as hardy and courageous as the determined spirits who climbed steep mountain trails with heavy backpacks in their quest for gold in Alaska and the Yukon.

HOMEWARD JOURNEY

After a full day's drive, we arrived at Mountain Shadows RV Park, Wells, Nevada. The campground was lovely and well landscaped with a clean laundry and an exceptionally hospitable woman in the office. While I did three loads of laundry, Paul made sure all was well with the motorhome by checking the tires, looking for signs of any type of fluid leak, and cleaning the windshield.

On Friday morning, August 13, we again took I-80, this time from Wells, Nevada, across the border into Utah toward Salt Lake City. En route, we came upon the famous Bonneville Salt Flats, which is the location for official automobile race records. We parked the motorhome and I soon stood on the deck of an observation tower scanning that enormous, level, white area. Imagine all that salt lying there like a sheet on the ground. I chuckled as I thought, in the winter when it snowed in Utah, they had snow on salt instead of salt on snow as we did in Maryland.

At noon, we ate lunch in the motorhome at a sunny parking area west of Salt Lake City, then we continued on I-80 into Wyoming. By the time we reached Little America, Wyoming, the temperature had soared to 98 degrees, but by the time we reached the KOA Kampground at Rock Springs, Wyoming, in late afternoon, it had gone down to 86 degrees under sunny skies. It was quite different from the chilly breezes on the shore of the Arctic Ocean at Barrow.

The next day we would travel east across southern Wyoming to I-25 and head south to Denver, Colorado, where we wanted to visit close relatives.

Other famous people had already come to Denver the week we visited. When we arrived, Pope John Paul II was in town. President Clinton and his family had been there earlier that week. We arrived on Saturday, August 14, in the late afternoon. We weren't sure if we would be able to get through the barricaded streets without a pass because of strong security for the pope. But it turned out that was not a problem. We were in town to see Paul's sister Hazel and her husband, the Reverend Albert Guyer, in their latest home, which we had never visited.

When I knocked on their screen door on that sunny afternoon, the fragrance of a cake being baked wafted toward me—an indication of the warm visit that we would have. After deciding that where we were parked was okay, we ran our heavy, black, electric cord across their lawn into an electrical outlet on the outside of their house. One of the great things that we enjoyed about the motorhome was being able to visit people and yet stay in our own bed at night, which is what we did in Denver.

On Sunday morning, August 15, Hazel and I walked on their nearby greenbelt to stand beside the pilgrimage route of thousands of youth from around the world. They walked past from downtown Denver to participate in a World Youth Day papal mass at Cherry Creek State Park, a few blocks away. We shook hands and said "good morning" to some as they passed by. Their replies came in different languages.

A delightful part of our time in Denver was getting acquainted with the children of our nephew Stephen Guyer and his family. His young twins, Stephanie and Christopher, examined thoroughly all parts of the motorhome and took turns filming with our videotape recorder. Steve himself had attended the papal mass with an estimated 375,000 people, the largest public gathering in Colorado history, and gave us an interesting account of the experience. Not a Catholic himself, he was director of music for St. Luke's United Methodist Church in Highlands Ranch.

The next day, Monday, Al took me downtown to the Colorado History Museum where I beheld the ornate and sacred Vatican treasures, a rare opportunity.

We left the warm and generous hospitality of these family members in Denver in the early morning on Tuesday, August 17. Skies were overcast and it was a chilly 52 degrees in that mile-high city. I sensed once again cool Arctic-like air.

By the time we arrived at our campground in Russell, Kansas, that evening, it was sunny and the temperature was 92 degrees. We noted

Homeward Journey

that this town was the hometown of former Senator and presidential candidate Bob Dole.

By early afternoon, Wednesday, August 18, we pulled up beside the Friendship Child Care home in Hutchinson, Kansas. A young woman, Virginia Cain, from our home church was spending a year in Brethren Volunteer Service as a child care worker. Paul and I were her deacons. She had never been so far away from home for such a long time before—it may as well have been Alaska. She came flying across the yard toward us and soon we were hugging and sharing the joys of friendship. She took us inside and introduced us to the staff and some of the children. She was able to take a break and we sat in one of the classrooms enthusiastically exchanging news and experiences. What a happy time that was!

From Hutchinson, we returned to I-70 and moved on through northwest Missouri on I-35 to Moscow, Iowa, arriving in late afternoon, Thursday, August 19. It was here that the HWH Corporation relocated the rear hydraulic jacks on the motorhome, let us stay overnight on their grounds while they did so, and treated us to lunch, all at no charge.

In nearby Davenport, Iowa, Lujacks Chevrolet inserted a bolt in our transmission bracket, also at no charge.

By Saturday morning, August 21, we left Davenport on I-80. We crossed the cornfields and farmlands of Illinois and, on the south side of Chicago, entered the toll highway with its many lanes of traffic. We knew definitely that we were back in the Lower 48. We had encountered no toll roads in British Columbia, Yukon Territory, or Alaska and usually only two lanes of traffic on their highways. We continued into the northern part of Indiana on I-80 to the exit for Elkhart. That evening, we began a three-night stay at Elkhart Campground. Our mission was to get a cracked bracket and loose bolt fixed at the Mor-Ryde, Inc., facility. Unexpectedly, an air pump associated with the engine emission system failed as we parked in a shopping mall in Elkhart. This meant locating, purchasing, and installing a new one. We purchased two air pumps at $513.20, one for replacement and one spare.

On Tuesday, August 24, we visited the Holiday Rambler® customer service people in Wakarusa, Indiana, to discuss their thoughts on repairing the windshield with the ding, which had grown larger, and several minor items. That night we stayed at the Holiday Rambler Recreational Vehicle Club, Inc. (HRRVC), camping area in Wakarusa. As we were members of HRRVC, there was no campground fee.

When we left that area early on Wednesday morning, we returned to Elkhart. There, we stopped at McDonald Equipment, where a technician repaired a pinched wire in the starting circuit of our Onan auxiliary generator at no charge.

In less than an hour, we were on our way again, taking U.S. 31 south past Indianapolis to the Columbus Woods-n-Water Kampground. After dinner in the motorhome, we headed for Columbus to visit Paul's nephew, also named Paul; his wife, Donna; and their two children, Mark and Elyse Guyer. Paul worked for Electronic Data Systems as a systems software engineer at the Columbus Data Center. Donna's career was taking off at Cummins Engine Company as director of materials for the Fuel Systems Business. She had gone back to college and was close to earning a master of business administration degree.

They knew we were coming and gave us a warm reception. Before we went inside their new ranch-style home on that balmy evening, Mark, 10, performed difficult maneuvers as he rode his bicycle. Not to be outdone, eight-year-old Elyse asked us to watch as she agilely climbed high up into a shade tree and came down just as skillfully.

Inside the house, the children showed us their rooms, pointing out their "treasures." Near the end of our lively visit, Donna lit the candles on a birthday cake, turned out the electric lights, and we all sang the happy birthday ditty to Paul Guyer. It was a short but meaningful visit. We drove back to the campground in the dark.

We had made our last motorhome repair stop and our last visit with friends and relatives. Our travels had amazingly included all the visits and stops that we had hoped for. Thankfully, no emergencies occurred to cut short our trip. In a day or so, we'd be home.

· 29 ·

Reflections

WE FIGURED it was about 600 miles home from Columbus—too many miles for one day's travel, for us at least. We liked to be on the road, but not for long days of it and not too many days of driving in a row. We found it worked best for us to take a day or two off to "catch up" with ourselves. We had done that the two nights in Elkhart. Now we were ready for two more days of travel until we reached our home in Maryland.

When we left Woods-n-Water campground on Thursday, August 26, a little after eight o'clock, we took Route 46 to I-74 as it crossed Indiana and joined I-275, which circled north of Cincinnati and led us into I-71. After a rest stop near Kings Island, we continued on I-71 northeast, circled the south side of Columbus, Ohio, on I-270, and made an exit onto I-70 east across Ohio. After a rest stop in Ohio for lunch, we continued on I-70 to Wheeling, West Virginia, where we filled the gas tank. From Wheeling we drove on I-70 into the southwestern corner of Pennsylvania, connected with I-79, and then with I-68 near Morgantown, West Virginia.

Soon we found our way to Sand Springs Camping Area, a few miles from Exit 15 off I-68 where we had stayed before on another trip. Paul pulled the motorhome into a lovely, wooded, spacious site.

281

Hardly anyone else was parked on the grounds. It was an inspirational area, and I explored the campground roads, listening to birds, enjoying the woods, and being thankful for the safe travel on the roads of North America that brought us happily to that place.

Before leaving the Sand Springs Camping Area the next morning, I left a message for our son, Jeff, at his business office, saying that we expected to be home that day, but that we would have plenty to do and did not want to interfere with any anniversary plans that he and Nancy might have. (It was their fifth wedding anniversary.) Then it was back to I-68 and less than 200 miles home.

As we rode toward Sideling Mountain, I knew that I could not just ride past without stopping. It was the first stop that the Graybeals and we had made on our trip to Alaska three months earlier. Since it was also lunch time, Paul pulled into the parking area on our side of the highway, where I stepped outside into the warm sunshine. So many memories flooded my mind about our trip that it was impossible to identify them all. Since we were parked on the opposite side of the wide highway from the visitor center, I decided not to go back to see that again. I was content just to walk around outside and be in touch with the place where we had first stopped. We ate lunch and watched other travelers come and go.

Soon familiar scenes passed by. We stopped in Frederick, Maryland, for one last big gulp of gas for the motorhome. And then it was Walkersville, Woodsboro, Taneytown, and Westminster.

How strange to go up the hill to our house after being away so long. No bands played, no people shouted from the roadside—just as pioneers and gold seekers to Alaska went unheralded. Just the two of us returning in our own time at our own pace. Returning, then turning into our driveway, stopping. Paul turned off the engine. How quiet it was. I asked for the odometer reading. "56686," he announced. I wrote it in the travel log. And beside it, "Ar. HOME!!! Time—2:20. Driver—Paul. Weather—Sunny 90 degrees." Paul waited until I did the math. We had driven 14,506 miles during the three-month trip.

I turned in the passenger seat, stepped off the carpeted hump, picked up my white handbag and a bag of laundry, and headed for the house. Paul walked ahead to unlock the garage and house doors.

The sidewalk seemed so stationary. My body was still riding, even as my feet walked. We entered the house through the adjoining garage.

"Hi, House! Did you miss us? I see you took good care of yourself," I said as I walked down the hallway toward the dining room. On special occasions, I love to talk to the house when I'm leaving or coming back. It was just as I had left it, except for the natural accumulation of dust, not visible unless you ran a finger over the furniture.

I'm not sure when I started it, but sometime on the trip home, I began a to-do list of tasks for when we got home. That list was in my hand. It would keep me focused even as I dilly-dallied or reminisced about our travels at times. It would take away the confusion of trying to do everything first. First on my list was calling Jeff and Nancy and some friends to let them know we were home safely. Then would come other tasks.

This had been our longest trip yet in the almost six years we'd had the motorhome. Only time would tell where and when and for how long our next trip would be and whether it would be just the two of us or with a caravan. Even though I was apprehensive before the trip, with the fantastic experiences of that Alaskan adventure, I knew I could travel with an RV group again and have a wonderful time!

Epilogue

AND SO our Alaskan tour had ended, but the memories would brighten our thoughts forever. My initial questions had been answered. It was immensely satisfying to go as far north (Barrow) and west (Pacific Ocean) as I could go in the United States. We had already been to southern Florida and Texas and had splashed in the Atlantic Ocean at New Jersey, driven the coastal road of Nova Scotia, and crossed both Canada and the United States.

The tour itself was exceptional. Karen and Scott gave accurate and precise directions as wagonmasters. They worked as a team in preparing the way for us. Don and Laurie provided mechanical security as well as congeniality. Using suggestions from the wagonmasters, information from *The MILEPOST®*, or advice from another caravaner on the CB, we could decide as we went along where we wanted to stop and sightsee. Some days, we would stop at the same places as others in our group. Some days, other caravaners would pass us on the road; rarely did we pass them. Some days, we would not see the others until we rendezvoused at a sightseeing stop or a campground. Mostly, the Graybeals and we traveled by twos on the road, often with the Beelers behind or ahead and with the tailgunners within radio range behind us.

I discovered that I liked touring by caravan—the security of a tailgunner, the advance preparations of the wagonmaster, the camaraderie of the group, the opportunity to see and do more than one might on one's own, the reserved seats at shows, and the new friends.

We all returned safely to our homes. None of our RVs were ruined by the rough roads, although some, including ours, had dings in the windshield. Our insurance covered the cost of replacing the windshield at our local Holiday Rambler® service center. Although rough roads caused our vehicles to "bottom out" at places, we had safe travel.

As for fitting into the group, after our initial getting-acquainted period, I felt right at home with everybody, and I hope everyone felt that way about me. I did not grow weary at all from being with the

Epilogue

same group of people every day. They were sociable, friendly, and upbeat, which made it easy to talk with them.

Although there is always more to learn about a place, my recent education about Alaska had at least brought me up-to-date. It was indeed a massive territory with majestic mountains and great glaciers and endless miles of snowy tundra. But it also was green with lots of lakes. While it was true that its few villages and towns were scattered, it was not true that most people in them were Eskimos. People went to Alaska from all over the world—to make their fortunes and to get away from the hectic pace where they lived. I liked the Eskimos that I met in Barrow and felt an affinity for them as well as for the Athabascan Indians in Fairbanks.

Anchorage and Fairbanks *did* have high-rise buildings. The 1800s milieu existed in historic towns chiefly to attract tourists. Supermarkets had mostly replaced the old general stores—even in Barrow!

I saw for myself the Trans-Alaska pipeline running from Prudhoe Bay to Valdez, its installation in compliance with the Environmental Protection Agency requirements for preserving the soil and the wildlife. Prince William Sound had no oil slick on it.

As I had imagined, prices were generally high, seals played on ice floes and swam in the water, many Eskimos wore parkas and mukluks, extremely cold temperatures did exist in the winter in northern Alaska, the short summer did bring wildflowers and long daylight hours, the DEW line site remained in operation at Barrow, miners still worked their claims and panned for gold, Mount McKinley was indeed majestic, and I did sense the pioneer in people—the spirit of risk taking and helping one another.

Contrary to my initial picture, I learned that igloos existed only on the frozen ocean during whaling expeditions and not on land; dogsleds were often replaced by all-terrain vehicles; and Eskimos had cemeteries, which said to me that their older people who were ready to die no longer floated out to sea on an ice floe.

We were not attacked by grizzly or polar bears. We did not get marooned by a mud slide. Our good health held out for the 44-day tour and my sinusitis and Paul's sore throat were cured in a week or two because we had no trouble finding a doctor in British Columbia. We didn't miss any planned activity on the tour because of ill health. Traveling as we did in our RV was comfortable; one of us could rest en route while the other drove so that we did not get overly tired. In addition, when traveling with other RVers, there's a kind of unwritten code that you can decide to take a nap instead of visiting and everyone understands.

Although the Graybeals and we traveled together and often ate together at group events, we still related to the others in the group on bus rides, in restaurants, at shows, on boat rides, visiting museums, shopping, and at departure meetings. We all accepted one another regardless of the size or cost of anyone's RV. Smoking and drinking alcoholic beverages were no problem, because only one couple smoked, which they politely did away from group activities, and most of the group did not drink alcoholic beverages. We had no loud, boisterous, late-night drinkers in the group. We all felt friendly toward each other—even though we had no knowledge of anyone's status back home. We lived in the moment and that called for experiencing together as equals our adventure in Alaska.

We had no extravagant spenders of money. The only slight pressure I felt came when optional tours or shows were offered, but people made up their own minds and were mature enough to say no if they didn't want to go.

As for my concerns about Sunday worship when we were on the road and unable to go to church, after my conversation with Lib on Homer Spit, Paul and I had devotions at our dinette table together—reading scripture, talking about its meaning and application, and praying.

In due time, I totaled the logs.

EPILOGUE

ALASKA TRIP STATISTICS

Total cost of trip:	
Original tour package ($4,995 + 589 for ferry)	$5,584.00
Gasoline expense:	
(includes both U.S. and Canadian purchases adjusted for the exchange rate)	$2,421.45
Other expenses:	
shows, extra tours, shopping, repair parts, food, etc. (includes both U.S. and Canadian purchases adjusted for the exchange rate)	$6,748.74
	$14,754.19
Days en route:	92 days
Started on 5/28/93 at 7:39 A.M.	
Returned home on 8/27/93 at 2:20 P.M.	
Total mileage:	14,506.00
Total gallons of gasoline:	1,738.57
Miles per gallon of gasoline	8.34
Average price per gallon of gasoline in U.S	$1.22
Average price per gallon of gasoline in Canada ($.56 per liter; adjusted for exchange rate)	$2.56

When all was said and done, my original questions about how I would relate to the people, places, and the tour itself were answered affirmatively. My good feelings about the trip were further reinforced by the ready response to a round robin letter (circulated from person to person with each adding their own letter containing news or comments) started by Mary Jo Cornell after we all got home, and by the quick yeses given to John Graybeal when he later suggested and arranged a week's reunion of our Alaskan tour group. What a happy gathering that was! We continue the round robin letter, the reunions, and sending holiday greetings. Some of our group, who didn't know each other before the Alaskan tour, now vacation together. Best of all, the friendship network of each of us has spread—all because we were RVers and took an RV caravan tour.

Until we meet again, by the written page or by your travels on the road, perhaps by RV caravan, I wish you the best of times.

Appendix

Is It a Rally or a Caravan Tour?

What's the difference between a rally and a caravan tour? Many RV clubs offer both activities. Rallies are gatherings in one location for the purpose of learning, socializing, and having a vacation. You travel to that location and park your RV for several days or more. During that time, your host club offers food, entertainment, and education. The club may offer optional bus tours of the surrounding area after which you usually return at night to your own RV at the rally location.

A caravan tour is designed by an RV club or a commercial caravan tour company to explore a selected area of the world. The host organization provides leaders, plans the itinerary, and makes advance group reservations for campgrounds, meals, cruises, and shows for a fee payable in advance. Caravan tours may run from a few weeks to a few months. Caravaners usually travel in their own RVs, using buses, ferries, airplanes, and trains as appropriate auxiliary transportation. When on the road, caravaners travel in groups of two or three rather than as a convoy.

Who Offers RV Caravan Tours?

As of press time, the following groups were offering tours to the places indicated. You may enjoy looking in your local library or bookstore for books and magazine articles and advertisements on the subject of RV Caravan Tours. Or as an RV owner, you may want to inquire at the headquarters of your brand-name vehicle club or other RV association.

Clubs and Associations

National camping clubs and recreational vehicle owner associations represent RVers by getting them together for national and regional rallies and conventions, educating them, and keeping them current with maintenance and other information. Many of them also offer RV caravan tours. Listed below are some of these groups.

The Escapees RV Club offers such educational and support services as a magazine, rallies, educational gatherings, a blood bank program, economical places to park, and Continuing Assistance for Retired Escapees (CARE), which allows members to continue living in their own RVs while receiving the assistance they need to remain independent. While Escapees does not sponsor or conduct RV tours or caravans, it publishes classified ads in its bimonthly magazine, *Escapees for the Serious RVer,* from independent businesses that provide caravan tours.

Escapees, Inc.
100 Rainbow Drive
Livingston, Texas 77351
(888) 757-2582
(409) 327-8873
Fax (409) 327-4388
Web site: http://www.escapees.com

Family Campers & RVers (FCRV) is a not-for-profit, member-owned, recreational camping organization with some 20,000 members. Formerly known as the National Campers & Hikers Association, it offers a wide range of educational, service, and recreational programs as well as "Travalongs" for its members who like to travel to new places with fellow members.

Family Campers & RVers
4804 Transit Road, Building 2
Depew, New York 14043
(800) 245-9755
Phone/Fax (716) 668-6242

Family Motor Coach Association, which is for motorhome owners only, itself does not offer RV caravan tours but does work with caravan tour companies who offer FMCA members special tours that are tied in with FMCA conventions and other special FMCA events. It also has ads for caravan tours in its magazine *Family Motor Coaching*.

Family Motor Coach Association (FMCA)
8291 Clough Pike
Cincinnati, OH 45244
(513) 474-3622
(800) 543-3622

The Good Sam Club, with a membership of approximately 1 million RV owners, offers RV caravan tours called "Caraventures" to Canada, Alaska, Baja California (Mexico), and Nova Scotia.

The Good Sam Club
2575 Vista Del Mar Drive
Ventura, CA 93001-3920
(805) 667-4100
(800) 234-3450

APPENDIX

Loners on Wheels, an RV organization composed of nearly 3,000 single campers, does not sponsor, underwrite, or organize tours and caravans. They do, however, offer their members who organize such events the opportunity to announce them in their newsletters. A recent newsletter offered its members a caravan and river boating tour in Northwest Canada and two different caravan tours to Mexico.

Loners on Wheels, Inc.
P.O. Box 1355
Poplar Bluff, MO 63902
Fax (573) 686-9342

The National Recreational Vehicle Owners Club (NRVOC), the International Family Recreation Association (IFRA), and Van Conversion Owners International (VCOI) offer a wide variety of caravan tours, rallies, and "Funfest Events" to their members. In addition to events and activities for members, they also allow members to invite their friends who are nonmembers to events described as a "Buddy Event." They offer a variety of events and activities to accommodate the various methods of recreational and leisure travel—car, bus, RV, tent camper, and van conversion. Their caravan tours include a trained trail host.

The National Recreational Vehicle Owners Club
P.O. Box 520
Gonzalez, Florida 32560-0520
(904) 477-7992
(904) 479-8393
Fax (904) 479-8393
E-mail: nrvockws@spydee.net

RVing Women, Inc., is an organization for women who are recreational vehicle enthusiasts whether or not they own an RV. Their purpose is to inform, support, and network among members in order to expand their horizons, seek new adventures, and try new experiences. In addition to other benefits such as classes and seminars on the care and maintenance of RVs, they offer rallies, special events, and caravan tours to such places as the Oregon coast and Alaska. They may be reached at the following address:

RVing Women, Inc.
P.O. Box 1940
Apache Junction, AZ 85217
(888) 557-8464
(602) 983-4678

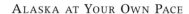

Fax (602) 982-6125
Web site: http://www.RVingWomen.com
E-mail: RVingWomen@Juno.com

S*M*A*R*T stands for Special Military Active Retired Travel Club, Inc., with membership presently limited to retirees and active-duty personnel from the United States and Canada and associate membership for widows and widowers of persons eligible for membership. Its objectives are to provide comradeship, seminars, and workshops on RVing; assist military installations in improving and expanding their campgrounds, sponsoring annual musters (rallies), and social and recreational activities, including RV caravan tours to such areas as the Northwest, the Calgary Stampede, Australia/New Zealand, the British Isles, Baja California, the Copper Canyon, and others.

S*M*A*R*T
Special Military Active Retired Travel Club, Inc.
600 University Office Blvd., Suite 1A
Pensacola, FL 32504
(904) 478-1986
(800) 354-7681

The Wandering Individuals' Network, Inc. (WIN), is an organization for single RVers. Members must be under 70 at the time of joining, but may remain as long as they wish. WIN members may host gatherings or lead caravans anywhere and anytime they wish after giving three months' notice to the newsletter editor who gets the word out. WIN recently added four- to six-month caravans called "Circuits" that provide members an opportunity to travel at a reasonable cost through designated regions such as the Rocky Mountains with stayovers of varying lengths of time en route.

Wandering Individuals Network, Inc.
P.O. Box 2010
Sparks, NV 89432-2010

Caravan Tour Operators

You may want to obtain information from commercial companies such as the following that offer RV tours. The places shown in parentheses are not meant to be a complete listing, only an indication of the tours offered by the company. Indeed, the tour destinations often change from year to year.

A Adventure RV Tours (Mexico and Panama)
(800) 455-8687

APPENDIX

Adventure Caravans (Mexico, Alaska, Canada)
(800) 872-7897

Adventure World RV Tours
The Seachest
Broad Park, Oreston Plymouth PL9 7QF
United Kingdom

All About Travel (Provides rental motorhomes for caravan tours of Alaska)
Post Office Box F
6040-A Lake Isabella Boulevard
Lake Isabella, CA 93240
(800) 882-5652
(760) 379-5661
Fax: (760) 379-4239
E-mail: allabouttravel@lightspeed.net
Web site: http://www.bosonline.com/~allabouttravel/

Caravanas Voyagers® (Mexico)
1155 Larry Mahan Street, Suite H
El Paso, TX 79925
(800) 933-9332

Carefree Caravans (Texas, Southern United States, New England, the Great West, Alaska)
(800) 698-9390

Carnival RV Caravans (Mexico, Calgary Stampede)
(800) 556-5652

Creative World Rallies and Caravans (Cajun Country, Michigan lakes area, Canada, Cheyenne frontier, Alaska, Australia/New Zealand, New England, a circle that includes Las Vegas, Grand Canyon [north Rim], Bryce Canyon, and Mesa Verde)
4005 Toulouse Street
New Orleans, LA 70119
(504) 486-7259
(800) 732-8337
E-mail: info@Rv-fun.com
Web site: http://www.rv-fun.com

El Dorado Tours, Inc.
RV Caravan Tours
P.O. Box 1145
Alma, AR 72921
(800) 852-2500
(501) 632-6282
Fax (501) 632-4968
E-mail: meikle@concentric.net
Web Site: http://www.cris.com/~meikle/

Fantasy Caravans to Mexico (Mexico, Alaska, Canada)
(800) 952-8496

Overseas Motorhome Tours, Inc. ("Tulips and Alps"—Holland, Belgium, Austria, Germany, Liechtenstein, Switzerland; "Viking Trails"—Denmark, Sweden, Norway, Finland, Germany; "Alpine Heights"—Switzerland, Germany, Austria, Liechtenstein, Italy, France; "Romantic Italy and France"—Italy, France, Germany, Austria, Monaco)
222 K South Irena Street
Redondo Beach, California 90277
(800) 322-2127
Fax (310) 543-2590
E-mail: omtusa@earthlink.net
Web site: http://www.omtinc.com

Pan American Motor Tours (Mexico)
511 Wilbur Avenue, Unit 4
Antioch, CA 94509-2186
(510) 778-8874
Fax (510) 778-9674
E-mail: info@panamtours.com

Penasco RV Club (Northern Mexico)
(800) 850-9248
Web site: http://www.penascorvclub.com/

Point South RV Tours (Alaska, Canada, Mexico, and Panama)
(800) 421-1394

APPENDIX

Reli Custom RV Tours (Australia/New Zealand)
(800) 409-7354
Web site: http://www.daylanns.com/reli/

Tracks to Adventure (Copper Canyon, Alaska, Canada, New Zealand/Australia, the Civil War area, national parks and monuments in Colorado, Arizona, Utah, and Wyoming; "Pilgrims to Patriots" in northeastern United States, Lighthouse and Shipwreck tour on East Coast of United States, the Smoky Mountains, and the Oregon Trail)
2811 Jackson, Suite K
El Paso, TX 79930
(800) 351-6053
(915) 565-9627
Web site: http://www.trackstoadventure.com/

Woodall's World of Travel Tours (Alaska; Calgary Stampede; Nova Scotia; national parks; "Canadian Sunsets"—Ottawa, Montreal, St. Lawrence Seaway, Gaspe Peninsula, Quebec, New Brunswick shoreline, and Prince Edward Island; Cheyenne Rodeo; New York City; "North Woods"—Michigan and Wisconsin, and Mackinac Island; and "New England Fall Colors"—New York, Vermont, New Hampshire, Maine, Massachusetts, and Connecticut)
6756 S. Greenville Road
P.O. Box 247
Greenville, MI 48838
(616) 754-2251
(800) 346-7572
Web site: www.woodalls.com

Brand Name Clubs That Offer RV Caravan Tours

Many brand name clubs offer RV caravan tours. A sampling of these is listed below.

Holiday Rambler RV Club (HRRVC) offers its members, owners of Holiday Rambler® vehicles, caravan tours to such places as the Cajun country; "Mississippi River Road" from Greenville, Mississippi up to St. Louis, Missouri to Hannibal, Missouri; "Canyonlands" in western United States; Great Smoky Mountains; New England; Indian Nations of Oklahoma to Pueblo, Colorado; Big Sky Country; Alaska; Western Canada; Eastern Canada; Newfoundland, Labrador; and several locations in Europe. For more information, contact the following address:

295

Holiday Rambler RV Club
P.O. Box 587
Wakarusa, IN 46573
(219) 862-7330
Fax (219) 862-7390
E-mail: holidayclub@star-link.net

Jayco Jafari International Travel Club develops and operates rallies and caravans that are exclusive to Jayco Jafari Club members.

Jayco Jafari International Travel Club
P.O. Box 192
Osceola, IN 46561-0192

Newmar Kountry Klub for owners of Newmar recreational vehicles provides fun rallies, special events, and caravans to many places in North America. The address is as follows:

Newmar Kountry Klub
P.O. Box 30
Nappanee, IN 46550-0030
(219) 773-7791
E-mail: newmarklub@aol.com

The Wally Byam Caravan Club International, Inc. (WBCCI) is for owners of Airstream Company recreational vehicles. It offers caravans to Mexico, Canada, Alaska, and even overseas to such places as Australia, Great Britain, Germany, and Finland among others. Its caravans are staffed and led by club members who are trained volunteers and who have traveled extensively. This enables travelers to see more and spend less than on other caravans. When traveling to foreign destinations, the caravaners usually rent local recreational vehicles. The WBCCI address follows:

Wally Byam Caravan Club International, Inc.
803 E. Pike Street
P.O. Box 612
Jackson Center, OH 45334-0612
(937) 596-5211
Fax (937) 596-5542

Winnebago-Itasca Travelers (WIT) offers many exciting caravan tours. A participant must be a member of WIT and arrive in a Winnebago Industries product.

Winnebago-Itasca Travelers
P.O. Box 268
Forest City, IA 50436-0268
(515) 582-6874
(800) 643-4892
Fax (515) 582-6703

Publications

The following are guidebooks for overseas travel:

Real Exploring—British Isles
Real Exploring—France
Cimino Publishing Group Incorporated
P.O. Box 174
Carle Place, New York 11514
(516) 997-3721

Exploring Europe by RV by Dennis and Tina Jaffe
The Globe Pequot Press, Inc.
P.O. Box 833
Old Saybrook, CT 06475-0833
(203) 395-0440
Fax (203) 395-1418

The following periodicals are some that list RV caravan tours in their classified sections:

Escapees: For the Serious RVer
100 Rainbow Drive
Livingston, Texas 77351
(888) 757-2582
(409) 327-8873
Fax (409) 327-4388
http://www.escapees.com

Highways
Motorhome
TL Enterprises, Inc.
2575 Vista Del Mar Drive
Ventura, CA 93001-2575
(805) 667-4100
(800) 234-3450

Alaska at Your Own Pace

Questions for Caravaners

The following are questions that you may want to ask before you sign up for a caravan tour:

- What kind of insurance do I need on my RV?
- How much will the basic tour cost?
- What are the optional activities and what is their overall approximate cost?
- What costs does the tour *not* include?
- Does the tour operator offer trip cancellation insurance?
- What happens if I sign up and cannot go at the last minute?
- What happens if the people on the tour do not relate well with one another?
- Do we get to meet the other people on the tour ahead of time or know who they are?
- What happens if my RV breaks down and can't be repaired?
- What happens if I have to leave the tour before it is over and return home?
- Will there be time in the schedule and places for me to get my hair (or nails) done each week?
- What are the roads or highways like?
- We would like to go to _____; is this an option on the tour?
- Will we get a detailed itinerary before we leave home to go on the tour?
- How much film should I bring along?
- Will the tour information packet have a checklist of what clothes to take and what things to do before leaving, such as checking with our medical insurance provider on how to handle illness on the road?
- Where and when do we meet for the beginning of the tour?
- When do we need to make the initial deposit and final payment?
- May I bring my pet along?
- Where may I receive mail en route?
- Do I need to do anything in particular to protect my RV from road conditions?
- May I bring a tow car with my motorhome?
- If we will be on a ferry with our RV overnight, what do we need for staying in the ferry boat cabin?
- Are the wagonmasters and tailgunners competent and experienced?
- Will the tour operator provide three names and telephone numbers of references?
- How will we know where to go each day?
- How many meals will be provided? What are they? Will there be potlucks? (The answer determines what food I need to have on board the RV.)
- Will we do any boondocking (dry camping)? If so, how often and when?
- Do I have protection against price increases?

APPENDIX

Preparing to Travel

Your caravan tour company will normally inform you of requirements for travel in the area where you will be going. In addition, organizations such as Family Motor Coach Association provide rather detailed checklists for RVers about to start out on a big trip for the season.

The following are the checklists that Paul and I use before starting on a long journey. They developed from the original checklist that I made when our motorhome was brand new and we were deciding what to keep on board. The checklists—one for Paul and one for me—therefore include what we normally try to keep in stock in the motorhome as well as reminders of what relevant items to take along on each excursion. Paul and I each scan our lists before heading out. They may seem like long lists, but eventually you will be able to scan parts of it quickly because you know that a listed item is already on board or that you have done a particular detail. Using the checklists gives us the satisfaction of knowing that when we pull out of the driveway we have on board what we will need (or else know what we want to get along the way) and that our affairs at home are handled.

Motorhome Checklist—Bernice

Kitchen and Dining Area Supplies and Equipment

Place settings for eight - microwavable, nonbreakable dishes
Silverware for four
Acrylic tumblers
Plastic knives, forks, spoons
Plastic cereal bowls
Paper plates
Paper cups
Paper napkins
Placemats for eight
Tablecloth and seat covers for picnic table
Paper towels (two rolls for kitchen; one roll for windshield)
Bottle opener
Spatula
Butcher knife
Paring knife
Serrated-edge knife
Sieve spoon
Measuring spoons
Measuring cups
Ice cream dipper
Dishcloth

Tea towels (four)
Hand towels, turkish (four)
Cleansing/scouring powder
Dishwashing liquid
Liquid hand soap
Laundry detergent
Spot-and-stain remover
Fabric softener sheets
Quart plastic pitcher
Electric can opener
Windowpane cleaning liquid spray
Waxed paper (one roll)
Plastic wrap (one roll)
Aluminum foil - one roll
Sandwich plastic bags
Freezer plastic bags
Trash bags to line wastebasket
Clothespins (twelve)
Clothesline
Matches
Candles for light
Candles for birthday cakes
Plastic water bucket (one- or two-gallon size)
Plastic wash basin
Steel wool pads
Plastic scrubber for removing dried-on foods from cookware
Hot mats (four)
Oven mitts (two)
Fly swatter
Tape measure
Pen flashlight
Wastebasket
Pens
Pencil with eraser
Eraser
Pencil sharpener (hand-held)
Memo pad for writing grocery lists
Scissors
Needle
Thimble
Sewing thread

APPENDIX

Bathroom Supplies and Equipment
Prescription medicines
Bathroom tissue
Chemical to deodorize holding tank
Baking soda for toilet (alternative for chemical above)
Toilet-bowl brush
Facial tissues (at least three boxes—one each for bath, bedroom, passenger seat)
Headache tablets
Antiseptic
Self-stick bandages
Cough drops
Upset stomach liquid or tablets
Calcium tablets
Enema preparation
Fever thermometer
Bath powder
Moleskin
Cotton tips
Petroleum jelly
Lip balm
Rubbing alcohol
Shampoo
Hair dryer (electric)
Extension cord
Insect repellent
Toothbrush
Toothpaste
Dental floss
Razor
Shaving cream
Aftershave lotion
Hair pick
Comb
Spring clips for hair (four)
Shower cap
Deodorant
Moisturizing cream
Foundation liquid
Rouge
Makeup brushes

Lipstick
Hair spray
Nail clippers
Nail file
Nail polish
Nail polish remover
Magnifying mirror
Tweezers
Nail scissors
Wash cloths (four)
Hand towels (four)
Body towels (four)

Bedroom Supplies and Equipment
Pillows (two)
Sheets (two queen size)
Thermal blanket (one queen size)
Thermal bedspread (one queen size)
Mattress cover (one queen size)
Goose-down comforter (store in overhead cabinet until needed)
Bible
Dictionary
Resource books for hobbies such as writing, crafts

Wardrobe Accessories and Equipment
Hangers in each closet (four)
Hats
Lightweight boots that go over shoes
Winter boots
Umbrellas
Bathrobe
Laundry bag

Where we are going determines what other clothes we take, such as blouses, shirts, pants, skirts, coats, jackets, sweaters, shorts, vests, and shoes. I always take a raincoat and plastic rain cap. We add from our house wardrobe the everyday items such as underwear, socks, hose, shoes, pajamas, bedroom slippers, and jewelry.

Handbag Items

I use a handbag large enough to hold my camera if necessary and add the following:

House keys
Motorhome keys

APPENDIX

Car keys
Credit card (as few as possible—carrying only one is recommend by safety experts)
Plastic rain cap
Hair care instructions for hairstylists en route
Wallet with driver's license

Living Room Supplies and Equipment
Sofa pillows (two)
Afghan
Stationery
Tablets of lined paper
Games (playing cards and others)
Magazines
Home telephone directory
Address book
Stamps (for both first class letters and postcards)
Broom for sweeping scatter rug and awning outside
Whisk broom
Journal
Trip log chart
Files from the house as relevant
Laptop computer
Printer that works with computer
Paper and envelopes for printer

Driving Area Supplies and Equipment
Sunglasses
Calculator
Audio cassette tapes
Cellular telephone
Binoculars
Map of each state we'll be going through
Atlas
Campground directory (to locate campgrounds)
Reservation confirmations or information
Tour books
Magnifying glass
Proof of vehicle insurance

To Do Before Leaving Home

Turn on refrigerator a few days before leaving to be sure it works, to begin freezing ice cubes, and to load frozen foods.

Load electric toaster if we're going on a long journey and we think we'll want toasted bread.

Leave license plate number of RV with appropriate person.

Leave telephone numbers and addresses of stops en route with appropriate person.

Leave obituary file (in obvious place and be sure appropriate person has a house key and knows location of important papers). The obituary file contains our instructions in the event of death.

Make arrangements for mail - (1) Use mail forwarding service or (2) ask appropriate person to handle mail while you are away or (3) arrange with post office to forward or hold mail.

Get maps and tour books as needed and place in passenger seat area.

Call neighbors on either side of house and perhaps across the street to let them know your departure and return dates. Also notify police of these dates.

Get groceries or load RV from what you have on hand. We usually follow our normal eating patterns when on the road: (1) breakfast consists of cereal, fruit, and skim milk; (2) lunch consists of a sandwich, fruit, and dessert; and (3) dinner of a meat, two vegetables, fruit, bread, and dessert. For snacks on the road, we choose pretzels and graham crackers. The following is our typical grocery list:

    Milk
    Bananas
    Cereal
    Peanut butter
    Canned fruit
    Canned soups
    Jelly
    Canned beef stew
    Canned spaghetti and meatballs
    Canned vegetables (small cans)
    Puddings in individual servings
    Cranberry juice
    Sodas in individual bottles with screw caps
    Graham crackers
    Soda crackers
    Frozen dinners
    Frozen meats

Ice cream
Bread or rolls
Margarine or butter
Vegetable oil cooking spray
Salt (can keep on board)
Sugar (can keep on board)
Flour
Eggs
Coffee for guests
Granola bars
Individual cakes or cookies

Motorhome Checklist—Paul

Bathroom Supplies and Equipment
Toothbrush
Toothpaste
Razor
Shaving cream
Aftershave lotion
Comb
Prescription medicines

Wardrobe Accessories and Equipment
Bathrobe
Coveralls
Yellow slicker
Baseball caps
Short-sleeved shirts
Long-sleeved shirts
Jeans
Sport trousers
Sport shorts
Sweaters
Tee-shirts
Shorts
Swim trunks
Socks
Handkerchiefs
Belts
Shoes
Hiking boots

Driving Area Supplies and Equipment
House keys
Motorhome keys
Credit and debit cards
Senior and campground discount cards
Registration card for motorhome
Flashlight
Sunglasses
Swiss army knife

Living Room Area
Files from house you want to take along
Magazines from house you want to take along

Outside Storage Supplies and Equipment
Folding lawn chairs (two)
Mud rug for outside entrance steps to motorhome
Antifreeze for water system
Applicable tools such as
    screwdrivers
    pliers
    socket wrenches
    adjustable wrenches
    ignition wrenches
    Tire-changing equipment
    Electrical repair equipment
    Spare belts
    Spare coolant
    Spare fuses
    Spare hoses
    Spare in-line gasoline filter

To Do Before Leaving Home
Check on gasoline for motorhome and tow car—fill tanks as needed
Check on propane gas
Obtain supply of oil for motorhome engine
Obtain supply of oil for tow car engine
Stop newspaper
Get cash in $20 bills
Make sure funds are in account for debit card
Pay ahead the following:
    house and car insurance
    gasoline service bill

- gas and electric bill
- telephone bill
- fuel oil bill

Lubricate chassis
Change oil and oil filter of motorhome engine and refill, if necessary
Change transmission oil and filter and refill, if necessary
Check auxiliary generator to be sure it operates and check oil level and change as noted in manual
Check front wheel bearings and brake pads
Check radiator
Check furnace to be sure it works properly
Check water heater to be sure it works properly
Check tires (spare also)
Check all lights outside and inside to be sure they work
Check batteries
Take along any additional specialty tools that might be needed
Take along books and literature that may be needed for maintenance or repair
Check power-steering fluid
Check brake fluid
If going to another country, follow instructions of tour company
Get proof of vehicle coverage from RV insurance provider

ALASKA AT YOUR OWN PACE

Itinerary for Our Alaska Trip

During the first two weeks, we traveled with our friends the Graybeals from our homes in central Maryland to Vancouver, British Columbia. That part of the three-month journey took us through the states of West Virginia, Pennsylvania, Ohio, Indiana, Illinois, Wisconsin, Minnesota, North Dakota, Montana, Idaho, and Washington.

For our 44-day trip our evening destinations were as follows:

Day 1	Cache Creek RV Park & Campgrounds, British Columbia
Day 2	Barkerville
Day 3	Prince George
Days 4 and 5	Dawson Creek
Day 6	Fort Nelson
Days 7 and 8	Muncho Lake
Day 9	Watson Lake, Yukon Territory
Days 10, 11, and 12	Whitehorse
Day 13	Moose Creek Provincial Campground
Days 14 and 15	Dawson City
Day 16	Tok, Alaska
Day 17	Fairbanks
Day 18	Barrow
Day 19	Fairbanks
Days 20 and 21	Healy
Days 22, 23, and 24	Anchorage
Days 25 and 26	Kenai
Days 27 and 28	Homer Spit
Days 29, 30, and 31	Seward
Day 32	Palmer
Days 33, 34, and 35	Valdez
Day 36	Tok
Day 37	Kluane Lake, Yukon Territory
Days 38, 39, and 40	Skagway, Alaska
Days 41 and 42	Alaska Marine Highway ferry
Day 43	Smithers, British Columbia
Day 44	Prince George, British Columbia

The return route took us down the west coast of British Columbia, Washington, Oregon, and California then inland through Nevada, Utah, Wyoming, Colorado, Kansas, Missouri, Iowa, Illinois, Indiana, Ohio, Pennsylvania, West Virginia, and home to north-central Maryland.

Glossary

Black water. Waste (sewage) from the toilet that is flushed into a black water holding tank, usually located beneath the main floor of the RV.

Boondocking. Camping in an RV without benefit of electricity, freshwater, and sewer utilities. Boondockers should follow the rules of courtesy and the local laws about where to camp. The term came originally from people who parked (or docked) out in the "boonies" (boondocks—remote rural areas, back country, backwoods, sticks) where there were no hookups or other luxuries such as swimming pools.

Cabover. That part of the RV's body that extends over the cab and is used for a bedroom or storage. This RV is known as a Type C or Class C motorhome.

Campfire. A gathering around an outdoor fire for warmth, to enjoy roasting or toasting food, and for sociability.

Campground. A place to camp usually with designated sites for RVs or tents. A campground may be private or public and usually has a user fee. It also usually has a host, manager, or owner who administers the policies or rules of the campground.

Campground directory. A listing of available campgrounds with descriptions of facilities available and directions to find them.

Campground association. An organization of independent campground owners or of campground chains.

Camping club. An organization established for certain benefits related to RVing for its members. Some camping clubs are for people with a variety of RVs, some are for owners of specific brands of RVs.

Camping group. A group of RVers who get together for camping weekends or trips and social events on an informal basis, with a volunteer wagonmaster who makes reservations for campgrounds, collects deposits, and arranges social events.

Campouts. A group camping together at a specific location.

Caravan tour. A group of travelers using a specific mode of transportation such as RVs to explore a selected area of the country. Caravan tours may run from ten days to two months and are hosted by a tour company that usually provides a wagonmaster.

Checklist. A list of items or tasks used by RVers to be sure they have all items necessary on board and have completed necessary tasks.

Coach. Another name for a motorhome.

Convention. A gathering of the members of a trade, campground owners, or camping club, usually held annually to discuss and take action on matters of common concern. Often educational seminars and entertainment are included.

Conversion vehicle. A vehicle such as a van, truck, or sport-utility vehicle, manufactured by an automaker and then modified by a company that specializes in customizing vehicles. The modifications may include sofas, windows, carpeting, paneling, seats, and accessories.

Docking. Parking an RV at a place for overnight or longer.

Dropoff. A very steep descent alongside a road or highway.

Dry camping. Another name for boondocking. See Boondocking.

Dumping. To empty out, as in draining the holding tanks of an RV. Dumping is accomplished by removing the outlet safety cap and attaching a flexible hose to the outlet located on the RV holding tanks, inserting the opposite end of the flexible hose into a dumping station inlet pipe, usually located in a concrete station opening. See Holding tanks.

Dump station. Usually a concrete pad with an inlet opening connected to an underground sewage system at a campground or other facility offering dumping service to RV travelers.

Fifth-wheel trailer. Similar to a travel trailer except that its construction lends itself to a bi-level floor plan. It is normally pulled by a pickup truck–style vehicle equipped with a fifth-wheel hitch fastened to the bed of a truck.

Folding camping trailer. A camping unit on wheels with collapsible walls that fold inward so that it can be towed by a car, van, or truck. Also known as a pop-up.

Freshwater. Water suitable for human consumption.

Full-timing. Living in one's RV all year long. These RVers are known as full-timers.

Galley. The kitchen of an RV.

Gray water. Used water that drains from the kitchen and bathroom sinks and the shower into a holding tank, called a gray water holding tank, that is located under the main floor of the RV.

GCVW. Gross combined vehicle weight, a figure such as 19,000 pounds that is the maximum weight allowed for a fully loaded RV, including cargo, fluids, passengers, and towed vehicle.

Holding tanks. Tanks located on the RV, normally on the underside, that store freshwater, gray water, and black water. See Freshwater, Black water, and Gray water.

Hooking up. Connecting the RV to a supply of electricity and water and to the sewer receptacle at a campground or other site.

KOA. Kampgrounds of America, a franchise chain of RV parks in North America that offers camping facilities to vacationers and overnighters.

APPENDIX

Long-term visitor area (LTVAs). Places in the United States, particularly in Arizona and California, under the administration of the Bureau of Land Management for the United States Department of the Interior that offer camping free or at low charge for up to six months.

LP gas. See Propane.

Membership parks. Profit-making organizations of affiliated RV parks that provide their members camping sites after the member has paid a membership fee and annual dues or maintenance charges.

Marine highway ferry. A boat or ship that sails on a waterway and transports cargo and passengers.

Mobile home. A large house trailer designed to stay in one place that can only be moved by the proper towing vehicle. Usually 10 or 12 feet in width. It is not to be confused with a motorhome.

Monitor panel. A panel usually with lights and switches for checking the battery charge, space in waste tanks, LP gas, amount of freshwater in that tank, water pump operation, and other systems.

Motorhome. A self-propelled vehicle on wheels that serves as both transportation and home. It is built on a specially designed chassis and includes holding tanks and electrical, water, and sewage hookup connections. It provides complete living facilities. There are three types or classes of motorhomes: Type A or Class A looks similar to a bus, Type B or Class B is a van camper, and Type C or Class C is known as a cabover.

Park. Another name for a campground. See Campground. Also, an area of land set aside by a city, state, or nation, usually in its mostly natural state, equipped with facilities for rest and recreation for the public to enjoy.

Parking. Locating an RV in a site at a campground or other similar facility. See Docking.

Park-model trailer. A spin-off of a recreational vehicle and a mobile home. It is a maximum of 8-feet wide and 40 feet long, which is within the towability limits for an RV and may be parked in an RV park. Park-models have many options that movable RVs do not, such as regular appliances and furniture instead of built-ins. People who winter in one place other than their home location often opt for a park-model for their temporary living quarters.

Potluck. A group meal to which participants bring various foods to be shared.

Propane. Also known as LP gas. A colorless, flammable, liquefied, petroleum gas that provides fuel to the furnace, refrigerator, water heater, and stovetop range in RVs. Most campgrounds offer this product. Although our LP gas tank holds 21.8 gallons, it is never filled more than

311

80 percent because the liquefied gas requires space to vaporize before leaving the tank.

Pull-through or pull-through site. These sites allow the driver of an RV to pull into the space, hook up, camp, and depart by simply pulling ahead onto a campground road, rather than having to back into a space or site. Sometimes they are called drive-throughs.

Rally. A coming together of many members of a club or organization for a common effort or action. It is usually of shorter duration than a convention.

RV or recreational vehicle. A vehicle used for recreational purposes, such as camping, and usually equipped with living facilities. An RV can be a motorhome, fifth-wheel travel trailer, travel trailer, folding camping trailer, truck camper, or conversion vehicle.

Resort. A place where people go to relax, rest, and enjoy recreation facilities. A camping resort usually has more than the usual campground amenities, such as whirlpools, golf courses, craft rooms, planned social events, tennis courts, and others.

Rig. Another name for a recreational vehicle.

RV trade association. An organization of the manufacturers, dealers, and renters of RVs whose purpose is to promote high industry standards and to provide education to the public and to its members.

RV show. An exhibition of recreation vehicles and associated products, usually held in a large building, but sometimes held outdoors, during a long weekend or on two consecutive weekends for the purpose of education, display, and sales. Attending an RV show is an enjoyable way to learn about RVs. They are held in most major cities.

Self-contained. An RV that has holding tanks for the gray water (bath and dish water) and for the black water (sewage).

Slide-out. A portion of an RV that can be extended from the main body in order to create larger interior space. During travel on the road it is kept within the main outside dimensions of the RV.

Snowbirds. A term applied to RVers who travel seasonally to find good weather, often spending months in one campground or resort. The name applies to people leaving hot summer temperatures in the south for northern cooler ones as well as to people leaving cold winter temperatures in the north for balmy ones in the south. Some people prefer the term "winter tourists" instead.

Tailgunner. A person designated to assist mainly with mechanical problems of RVs during a caravan tour.

Tow car. A vehicle such as an automobile, van, or pickup truck that either pulls or is pulled by an RV. Motorhomes often pull small cars or trucks behind them for use for short errands or sightseeing in cities.

Travel trailer. A hard-sided unit on wheels towed by an automobile, van, or truck that usually contains living quarters. It is hitched to the towing vehicle.

Truck camper. A hard-sided portable unit of living quarters designed to be mounted on the bed or chassis of a pickup truck.

Unhooking. Disconnecting the electric cord from the campground outlet and storing the cord in its compartment in the RV, disconnecting the water hose from the campground faucet and storing the hose in its compartment in the RV, and disconnecting and stowing the black water hose. See Dumping.

Unit. Another name for a recreational vehicle.

Van camper. A panel-type vehicle that includes at least two of the following conveniences: kitchen, sleeping, and toilet facilities. The RV manufacturer of this vehicle must also include 120-volt hookup and city water hookup connections, and freshwater storage. This type of RV is known as a Type B or Class B motorhome.

Wagonmaster. A leader, either hired or chosen, who guides a caravan of recreational vehicles on a trip. The wagonmaster usually makes advance reservations for campgrounds, shows, cruises, sightseeing, and group meals.

Index

addresses
   caravan tour operators, 292–295
   clubs/associations, 289–297
   publications, 297
Alaska Highway, 46, 65
Alaskaland, 135
Alaska Marine Highway ferry, 241–247
   additional fees for, 7
Alaskan trip statistics, 287
Alcan Highway. *See* Alaska Highway
Alyeska Terminus, 215
Anchorage, 179–181
Arctic Ocean, 146–147
associations, list of camping and recreational vehicle, 289–297
Athabascan Indians, 164–165
auxiliary generators, 62, 204

Barkerville, 59–60, 63–64
Barrow, 4, 136–161
bathroom equipment checklist, 301–302, 305
bedroom equipment checklist, 302
black water, dumping, 57, 105–106
blanket toss, 151
boondocking, 62. *See also* dry camping; wilderness camping
border crossing, 124
bottoming out, 228
brand name clubs for caravan tours, list of, 295–297
Butcher, Susan, 164

caravan tour operators, list of, 292–297
caravan tours. *See* RV caravan tours
CB radio, communicating with, 22
checklists, 8, 299–307
Chicken, 129

clubs, list of camping and recreational vehicle, 289–295
clubs for caravan tours, list of, 295–297
Columbia Glacier, 213
Cook, James, 182
costs
   additional fees, 5, 7
   base price of Alaska tour, 3
   breakdown of Alaska trip, 287
crossing the border, 124
customs, 124

Dawson, George Mercer, 70
Dawson City, 120–123
Dawson Creek, 70–71
Denali National Park, 170–176
DEW (distant early warning) site, 145
dining/kitchen area equipment checklist, 299–300
driving area equipment checklist, 303, 306
dry camping, 57, 62
   preparing for, 104–105
dumping, black/gray water, 57, 105–106

Earthquake Park, 180
electricity, hooking up for, 18
Emerald Lake, 233–234
equipment
   bathroom, 301–302, 305
   bedroom, 302
   driving area, 303, 306
   kitchen/dining area, 299–300
   living room, 303, 306
   outside storage, 306
   personal items, 302
   wardrobe, 302, 305

INDEX

Eskimos
   arts and crafts demonstrations, 151–155
   religion, 150
Exit Glacier, 196–197
Exxon Valdez, 213, 214

Farewell to Alaska (poem), 258–262
fees. *See* costs
Five Fingers Rapids, 111
Fort Nelson, 79

gas filter, problems with clogging, 77–78
gas mileage, increasing, 9–10, 105
generators, 62, 204
global warming, 197–198
glossary, 309–313
gold, panning for, 123
gray water, dumping, 57, 105–106
grocery list, 304–305. *See also* checklists; equipment
GuggieVille, 123

Harding Ice Field, 197
health care coverage, 9
Hell's Gate, 52–54
Holiday Rambler Recreational Vehicle Club, Inc. (HRRVC), 280
Homer Spit, 188
husky dogs, 198–200

Iditarod, 164, 179–180, 201
igloos, 286
insurance, health, 9
itinerary, 308

Keystone Canyon, 211–212
kitchen/dining area equipment checklist, 299–300
Kluane Lake, 232

living room equipment checklist, 303, 306
log books
   maintenance, 10
   trip log, 14
loonies, 98
LP gas detectors, 105

maintenance, wheel bearings, 222
maintenance log, 10
Mall of America, 21–22
Marmot Rock, 173
Midnight Dome, 122
The MILEPOST®, 46
mileposts, 46
Miles Canyon, 99
Minter Gardens, 51
Mount McKinley National Park. *See* Denali National Park
Musk Ox Farm, 206–207

Nenana River, 168–169
Northern Splendour Reindeer Farm, 109–110
North Pole, 134–135

outside storage equipment checklist, 306

Palmer, 205–206
panning for gold, 123
passing, safety, 13
Pennock, Homer, 188
personal items checklist, 302–303
Petersburg, 244
pipeline, Trans-Alaska, 133, 215, 216–217
Portage Glacier, 183–184
Portage Lake, 182–184
Pouce Coup, 71

315

preparations for traveling, 18, 222, 299–307
pressure regulators, 267
Prince William Sound, 212–215
publications, list of, 297

qiviut, 206–207

rafting, 168–169
rallies, 291
ratings, of campgrounds, 41
reindeer, 109–110
restrictions, on lengths of vehicles, 31
Resurrection Bay, 193
RV caravan tours, 2, 290–297
  questions to ask before choosing, 298

Seldovia, 189–190
Service, Robert, 116, 121
Seward, 192, 200–201
Shields, Mary, 164
Sideling Hill Exhibit Center, 16
Signpost Forest, 89, 92–93
Skagway, 233, 235, 236, 238–239
S.S. *Klondike*, 100
sternwheeler cruise, 163–165
supplies. *See* equipment

tailgunners, 5
Top of the World Highway, 124
totem poles, 248

Trailer Life Campground/RV Park & Services Directory, rating system of, 41
Trans-Alaska pipeline, 133, 215, 216–217
traveling
  preparations for, 18
Turnagain Arm, 181–182

upgrades to motorhome
  accessories, 10
  storage space, 15
  transmission overdrive unit, 9–10
Valdez oil spill, 213
volcanos, 180

wagonmasters, 5, 76
wardrobe equipment checklist, 302, 305
water (drinking/bathing)
  hooking up for, 18
  pressure regulators, 267
water (waste)
  dumping, 57, 105–106
Watson Lake Signpost Forest, 89, 92–93
whaling, 145
Whitehorse, 98
wilderness camping, 74. *See also* dry camping
Wrangell, 245–246

Yukon River, 99